RETRIEVING THE AMERICAN PAST

A CUSTOMIZED U.S. HISTORY READER

EDITED BY
Mr. Albert Churella
Early U.S. History
HIS. 2111
Southern Polytechnic State University
Social and International Studies

PEARSON CUSTOM PUBLISHING

Director of Database Publishing: Michael Payne
Sponsoring Editor: Natalie Danner
Development Editor: Katherine Gretz
Editorial Assistant: Samantha A. Goodman
Marketing Manager: Nathan L. Wilbur
Operations Manager: Eric M. Kenney
Database Project Specialist: Christopher Milot

Cover Art: Christie's Images, Long Island City, NY
Granger Collection, New York, NY

Printed in the United States of America

10 9 8 7 6 5 4 3 2 1

0536872309
BA 5567

PEARSON CUSTOM PUBLISHING
75 Arlington Street, Suite #300/Boston, MA 02116
Pearson Education Group

CONTRIBUTORS

Senior Editor
Saul Cornell

Managing Editor
John Day Tully

Copy Editor
Ann Heiss

Assistant Managing Editor
Douglas M. Paul

Contributing Editors

Tyler Anbinder
Kenneth J. Andrien
Jean Harvey Baker
Michael Les Benedict
Mansel Blackford
Paul C. Bowers
Rowland Brucken
John D. Buenker
John C. Burnham
Joan E. Cashin
William R. Childs
Albert J. Churella
Steven Conn
Saul Cornell
Nick Cullather
Jeanette Davis
Merton L. Dillon
Daniel Feller
Charles Coleman Finlay
Emily Greenwald
Mark Grimsley
Bernard N. Grindel
Peter L. Hahn
James Hansen
Susan M. Hartmann
Mary Ann Heiss
Earl J. Hess
Michael J. Hogan
R. Douglas Hurt

Bruce Karhoff
Michael Kazin
Terence Kehoe
K. Austin Kerr
Frank Lambert
Valerie Mendoza
James McCaffrey
Allan R. Millett
Pamela J. Mills
Daniel Nelson
Margaret E. Newell
Josef Ostyn
Carla Gardina Pestana
Patrick D. Reagan
Randolph A. Roth
Hal K. Rothman
John A. M. Rothney
Leila J. Rupp
Richard D. Shiels
David Sicilia
C. Edward Skeen
Amy L. S. Staples
David L. Stebenne
David Steigerwald
Marshall F. Stevenson, Jr.
Warren R. Van Tine
Christopher Waldrep
J. Samuel Walker

Contents

What Was Progressivism?

John D. Buenker

INTRODUCTION

The first two decades of the twentieth century were permeated with a bewildering variety of movements designed to "reform" virtually every aspect of American life and to promote "progress." Among it most important achievements on the municipal level were the city manager and commission forms of government, the municipal ownership or government regulation of public utilities, housing codes, anti-pollution ordinances, city planning and zoning, public health agencies, juvenile courts, playgrounds, vocational and adult education, and social settlements. On the state level, these movements produced industrial health and safety measures, workmen's compensation, the restriction of child labor, protective legislation for female workers, mothers' pensions, direct primary elections, initiative, referendum, and recall, income and inheritance taxes, and business regulation, among other initiatives. Nationally, they generated the 16th, 17th, 18th, and 19th amendments to the U.S. Constitution, conservation of natural resources, pure food and drug laws, anti-trust and regulatory measures, tariff reduction, the Federal Reserve and Federal Trade Commissions, child labor legislation, the Country Life Movement, to name but a few of the more celebrated reforms. So pervasive was the rhetoric and reality of "reform" and "progress" that President William Howard Taft received less than 25 percent of the popular vote during the 1912 election because he was the only one of the four candidates perceived to be "unprogressive."

Not surprisingly, contemporaries and historians alike have almost universally designated this highly interesting and exciting period "the Progressive Era", even though they have continued to *argue over its origins, nature, motivations, goals , accomplishments, duration, and legacy. In particular, they have disagreed long and loud over the question of whether the Progressive Era's myriad activities and achievements can be attributed to the existence of a reasonably coherent ideology called "progressivism," a philosophy that fell somewhere between laissiez-faire liberalism and some form of socialism or statism. This module constitutes an attempt to present a representative sampling of attempts by modern-day historians to define or explain the elusive concept of "progressivism", followed by a selective presentation of some of the most useful documentary evidence in the form of writings by prominent "progressives" and platforms or programs of important activist organizations. As you read and critique them, begin to formulate your own definition of "progressivism."*

WHAT WAS "PROGRESSIVISM"?: SCHOLARS' INTERPRETATIONS

For almost three-quarters of a century, historians have struggled to define the protean concept of "progressivism." Their disagreements have produced some of the most hotly contested debates in twentieth century American historiography, especially since the 1960s. What follows are selections from the works of seven modern-day scholars who have grappled with the complexities and pitfalls inherent in that frequently frustrating task. As you read and analyze these selections, determine whether they are all asking the same question and focusing on the same phenomenon. What kind of evidence do they cite in proof of their contentions?

A Babel of "Progressive" Tongues

Taking as his point of departure two essays—his own "The Progressive Era: A Search for a Synthesis," **Mid-America,** *51(July, 1969): 175-193 and Peter Filene's "An Obituary for 'The Progressive Movement',"* **American Quarterly,** *22(Spring,1970): 20-34—John D. Buenker argues that the prodigious efforts of historians to agree upon a meaning of the term "progressivism" have largely resulted in a plethora of definitions that are either so generic as to be meaningless or so ambiguous and contradictory as to "foreclose the possibility that members of the same movement could hold them simultaneously." Instead, he urges historians to conceive of progressivism as a series of dynamic coalitions interacting around a series of complex issues resulting from massive and rapid changes in the economy and society. This excerpt is taken from John D.*

Buenker, John C. Burnham, and Robert M. Crunden, Progressivism, *(Cambridge, MA: Schenkman, 1977), 31-35.*

The Progressive Era, Peter Filene wrote in "An Obituary for the 'Progressive Movement,'" "seems to have been characterized by shifting coalitions around different issues, with the specific nature of those coalitions varying on federal, state and local levels, from region to region and from the first to the second decade of the century." Although this positive definition of the dynamics of progressive reform has received scant notice compared to Filene's systematic dissection of the movement concept and his bold conclusion that "the progressive movement never existed," both logic and the mounting weight of evidence demonstrate that the notion of shifting coalitions provides a much more comprehensive explanation of the period than the one that he laid to rest. Viewing the era as the work of shifting coalitions rather than of a single movement has the potential for reconciling most of the currently conflicting interpretations and of encompassing nearly all of the groups, values and programs that were plainly at work.

The proponents of the "progressive movement" interpretation have generally centered it in an amorphous middle class of professionals, intellectuals and businessmen, who were almost exclusively of British-American stock, well fixed, college educated and "touched by the long religious hand of New England." The numerous disputes that have arisen over motivation, background, programs, and results have usually been resolved under the umbrella of this movement, even though the evidence often defies such characterization. Since each scholar has assumed that the group under study was a microcosm of a larger, the logical tendency has been to project one's limited conclusions to cover the whole. This "preoccupation with the syndromes of middle class anxieties and prejudices," as Edwin Rozwenc has observed, "has served to distract attention from the content of progressive policies and the complex relations that comprised the political process during the Progressive Era."

Efforts to establish a common social type have proved to be largely unrewarding. "Progressive profiles" or "collective biographies" have established that many activist organizations were

Excerpts reprinted from *Progressivism,* by John D. Buenker, John C. Burnham, Robert M. Crunden, 1977, used by permission of Schenkman Books, Inc.

heavily populated by the native, Protestant middle class, but similar studies in numerous locations have demonstrated that these reformers differed little from many acknowledged conservatives of the day with respect to class, education, nativity, or similar considerations. As Samuel Hays has observed, "one cannot explain the distinc- tive behavior of people in terms of characteristics which are not distinctive to them." Nor have these profiles proved that their subjects had the influence, political skills and votes to enact legislation. Other scholars have uncovered evidence of reformist activity among segments of society that not even the most elastic definition of a native, Protestant, middle class movement could possibly encompass. The urban, foreign stock working class, a segment of society formerly held to be part of the "potent mass that limited the range and achievements of the American Progressive," has been shown to have contributed significantly to the success of reform in several key industrial states. A significant role in at least some areas has been claimed for midwestern German-American Catholics, Socialists, organized labor, social and business elites and former Populists, all of whom fall outside the pale of a native, Protestant, middle class movement. "Movements with tolerable progressive credentials," Lewis Gould has recently written, "have been found in the agrarian South, among machine politicians in the city, within technical and professional groups, the military, the arts, as well as in the more familiar environs of middle-class America."

Small unit electoral analyses in three states have produced solid evidence that the constituencies backing reform candidates and measures in those states were neither homogeneous nor constant. Michael P. Rogin and John L. Shover have shown that Hiram Johnson and the republicans in California had two constituencies-the first urban, middle class and interested in business regulation and electoral reform, the second increasingly foreign stock and working class and attracted by labor and welfare measures. In Colorado, James L. Wright has argued, the Progressive Party vote was urban, middle class, and native, but it was not very "progressive", since the vote for it correlated badly with referenda on all reform measures except prohibition and resembled the Ku Klux Klan vote of 1924. Support for acknowledged reform measures came instead from the former hotbeds of Populism, especially among union labor and mine workers who voted heavily Socialist and Democratic during the Progressive Era. In Wisconsin, Roger Wyman has concluded, urban middle class and upper middle class wards leaned toward stalwart candidates, while Scandinavians, farmers, and German urban workers provided much greater electoral support to La Follette and his successors. "In terms of both program and support", Wyman insists, "progressivism was an extremely complex and amorphous movement, held together by tenuous political alliances which had ethnic, economic, geographic, and personal roots."

Nor have efforts to discern a common set of values or a coherent program among acknowledged reformers proved any more fruitful. Even among native, Protestant, middle class activists, such attempts have either produced ideas so general as to be held by practically everyone or so ambiguous, and even contradictory, as to foreclose the possibility that members of the same movement could hold them simultaneously. Some have viewed its members as motivated primarily by idealism and altruism. The status revolution school has seen them seeking to recoup the prestige lost by the rise of big business and the urban masses. Yet another group, equally committed to the movement concept, has discovered not an old elite trying to reassert lost values, but a new one, trying to affirm a new order. For them, reform meant the realization of such bureaucratic and professional goals as systematization, rationalization and efficiency, an outlook that bound them together against all those forces which represented unpredictability and instability. Even among a handful of prominent Progressive Era intellectuals, Daniel Levine found that "they did not share a body of fundamental assumptions about man, society, government and the good life." They "saw not the same social reality, but social realities of very different sorts." Virtually every significant issue of the era drove deep fissures into the ranks of the very group that was supposed to constitute the heart of the "progressive movement."'

Other segments of society pursued reform from far different value systems. Foreign stock reformers were motivated by a mixture of their Old and New World experiences. In the old country, the community, the village, the guild and the landlord had restricted their opportunity for socioeconomic advancement, but had also assumed some measure of obligation for their well-being. In those countries touched by the industrial revolution, its impact had been partially ameliorated by conservative social classes and institutions. The welfare state emerged much earlier in Europe than in the United States. In America immigrants benefited from the ministrations of the ward boss, the clergy, and the fraternal and benevolent societies that gave material aid and sought to preserve distinctive values and customs. Catholicism, Judaism, the eastern Orthodox religions, and Lutheranism had never adjusted to capitalist values as completely as had the various offshoots of Calvinism which were the major American denominations. Their clergy also generally preferred to leave alcohol, gambling, and other human vices to the individual conscience guided by the Church. Less influenced by the Enlightenment and the Protestant ethic, they had little faith in the perfectibility of man and society, bur they did believe in amelioration. "A coherent community structure, Herbert Gutman has found, "allowed these lower class, first-and-second-generation immigrants enough leverage to begin to humanize the emerging industrial system." Southern Populists, Socialists, and Midwestern Insurgents proceeded from still other value systems.

Nor was there a single "progressive" program. The label "progressive reform" has been affixed to efforts to increase popular political participation as well as to those to turn government over to a group of experts immune from electoral politics. Dealing with the problem of big business through trust-busting, through regulation, or through public ownership have all been designated as progressive solutions. Reformers have been portrayed as sympathetic to the rise of organized labor as well as hostile toward it, as fostering the growth of the welfare state as well as resisting it. Those who sought to legislate conformity to established cultural norms have been held equally progressive with those who opposed such measures. What was the "progressive" side of such issues as prohibition, Sunday blue laws, immigration restriction, disfranchisement and segregation? Some scholars have termed such cultural legislation as aberrational, while others have seen the same measures as a logical outgrowth of the reform impulse. Nomenclature, as David M. Kennedy has observed, "can be stretched over such vast expanses of time and temperament only at the expense of descriptive accuracy."

Despite these difficulties, most Progressive Era historians have held on to the concept of a movement. Some have sought to account for the apparent discrepancies by positing the existence of two or more such movements, each retaining a basic native, Protestant, middle class character. Thus there have been analyses of political versus social progressives, uncompromising versus middle-of-the-road progressives, traditionalists versus moderns, New Freedom versus New Nationalism, eastern versus midwestern-southern progressivism, and nativists versus cultural liberals. When historical evidence resists the historian so resolutely, Filene has argued persuasively, "one must question the categories being used." Small wonder that Levine has concluded that "the word 'Progressive' has been used in so many ways that it has lost all clear meaning except as a designation for a particular time period or a particular political party. As a description of either an ideology or a political program, I find it worthless and misleading."

Religion and Science Seek to Ameliorate Industrialism

Casting their nets broadly, Arthur S. Link and Richard L. McCormick define the basic characteristics of progressivism as a decision to accept and ameliorate modern industrialism, a desire to preserve the environment, and a disposition to intervene purposefully in the economic and social systems in order to impose a measure of order upon them. They identify its ideals as an amalgam of the tenets of evangelical Protestantism, on the one hand, and the natural and social sciences, on the other. The following selection is from Arthur S. Link and Richard L. McCormick, Progressivism, *(Arlington Heights, IL, 1982), 21-25.*

Progressivism was characterized, in the first place, by a distinctive set of attitudes toward industrialism. By the turn of the century, the overwhelming majority of Americans had accepted the permanence of large-scale industrial, commercial, and financial enterprises and of the wage and factory systems. The progressives shared this attitude. Most were not socialists, and they undertook reform, not to dismantle modern economic insti-

---

tutions, but rather to ameliorate and improve the conditions of industrial life. Yet progressivism was infused with a deep outrage against the worst consequences of industrialism. Outpourings of anger at corporate wrongdoing and of hatred for industry's callous pursuit of profit frequently punctuated the course of reform in the early twentieth century. Indeed, anti-business emotion was a prime mover of progressivism. That the acceptance of industrialism *and* the outrage against it were intrinsic to early twentieth-century reform does not mean that progressivism was mindless or that it has to be considered indefinable. But it does suggest that there was a powerful irony in progressivism: reforms which gained support from people angry with the oppressive aspects of industrialism also assisted the same persons to accommodate to it, albeit to an industrialism which was to some degree socially responsible.

The progressives' ameliorative reforms also reflected their faith in progress-in mankind's ability, through purposeful action, to improve the environment and the conditions of life. The late nineteenth-century dissidents had not lacked this faith, but their espousal of panaceas bespoke a deep pessimism: "Unless this one great change is made, things will get worse." Progressive reforms were grounded on a broader assumption. In particular, reforms could protect the people hurt by industrialization and make the environment more humane. For intellectuals of the era, the achievement of such goals meant that they had to meet Herbert Spencer head on and confute his absolute "truths." Progressive thinkers, led by Lester Frank Ward, Richard T. Ely, and, most important, John Dewey, demolished social Darwinism with what [Eric] Goldman has called "reform Darwinism." They asserted that human adaptation to the environment did not interfere with the evolutionary process, but was, rather, part and parcel of the law of natural change. Progressive intellectuals and their popularizers produced a vast literature to condemn laissez faire and to promote the concept of the active state.

To improve the environment meant, above all, to intervene in economic and social affairs in order to control natural forces and impose a measure of order upon them. This belief in interventionism was a third component of progressivism. It was visible in almost every reform of the era, from the supervision of business to the prohibition of alcohol. . . . Interventionism could be both private and public. Given their choice, most progressives pre-

One of the major reform movements of the Progressive era, the temperance movement underscored the willingness of reformers to resort to government interventionism to solve social problems. (Courtesy of the Library of Congress.)

ferred to work noncoercively through voluntary organizations for economic and social changes. However, as time passed, it became evident that most progressive reforms could be achieved only by legislation and public control. Such an extension of public authority made many progressives uneasy, and few of them went so far as Herbert Croly in glorifying the state in his *The Promise of American Life* (1909) and *Progressive Democracy* (1914). Even so, the intervention necessary for their reforms inevitably propelled progressives toward an advocacy of the use of governmental power. A familiar scenario during the period was one in which progressives called upon public authorities to assume responsibility for interventions which voluntary organizations had begun.

The foregoing describes the basic characteristics of progressivism but says little about its ideals. Progressivism was inspired by two bodies of belief and knowledge: evangelical Protestantism and the natural and social sciences. These sources of reform may appear at first glance antagonistic to one another. Actually, they were complementary, and each imparted distinctive qualities to progressivism.

Ever since the religious revivals from about 1820 to 1840, evangelical Protestantism had spurred reform in the United States. Basic to the reform mentality was an all-consuming urge to purge the world of sin, such as the sins of slavery and intemperance against which nineteenth century reformers had crusaded. Now the progressives carried the struggle into the modern citadels of sin-the teeming cities of the nation. No one can read their writings and speeches without being struck by the fact that many of them believed that it was their Christian duty to right the wrongs created by the processes of industrialization. Such belief was the motive force behind the Social Gospel, a movement which swept through the Protestant churches in the 1890s and 1900s. Its goal was to align churches, frankly and aggressively, on the side of the downtrodden, the poor, and working people-in other words, to make Christianity relevant to this world, not the next. It is difficult to measure the influence of the Social Gospel, but it seared the consciences of millions of Americans, particularly in urban areas. And it triumphed in 1908 in the organization of the Federal council of Churches of Christ in America, with its platform which condemned exploitative capitalism and proclaimed the right of workers to organize and to enjoy a decent standard of living. Observers at the Progressive party's national convention of 1912 should not have been surprised to hear the delegates sing, spontaneously and emotionally, "Onward, Christian Soldiers!"

The faith which inspired the singing of "Onward, Christian Soldiers!" had significant implications for progressive reforms. Progressives used moralistic appeals to make people feel the awful weight of wrong in the world and to exhort them to accept personal responsibility for its eradication. The resultant reforms could be generous in spirit, but they could also seem intolerant to the people who were "reformed". Progressivism sometimes seemed to envision life in a small-town Protestant community or an urban drawing room-a vision sharply different from that of Catholic or Jewish immigrants. Not every progressive shared the evangelical ethos, much less its intolerance, but few of the era's reforms were untouched by the spirit and techniques of Protestant revivalism.

Science also had a pervasive impact on the methods and objectives of progressivism. Many leading reformers were specialists in the new disciplines of statistics, economics, sociology, and psychology. These new social scientists set out to gather data on human behavior as it actually was and to discover the laws which governed it. Since social scientists accepted environmentalist and interventionist assumptions implicitly, they believed that knowledge of natural laws would make it possible to devise and apply solutions to improve the human condition. This faith underpinned the optimism of most progressives and predetermined the methods used by almost all reformers of the time: investigation of the facts and application of social-science knowledge to their analysis; entrusting trained experts to decide what should be done; and, finally, mandating government to execute reform. These methods may have been rational, but they were also compatible with progressive moralism. In its formative period, American social science was heavily infused with ethical concerns. An essential purpose of statistics, economics, sociology, and psychology was to improve and uplift. Leading practitioners of these disciplines, for example, Richard T. Ely, an economist at the University of Wisconsin, were often in the vanguard of the Social Gospel. Progressives blended science and religion into a view of human behavior which was unique to their generation, which had grown up in an age of revivals and come to maturity at the birth of social science.

All of progressivism's distinctive features found expression in muckraking-the literary spearhead of early twentieth century reform. Through the medium of such new ten-cent magazines as *McClure's, Everybody's,* and *Cosmopolitan,* the muckrakers exposed every dark aspect and corner of American life. Nothing escaped the probe of such writers as Ida M. Tarbell, Lincoln Steffens, Ray Stannard Baker, and Burton J. Hedrick-not big business, politics, prostitution, race relations, or even the churches. Behind the exposes of the muckrakers lay the progressive attitude toward industrialism: it was here to stay, but many of its aspects seemed to be deplorable. These could be improved, however, if only people became aware of conditions and determined to ameliorate them. To bring about such awareness, the muckrakers appealed to their readers' consciences. Steffens' famous series, published in book form as *The Shame of the Cities* in 1904, was frankly intended to make people feel guilty for the corruption which riddled their cities. The muckrakers also used the social scientists' methods of the careful and painstaking gathering of data-and with devastating effects. This investigative function-which was later largely taken over by governmental agencies-proved absolutely vital to educating and arousing Americans.

All progressive crusades shared the spirit and used the techniques discussed here, but they did so to different degrees and in different ways. Some voiced a greater willingness to accept industrialism and even to extol its potential benefits; others expressed more strongly the outrage against its darker aspects. Some intervened through voluntary organizations; others relied upon government to achieve changes. Each reform reflected a distinctive balance between the claims of Protestant moralism and of scientific rationalism. Progressives fought among themselves over these questions even while they set to the common task of applying their new methods and ideas to the problems of modern society.

Three Distinct Social Languages of Discontent and Vision

In this selection, Daniel T. Rodgers boldly asserts that progressive reformers "did not share a common creed or a string of common values, however ingeniously or vaguely defined." In place of the search for a common ideology of progressivism, he proposes the existence of three "clusters of ideas" or "social languages" in which reformers communicated and operated. This excerpt is taken from his "In Search of of Progressivism," Reviews in American History, *10 (1982):122-27.*

The obstacles in the way of getting progressive social thought straight have little to do with insufficient evidence; progressives

---

"In Search of Progressivism," by Daniel T. Rodgers, reprinted from *Reviews in American History*, 1982, Johns Hopkins University Press.

shared an inordinate faith in the word . . . and they preached and wrote with consuming zeal. One of the results, however, was a rhetoric thick with straw men and partisan exaggerations which can be safely read only with a sense of context and contest as strong as the progressives' own. "Social justice" is a case in point—a powerful Rooseveltian slogan in 1912 which, in the absence of anyone willing to defend "social injustice," worked its magic in large part through its half-buried innuendoes and its expansive indistinctness. The progressives' appeal to "the people" is a more complicated example of the phenomenon; but one of the reasons for the triumph of that particularly elastic phrase (as opposed to the term "democracy," for example) was that it allowed those who sincerely believed in a government serving the needs of "the people" to camouflage from voters the acute distrust many of those same persons harbored of political egalitarianism. Above all, when the progressives exaggerated, they were prone to exaggerate their triumph over what they belittled as the drift and pessimism of their predecessors, counting on their audiences not to inquire too closely into the relationship between the frenetically active, progress-imbued nineteenth century and the progressives' deliberate caricature of it. Yet in the lists of the characteristic ideological ingredients of progressivism compiled in the 1970s one could still find the terms optimism, activism, democracy, and social justice—too often with only a thin sense of the traps surrounding each of them. Like all partisans, the progressive publicists used words less to clarify a political philosophy than to build a political constituency. What their slogans meant lay not only in what they said but in what these slogans were designed to accomplish.

The trouble with comprehending "progressivism" as a list of beliefs is a deeper one, however, than the presence of some misleading or exaggerated elements on many such lists. The deeper problem stems from the attempt to capture the progressives within a static ideological frame. If the contradictory lists prove anything it is that those who called themselves progressives did not share a common creed or a string of common values, however ingeniously or vaguely defined. Rather what they seem to have possessed was an ability to draw on three distinct clusters of ideas—three distinct social languages—to articulate their discontents and their social visions. To put rough but serviceable labels on those three languages of discontent, the first was the rhetoric of antimonopolism, the second was an emphasis on social bonds and the social nature of human beings, and the third was the language of social efficiency.

These three did not add up to a coherent ideology we can call "progressivism." All three tended to focus that discontent on arbitrary, unregulated individual power-enough so to make the trust, the political boss, and the sweatshop terms of enormous bearing. But on a deeper level the three languages—full of mutual contradictions—did not add up at all. They had distinctly different historical roots, and they rose into currency and fell into disuse at distinctly different times. We can best imagine those who called themselves progressives as drawing from each of them—some more from one, some more from another—without undue concern for philosophical consistency. Together they formed not an ideology but the surroundings of available rhetoric and ideas—akin to the surrounding structures of politics and power—within which progressives launched their crusades, recruited their partisans, and did their work.

Of these languages, antimonopolism was the oldest, the most peculiarly American, and, through the first decade of the century, the strongest of the three. When Tom Johnson took on the streetcar franchises, when Frederic Howe plumped for municipal ownership of natural monopolies, when the muckrakers flayed the trusts, there was nothing essentially new in the grievances they dramatized or the language they employed. The disproportionately large number of single taxers in the early progressive crusades was clue enough that this line of attack on "privilege" and "unnatural" concentration of wealth ran back through the Populists, through Henry George, and on at least to Andrew Jackson. But this understanding of economics and politics in terms of graft, monopoly, privilege, and invisible government had almost always before been the property of outsiders; workers, farmers, Democrats, Populists. What was new in the Progressive years was that the language of antimonopolyism suddenly gained the acceptance of insiders: the readers of slick magazines and respectable journals, middle class family men, and reasonably proper Republicans. William A. White caught the point in 1905. "It is funny how we have all found the octopus, " he mused, when less than a decade earlier, backed up against the wall by Populism, his like had denied that animal's very existence. . . .

The second cluster of ideas from which the Progressives drew—the language of social bonds—was more specific to the Progressive years, and at the same time much less peculiarly American. To call it, in Thomas Haskell's terms, the discovery of "interdependence" runs a risk of misunderstanding. That human beings live in a web of social relations has never been open to doubt. Much of the thrust of academic social thought in the nineteenth century had, in fact, consisted of a finer and finer elaboration of what the term "society" meant. Still the most common explanations most Americans gave to political, economic, and social questions at the end of the century were couched in terms of largely autonomous individuals: poverty and success were said to hinge on character; the economy was essentially a straight sum of individual calculations; governance was a matter of good men and official honesty. Part of what occurred in the Progressive era was a concerted assault on all these assumptions, and, in some measure, an assault on the idea of individualism itself. That was what the era's "revolt against formalism" was all about: not a revolt against formal categories of thought, for progressive intellectuals were full of them, but against a particular set of formal fictions traceable to Smith, Locke, and Mill—the autonomous economic man, the autonomous possessor of property rights, the autonomous man of character. In its place, many of the progressives seized on a rhetoric of social cohesion. . . .

The last of the three clusters of ideas to arrive—so very different in outward form from the other two—was the one we associate with efficiency, rationalization, and social engineering. Some of the progressives never stomached the new bureaucratic language of budgets, human costs, and system, nor felt comfortable translating social sins into the new-fangled language of social waste. For others, however, the language of social efficiency offered a way of putting the progressives' common sense of social disorder into words and remedies free of the embarrassing pieties and philosophical conundrums that hovered around the competing language of social bonds. Like Charles Beard or John R. Commons they were ready to put their Ruskins and their Christian Sociology on the shelf in exchange for the stripped down language of social science—and for the new occupational niches available for social scientific experts. . . .

What made progressive social thought distinct and volatile, if this reading is correct, was not its intellectual coherence but the presence of all three of these languages at once. If we imagine the progressives, like most of the rest of us, largely as users rather than shapers of ideas, this was the constellation of live, accessible ways of looking at society within which they worked, from which they drew their energies and their sense of social ills, and within which they found their solutions. It did not give those who called themselves progressives an intellectual system, but it gave them a set of tools which worked well enough to have a powerful impact on their times. To think of progressive social thought in this way is to emphasize the active, dynamic aspect of ideas. It is also to admit, finally, that progressivism as an ideology is nowhere to be found.

Questions

---

1. *Which of the interpretations given by the modern-day scholars comes closest to providing a comprehensive explanation of the movement that each of the Progressive Era activists might accept? Are there any interpretations that at least some of the contemporary activists would reject?*
2. *Imagine a discussion among these three modern-day scholars. What areas of agreement and disagreement would likely emerge?*

DEFINITIONS OF
PROGRESSIVE ERA ACTIVISTS

To an unusual degree, the Progressive Era was blessed (or cursed) with a great number of perceptive and articulate activists, who saw themselves as operating in a wider universe according to a set of basic, widely understood, and highly regarded principles. Accordingly, they undertook to convey their sense of those ideas and values to their contemporaries, in order to justify their actions and to proselytize for converts. The more of those works one reads, the more one understands the reasons for the inability of modern historians to agree on the nature of progressivism, and the more one appreciates the complexity and diversity that characterized the era's reformist efforts. The following selections, taken from autobiographies, memoirs, or books intended to explain and advocate, are designed to demonstrate that the differences among modern day historians reflect an equally great disagreement among Progressive Era activists and interpreters.

The "Confession" of a Progressive Activist

One of the most energetic and prolific interpreters of progressivism was Frederic C. Howe (1867-1940), whose career began in a Cleveland settlement house in the 1890s and ended as consumer advocate for the Agricultural Adjustment Administration in 1935. In between, he served on the Cleveland city council and in the Ohio senate, was an adviser to progressive mayor Tom Johnson, acted as U.S. commissioner of immigration during the Woodrow Wilson administration, and wrote ten books on municipal reform and related subjects. In this selection from his

The Confessions of a Reformer, *(New York: Scribner's, 1925), 176-181, Howe describes his "conversion" to progressive activism and his devotion to "democracy."*

My text-book government had to be discarded; my worship of the Constitution scrapped. The state that I had believed in with religious fervor was gone. Like the anthropomorphic God of my childhood, it had never existed. But crashing beliefs cleared the air. I saw that democracy had not failed; it had never been tried. We had created confusion and had called it democracy. Professors at the university and text-book writers had talked and written about something that did not exist. It could not exist. In politics we lived a continuous lie.

I set down for myself principles that would constitute democracy. I applied biological processes to it. From some source or other I had come to believe that Nature was very wise, and that her rules, by which billions upon billions of creatures were able to live, must be a reasonably good guide for the organized state. I took the private corporation as a guide. Business had succeeded in America and it worked with very simple machinery. It was not bothered by a constitution; it was not balked by checks and balances; it was not compelled to wait for years to achieve what it wanted. Its acts were not supervised by a distant supreme court. The freedom of a private corporation was close to license; what its officials wanted done was done. Mayors, governors, legislatures, city councils had no such power. In many ways the corporation that disposed of the city's garbage had more freedom of action than had the municipality that employed it. Here was a suggestion of machinery that worked well, even if it did not work in the interest of the public.

Business men had been given one instrument, the people another. The one was simple, direct, and powerful; the other confused indirect, and helpless. We had freed the individual but imprisoned the community. We had given power to the corporation but not to the state. The text-books talked of political sovereignty, but what we really had was business sovereignty. And because the business corporation had power while the political corporation had not, the business corporation had become the state.

Nor had we followed what nature had to teach. We violated the instincts of man. Politics offered no returns to the man of talent, who wanted to see the fruit of his efforts. If business had been organized like the state, it would have been palsied. Business would have gone bankrupt under the confusion, the complexity, the endless delays which were demanded by the political state.

Taking the private corporation as a model, I evolved three basic principles; they were: Government should be easily understood and easily worked; it should respond immediately to the decision of the majority; the people should always rule.

Elaborated into a programme of constitutional change, these principles involved:

(1) The easy nomination of all candidates by petition. There should be no conventions. Direct primaries are the fountainhead of democracy.

(2) Candidates should print their platforms in a few lines on the election ballots. Voters would then know what a man stood for.

(3) The short ballot.

(4) The recall of all elective officials, including judges.

(5) The initiative and referendum on the Constitution, on laws, and on city ordinances.

(6) Complete home rule for cities. The city should be a state by itself, with power to do anything of a local nature that the people wanted done. A free city would be like the cities of ancient Greece, like the medieval Italian republics., like the cities of Germany to-day. It would inspire patriotism. Able men would be attracted to the task of administering it.

(7) The State Assembly should consist of but one body of not more than fifty members. It should be in continuous session for a four-year term, the governor sitting with it and responsible to it for the exercise of wide powers.

(8) The courts should have merely civil and criminal jurisdiction. They should have no power to interfere with legislation. Congress and the State legislatures should be the sole judges of the constitutionality of their acts. The British Parliament and the legislative bodies of other countries are supreme. America alone has created a third assembly-chamber that has an absolute veto of the popular will.

Such a government would be democracy. It would be simple and easily understood. There would be no confusion, no delays. In such a state the people would be free. And they would be sovereign. Under the existing system they were neither sovereign nor free. We had stripped the state of sovereignty; the first thing to do was to restore it. Under such a system we could have a boss if we wanted one. Certainly we should have leaders. But we could hold the leader to responsibility. Things could be done in the open. We should not be living the lie of the existing system, which was not democracy but eco-   nomic oligarchy.

The Revolt of the "Ultimate Consumer"

Hailed by fellow progressive intellectual Walter Lippmann as "by far the best trained economist in the progressive movement," Walter E. Weyl (1873-1919) received his Ph.D. under the mentorship of Simon Patten, worked for the U.S. Bureau of Labor Statistics, was a settlement house resident, and served as an adviser to the United Mine Workers. He was the founding editor of the New Republic *and wrote numerous books on labor, railroads, and immigration. According to a contemporary, Weyl "looked like a saint and fundamentally was one." In 1912, he published his most celebrated book* The New Democracy, *in which he proposed an agenda which would enable disadvantaged social groups, including consumers, regain control of the country from the "plutocracy." (New York, 1912), 249-253.*

When the trust raises prices, obtains valuable franchises or public lands, escapes taxation, secures bounties, lowers wages, evades factory laws, or makes other profitable maneuvers, it is diverting a part of the social surplus from the general community to itself. The public pays the higher prices, loses the franchises or lands, pays higher taxes, suffers in wages (and pays for the ill effects of low wages), and generally makes up dollar for dollar for all such gains. In all these things the people have a perceivable interest. The great mass is injured in its capacity of wage earner, salary earner, taxpayer and consumer.

Of these capacities that of the consumer is the most universal, since even those who do not earn wages or pay direct taxes consume commodities. In America to-day the unifying economic force, about which a majority, hostile to the plutocracy, is forming, is the common interest of the citizen as a consumer of wealth and incidentally as an owner of (undivided) national possessions. The producer (who is only the consumer in another role) is highly differentiated. He is banker, lawyer, soldier, tailor, farmer, shoeblack, messenger boy. He is capitalist, workman, money lender, money borrower, urban worker, rural worker. The consumer, on the other hand, is undifferentiated. All men, women, and children who buy shoes (except only the shoe manufacturer) are interested in cheap good shoes. The consumers of most articles are overwhelmingly superior in numbers to the producers.

Despite this overwhelming superiority in numbers, the consumer, finding it difficult to organize, has often been worsted in industrial battles. In our century-long tariff contests a million inaudible consumers have often counted less than has a petty industry in a remote district. The consumer thought of himself as a producer, and he united only with men of his own productive group. For a time there was a certain reason for such an alignment. It was a period of falling prices, of severe competition, in which the whole organization of industry favored the consumer. In fact, the unorganized and ruthless consumer was blamed -and rightly blamed (as he is still rightly blamed to-day)—for many of the evils of industry. The curse of the sweatshop and of the starving seamstress, sewing by candlelight, was fairly brought to the doors of the bargain-hunting housewife. The consumer, though acting singly, felt himself secure. Even when prices began to rise, consumers remained quiescent. There was greater difficulty in resisting price advances, because the loss to each individual from each increase was so infinitesimal. The reverse of the overwhelming numbers of the consumers was the small individual interest of each in each transaction. Wages affected a man far more sensibly than did prices. If a motorman's wages were reduced one cent an hour he might lose thirty dollars a year; a rise of ten cents in the price of shoes, on the other hand, meant a loss of, at most, two dollars a year. A man could not spend his lifetime fighting ten-cent-increases. The cure for high prices was high wages.

As prices continue to rise, however, as a result (among other causes) of our gradually entering into a monopoly period, a new insistence is laid upon the rights of the consumer, and political unity is based upon him. Where formerly production seemed to be the sole governing economic fact of a man's life, to-day many producers have no direct interest in their product. It is a very attenuated interest which the Polish slag-worker has in the duty on steel billets, but the Polish slag-worker and the Boston salesgirl and the Oshkosh lawyer have a similar interest (and a common cause of discontent) as consumers of the national wealth. The universality of the rise of prices has begun to affect the consumer as though he were attacked by a million gnats. The chief offense of the trust becomes its capacity to injure the consumer. Therefore the consumer, disinterred from his grave, reappears in the political arena as the "common man," " the plain people", "the taxpayer," "the strap-hanger," "the man on the street," and the "ultimate consumer." Men who voted as producers are now voting as consumers. . . .

To secure their rights as consumers, as well as to secure other economic interests, less in common, the people unite as citizens to obtain a sensitive popular government. They attain to a certain political as well as economic solidarity. This solidarity is by no means a complete unification of interest. There remain differences in agreement and discords in harmony. The middle classes are as much opposed to the trade-union as are the trusts, and the professional man is as anxious to secure a docile and cheap housemaid as the farmer is desirous of getting high prices for his wheat and paying low wages to his farm laborer. The elements of solidarity, however, being found in a common hostility to the plutocracy and a common interest in the social surplus, it becomes possible gradually so to compromise conflicting interests within the group as to secure a united front against a common enemy. The regulation of railroads in the interest of consumer and farmer   may be extended to the protection of the railroad worker; the conservation of natural resources may be linked to a similar policy of human conservation, to a campaign   against destitution, and to a progressive labor policy which will insure the health, safety, comfort, and leisure of all workers. By such internal adjustments within the wide democratic army the possibility of a sufficient, permanent solidarity is given.

The Essence of the Progressive Movement

Perhaps the first person to undertake a comprehensive interpretation of progressivism was New York attorney, professor, and political activist Benjamin Parke DeWitt (1889-1965). In his most famous work The Progressive Movement: A Non-Partisan, Comprehensive Discussion of Current Tendencies in American Politics, *(New York: Macmillan, 1915), he characterizes progressivism as a broad-based movement designed to purge self-interest from government, facilitate majority rule, and alleviate social and economic distress. The following excerpt is from pp. 3-5.*

The term "progressive movement" has been so widely used, so much discussed, and so differently interpreted that any exposition of its meaning and principle, to be adequate, must be prefaced by careful definition. To some comparatively few-the progressive movement stands for the attempt of one man, disappointed in his efforts to control his political party, to found another and return himself to power. To others, who are willing to concede that the movement is not confined to a single leader, it represents the efforts of a small body of self-seeking politicians to gain position and influence by making capital of a movement that is temporarily popular. To others, the movement expresses the effort of a few sincere but misguided enthusiasts to carry out an impossible and chimerical program of social reform through government and legislation. Some believe that the movement is partisan, limited to the party that bears its name; others believe that it is broader than any single party and that its supporters are found in political parties everywhere. Some believe it is new, fleeting, and evanescent, destined to disappear quickly from our political life; others hold that it is permanent, deep-seated, and fundamental, involving a modification and readjustment of our political theories and institutions.

Whatever difference of opinion may exist concerning the meaning of the progressive movement, every thinking man and woman must be convinced that the nation to-day is passing through a severe political crisis. After a period of unprecedented industrial and commercial expansion, during which time little or no attention has been given to the problems of government, the people have suddenly realized that government is not functioning properly and that radical changes are needed. Manifestations of this excitement and unrest are seen on every hand. Men write of a new democracy and a new freedom. In 1912 the vote of the Socialist party, the party of protest against existing conditions, almost reached the million mark; and in the same year a new political party, appealing to new ideals and new standards, polled four million votes. The Democratic party in the nation, after a stormy convention, nominated and elected as President, in 1912, a leader who insists upon high standards of public service; and the Republican party, chastened by defeat, and forced to recognize the present political tendencies, has already set about the work of party regeneration in many states. Everywhere there are evidences that the nation has passed into a new political era.

In this widespread political agitation that at first sight seems so incoherent and chaotic, there may be distinguished upon examination and analysis three tendencies. The first of these tendencies is found in the insistence by the best men in all political parties that special, minority, and corrupt influence in government-national, state, and city-be removed; the second tendency is found in the demand that the structure or machinery of government, which has hitherto been admirably adapted to control by the few, be so changed and modified that it will be more difficult for the few, and easier for the many, to control; and, finally, the third tendency is found in the rapidly growing conviction that the functions of government at present are too restricted and that they must be increased and extended to relieve social and economic distress.

These three tendencies with varying emphasis are seen to-day in the platform and program of every political party; they are manifested in the political changes and reforms that are advocated and made in the nation, the states, and the cities; and, because of their universality and definiteness, they may be said to constitute the real progressive movement.

The "Woman Mind" Transforms Society

Representative of many of the legion of "new women" who entered public life during the Progressive Era and made such vital contributions to its achievements was Rheta Childe Dorr (1866-1948). An investigative journalist for the New York Evening Post, *she crusaded for working women's protective legislation and woman suffrage, and was instrumental in the activities of the National Woman's Party and the General Federation of Women's Clubs. Acting as a spokesperson for the latter organization, Dorr wrote* What Eight Million Women Want, *(Boston: Small, Maynard & Co., 1910), in which, among other things, she proclaimed the philosophy of "municipal housekeeping" that animated many, but not all, of the era's feminists. The following selection is from pp.321-328.*

The woman mind is the most unchangeable thing in the world. It has turned on identically the same pivot since the present race began. Perhaps before.

Turn back and count over the club women's achievements, the things they have chosen to do, the things they want. Observe first of all that they want very little for themselves. Even their political liberty they want only because it will enable them to get other things—things needed, directly or indirectly, by children. Most of the things are directly needed—playgrounds, school gardens, child-labor laws, juvenile courts, kindergartens, pure food laws, and other visible tokens of child concern. Many of the other things are indirectly needed by children—ten-hour working days, seats for shop girls, protection from dangerous machinery, living wages, opportunities for safe and wholesome pleasures, peace and arbitration, social purity, legal equality with men, all objects which tend to conserve the future mothers of children. These are the things women want.

In my introductory chapter I cited three extremely grave and significant facts which confront modern civilization. The first was the fact of women's growing economic freedom, their emancipation from domestic slavery. I believe that women would not wish to be economically free if their instinct gave them any warning that freedom for them meant danger to their children. But no observer of social conditions can have failed to observe the oceans of misery endured by women and children because of their economic dependence on the fortunes of husbands and fathers.

Whatever may be the solution of poverty, whatever be the future status of the family, it seems certain to me that some way will be devised whereby motherhood will cease to be a privately supported profession. In some way society will pay its own account. If producing citizens to the State be the greatest service a woman citizen can perform, the State will ultimately recognize the right of the woman citizen to protection during her time of service. The first step towards solving the problem is for women to learn to support themselves before the time comes for them to serve the State. Through the educating process of productive labor the woman mind may devise a means of protecting the future mothers of the race.

The second fact, the growing prevalence of divorce, on the face of it seems to menace the security of the home and of children. So deeply overlain with prejudice, conventionalities, and theological traditions is the average woman as well as the average man that it is difficult to argue in favor of a temporary tolerance of divorce that a permanent high standard of marriage may be established. But to my mind any state of affairs, even a Reno state of affairs, looks more encouraging than the old conditions under which innocent girls married to rakes and drunkards were forbidden to escape their chains. It is not for the good of children to be born of disease and misery and hatred. It is not for their good to be brought up in an atmosphere of hopeless in harmony. What is happening in this country is not a weakening of the marriage bond, but a strengthening of it. For soon there will grow up in the American man's mind a desire for a marriage which will be at least as equitable as a business partnership; as fair to one party as to the other. He will cease to regard marriage as a state of bondage for the wife and a state of license for the husband. He will not venture to suggest to a bright woman that cooking in his kitchen is a more honorable career than teaching, or painting, or writing, or manufacturing. Marriage will not mean extinction to any woman. It will mean to the well-to-do wife freedom to do community service. It will mean to the industrial woman an economic burden shared. When that time comes there will be no divorce problem. There will be no longer a class of women who avoid the risk of divorce by refusing to marry.

The third fact, the increasing popularity of woman suffrage, I disposed of in the preceding chapter. Nothing that the women who vote have ever done indicates, in the remotest degree, that they are not just as mindful of children's interest at the polls as other women are in their nurseries and kitchens.

On the contrary, wherever women have left their kitchens and nurseries, whenever they have gone out into the world of action and of affairs, they have increased their effectiveness as mothers. I do not mean by this that the girl who enters a factory at fourteen and works there ten hours a day until she marries increases her effectiveness as a mother. Industrial slavery unfits a woman for motherhood as certainly as intellectual and moral slavery unfits her.

Women who are free, who look on life through their own eyes, who think their own thoughts, who live in the real world of striving, struggling, suffering humanity, are the most effective mothers that ever lived. They know how to care for their own children, and, more than that, they know how to care for the community's children.

The child at his mother's knee, spelling out the words of a psalm, stands for the moral education of the race—or it used to. A group of Chicago club women walking boldly into the city Bridewell and the Cook County Jail and demanding that children of ten and twelve should no longer be locked up with criminals; these same women, after the children were segregated, establishing a school for them, and finally these same women achieving a juvenile court, is the modern edition of the old ideal.

Woman's place is in the home. This is a platitude which no woman will ever dissent from, provided two words are dropped out of it. Woman's place is Home. Her task is homemaking. Her talents, as a rule, are mainly for homemaking. But Home is not contained within the four walls of an individual home. Home is the community. The city full of people is the Family. The public school is the real Nursery. And badly do the Home and the Family and the Nursery need their mother.

The Subjective Necessity
for Social Settlements

By all odds, the most famous and influential of all of the "new women" operating during the Progressive Era was Jane Addams (1860-1935). Variously dubbed an "American Heroine", "beloved lady", and "the only saint America has produced," she made Hull House in Chicago the prototype for American social settlements, was also a force in education, labor relations, immigration policy, and local and national politics. Addams was the first woman president of the National Conference of Charities and Correction and was the chief author of the "social and industrial justice" section of the platform of the Progressive Party in 1912. She also wrote twelve books and hundreds of articles interpreting the life of immigrants and poor people for middle-class readers. The following selection is taken from her book Twenty Years at Hull House, *(New York: Macmillan, 1910), pp. 115-27.*

This paper is an attempt to analyze the motives which underlie a movement based, not only upon conviction, but upon genuine emotion, wherever educated young people are seeking an outlet for that sentiment of universal brotherhood, which the best spirit of our times is forcing from an emotion into a motive. These young people accomplish little toward the solution of this social problem, and bear the brunt of being cultivated into unnourished, oversensitive lives. They have been shut off from the common labor by which they live which is a great source of moral and physical health. They feel a fatal want of harmony between their theory and their lives, a lack of coordination between thought and action. I think it is hard for us to realize how seriously many of them are taking to the notion of human brotherhood, how eagerly they long to give tangible expression to the democratic ideal. These young men and women, longing to socialize their democracy, are animated by certain hopes which may be thus loosely formulated; that if in a democratic country nothing can be permanently achieved save through the masses of the people, it will be impossible to establish a higher political life than the people themselves crave; that it is difficult to see how the notion of a higher civic life can be fostered save through common intercourse; that the blessings which we associate with a life of refinement and cultivation can be made universal and must be made universal if they are to be permanent; that the good we secure for ourselves is precarious and uncertain, is floating in mid-air, until it is secured for all of us and incorporated into our common life. It is easier to state these hopes than to formulate the line of motive which I believe to constitute the trend of the subjective pressure toward the Settlement. There is something primordial about these motives, but I am perhaps overbold in designating them as a great desire to share the race life. We all bear traces of the starvation struggle which for so long made up the life of the race. Our very organism holds memories and glimpses of that long life of our ancestors which still goes on among so many of our contemporaries. Nothing so deadens the sympathies and shrivels the power of enjoyment, as the persistent keeping away from the great opportunities for helpfulness and a continual ignoring of the starvation struggle which makes up the life of at least half the race. To shut one's self away from that half of the race life is to shut one's self away from the most vital part of it; it is to live out but half the humanity to which we have been born heir and to use but half our faculties. We have all had longings for a fuller life which should include the use of these faculties. These longings are the physical complement of the "Intimations of Immortality," on which no ode has yet been written. To portray these would be the work of a poet, and it is hazardous for any but a poet to attempt it.

I have seen young girls suffer and grow sensibly lowered in vitality in the first years after they leave school. In our attempt then to give a girl pleasure and freedom from care we succeed, for the most part, in making her pitifully miserable. She finds "life" so different from what she expected it to be. She is besotted with innocent little ambitions, and does not understand this apparent waste of herself, this elaborate preparation, if no work is provided for her. There is a heritage of noble obligation which young people accept and long to perpetuate. The desire for action, the wish to right wrong and alleviate suffering haunts them daily. Society smiles at it indulgently instead of making it of value to itself. The wrong to them begins even farther back, when we restrain the first childish desires for " do-in good" and tell them that they must wait until they are older and better fitted. We intimate that social obligation begins at a fixed date, forgetting that it begins with birth itself. We treat them as children, who, with strong-growing

Jane Addams founded Hull House in Chicago and became a major figure in the settlement house movement. Addams was also an active Progressive in local, state, and National Politics. (Courtesy of the Chicago Historical Society.)

limbs, are allowed to use their legs but not their arms, or whose legs are daily carefully exercised that after a while their arms may be put to high use. We do this in spite of the protest of the best educators, Locke and Pestalozzi. We are fortunate in the meantime if their unused members do not weaken and disappear. They do sometimes. There are a few girls who, by the time they are "educated", forget their old childish desires to help the world and to play with poor little girls "who haven't playthings." Parents are often inconsistent: they deliberately expose their daughters to knowledge of the distress in the world; they send them to hear missionary addresses on famines in India and China; they accompany them to lectures on the suffering in Siberia; they agitate together over the forgotten region of East London. In addition to this, from babyhood the altruistic tendencies of these daughters are persistently cultivated. They are taught to be self-forgetting and self-sacrificing, to consider the good of the whole before the good of the ego. But when all this information and culture show results, when the daughter comes back from college and begins to recognize her social claim to the "submerged tenth", and to evince a disposition to fulfill it, the family claim is strenuously asserted; she is told that she is unjustified, ill-advised in her efforts. If she persists, the family too often are injured and unhappy unless the efforts are called missionary and the religious zeal of the family carry them over their sense of abuse. When this zeal does not exist, the result is perplexing. It is a curious violation of what we would fain believe a fundamental law - that the final return of the deed is upon the head of the doer. The deed is that of exclusiveness and caution, but the return, instead of falling upon the head of the exclusive and cautious, falls upon a young head full of generous and unselfish plans. The girl loses something vital out of her life to which she is entitled. She is restricted and unhappy; her elders, meanwhile, are unconscious of the situation and we have all the elements of a tragedy.

We have in America a fast-growing number of cultivated young people who have no recognized outlet for their active faculties. They hear constantly of the great social maladjustment, but no way is provided for them to change it, and their uselessness hangs about them heavily. Huxley declares that the sense of use-lessness is the severest shock which the human system can sustain, and that if persistently sustained, it results in atrophy of function. These young people have had advantages of college, of European travel, and of economic study, but they are sustaining this shock of inaction. They have pet phrases, and they tell you that the things that make us all alike are stronger than the things that make us different. They say that all men are united by needs and sympathies far more permanent and radical than anything that temporarily divides them and sets them in opposition to each other. If they affect art, they say that the decay in artistic expression is due to the decay in ethics, that art when shut away from the human interests and from the great mass of humanity is self-destructive. They tell their elders with all the bitterness of youth that if they expect success from them in business or politics or in whatever lines their ambition for them has run, they must let them consult all of humanity; that they must let them find out what the people want and how they want it. It is only the stronger young people, however, who formulate this. Many of them dissipate their energies in so-called enjoyment. Others not content with that, go on studying and go back to college for their second degrees; not that they are especially fond of study, but because they want something definite to do, and their powers have been trained in the direction of mental accumulation. Many are buried beneath this mental accumulation with lowered vitality and discontent. Walter Besant says they have had the vision that Peter had when he saw the great sheet let, down from heaven, wherein was neither clean nor unclean. He calls it the sense of humanity. It is not philanthropy nor benevolence, but a thing fuller and wider than either of these.

This young life, so sincere in its emotion and good phrases and yet so undirected, seems to me as pitiful as the other great mass of destitute lives. One is supplementary to the other, and some method of communication can surely be devised. Mr. Barnett, who urged the first Settlement,—Toynbee Hall, in East London,—recognized this need of outlet for the young men of Oxford and Cambridge, and hoped that the Settlement would supply the communication. It is easy to see why the Settlement movement originated in England, where the years of education are more constrained and definite than they are here, where class distinctions are more rigid. The necessity of it was greater there, but we are fast feeling the pressure of the need and meeting the necessity for Settlements in America. Our young people feel nervously the need of putting theory into action, and respond quickly to the Settlement form of activity. Other motives which I believe make toward the Settlement are the result of a certain renaissance going forward in Christianity. The impulse to share the lives of the poor, the desire to make social service, irrespective of propaganda, express the spirit of Christ, is as Christianity itself. We have no proof from the records themselves that the early Roman Christians, who strained their simple art to the point of grotesqueness in their eagerness to record a "good news" on the walls of the catacombs, considered this good news a religion. Jesus had no set of truths labeled Religious. On the contrary, his doctrine was that all truth is one, that the appropriation of it is freedom. His teaching had no dogma to mark it off from truth and action in general. He himself called it a revelation - a life. These early Roman Christians received the Gospel message, a command to love all men, with a certain joyous simplicity. The image of the Good Shepherd is blithe and gay beyond the gentlest shepherd of Greek mythology; the hart no longer pants, but rushes to the water brooks. The Christians looked for the continuous revelation, but believed what Jesus said, that this revelation, to be retained and made manifest, must be put into terms of action; that action is the only medium man has for receiving and appropriating truth; that the doctrine must be known through the will.

That Christianity has to be revealed and embodied in the line of social progress is a corollary to the simple proposition, that man's action is found in his social relationships in the way in which he connects with his fellows; that his motives for action are the zeal and affection with which he regards his fellows. By this simple process was created a deep enthusiasm for humanity, which regarded man as at once the organ and the object of revelation; and by this process came about the wonderful fellowship, the true democracy of the early Church, that so captivates the imagination. The early Christians were preeminently nonresistant. They believed in love as a cosmic force. There was no iconoclasm during the minor peace of the Church. They did not yet denounce nor tear down temples, nor preach the end of the world. They grew to a mighty number, but it never occurred to them, either in their weakness or in their strength, to regard other men for an instant as their foes or as aliens. The spectacle of the Christians loving all men was the most astounding Rome had ever seen. They were eager to sacrifice themselves for the weak, for children, and for the aged; they identified themselves with slaves and did not avoid the plague; they longed to share the common lot that they might receive the constant revelation. It was a new treasure which the early Christians added to the sum of all treasures, a joy hitherto unknown in the world - the joy of finding the Christ which lieth in each man, but which no man can unfold save in fellowship. A happiness ranging from the heroic to the pastoral enveloped them. They were to possess a revelation as long as life had new meaning to unfold, new action to propose.

I believe that there is a distinct turning among many young men and women toward this simple acceptance of Christ's message. They resent the assumption that Christianity is a set of ideas which belong to the religious consciousness, whatever that may be. They insist that it cannot be proclaimed and instituted apart from the social life of the community and that it must seek a simple and natural expression in the social organism itself. The Settlement movement is only one manifestation of that wider humanitarian movement which throughout Christendom, but preeminently in England, is endeavoring to embody itself, not in a sect, but in society itself. I believe that this turning, this renaissance of the early Christian humanitarianism, is going on in America, in Chicago, if you please, without leaders who write or philosophize, without much speaking, but with a bent to express in social service and in terms of action the spirit of Christ. Certain it is that spiritual force is found in the Settlement movement, and it is also true that this force must be evoked and must be called into play before the success of any Settlement is assured. There must be the overmastering belief that all that is noblest in life is common to men as men, in order to accentuate the likenesses and ignore the differences which are found among the people whom the Settlement constantly brings into juxtaposition. It may be true, as the Positivists insist, that the very religious fervor of man can be turned into love for his race, and his desire for a future life into content to live in the echo of his deeds; Paul's formula of seeking for the Christ which lieth in each man and founding our likenesses on what seems a simpler formula to many of us.

In a thousand voices singing the Hallelujah Chorus in Handel's "Messiah," it is possible to distinguish the leading voices, but the differences of training and cultivation between them and the voices of the chorus, are lost in the unity of purpose and in the fact that they are all human voices lifted by a high motive. This is a weak illustration of what a Settlement attempts to do. It aims, in a measure, to develop whatever of social life its neighborhood may afford, to focus and give form to that life, to bring to bear upon it the results of cultivation and training; but it receives in exchange for the music of isolated voices the volume and strength of the chorus. It is quite impossible for me to say in what proportion or degree the subjective necessity which led to the opening of Hull-House combined the three trends : first, the desire to interpret democracy in social terms; secondly, the impulse beating at the very source of our lives, urging us to aid in the race progress; and, thirdly, the Christian movement toward humanitarianism. It is difficult to analyze a living thing; the analysis is at best imperfect. Many more motives may blend with the three trends; possibly the desire for a new form of social success due to the nicety of imagination, which refuses worldly pleasures unmixed with the joys of self-sacrifice; possibly a love of approbation, so vast that it is not content with the treble clapping of delicate hands, but wishes also to hear the bass notes from toughened palms, may mingle with these.

The Settlement, then, is an experimental effort to aid in the solution of the social and industrial problems which are engendered by the modern conditions of life in a great city. It insists that these problems are not confined to any one portion of a city. It is an attempt to relieve, at the same time, the overaccumulation at one end of society and the destitution at the other; but it assumes that this overaccumulation and destitution is most sorely felt in the things that pertain to social and educational advantages. From its very nature it can stand for no political or social propaganda. It must, in a sense, give the warm welcome of an inn to all such propaganda, if perchance one of them be found an angel. The one thing to be dreaded in the Settlement is that it lose its flexibility, its power of quick adaptation, its readiness to change its methods as its environment may demand. It must be open to conviction and must have a deep and abiding sense of tolerance. It must be hospitable and ready for experiment. It should demand from its residents a scientific patience in the accumulation of facts and the steady holding of their sympathies as one of the best instruments for that accumulation. It must be grounded in a philosophy whose foundation is on the solidarity of the human race, a philosophy which will not waver when the race happens to be represented by a drunken woman or an idiot boy. Its residents must be emptied of all conceit of opinion and all self-assertion, and ready to arouse and interpret the public opinion of their neighborhood. They must be content to live quietly side by side -with their neighbors, until they grow into a sense of relationship and mutual interests. Their neighbors are held apart by differences of race and language which the residents can more easily overcome. They are bound to see the needs of their neighborhood as a whole, to furnish data for legislation, and to use their influence to secure it. In short, residents are pledged to devote themselves to the duties of good citizenship and to the arousing of the social energies which too largely lie dormant in every neighborhood given over to industrialism. They are bound to regard the entire life of their city as organic, to make an effort to unify it, and to protest against its over-differentiation.

It is always easy to make all philosophy point one particular moral and all history adorn one particular tale; but I may be forgiven the reminder that the best speculative philosophy sets forth the solidarity of the human race; that the highest moralists have taught that without the advance and improvement of the whole, no man can hope for any lasting improvement in his own moral or material individual condition; and that the subjective necessity for Social Settlements is therefore identical with that necessity, which urges us on toward social and individual salvation.

Preaching the "Social Gospel"

Easily the most influential religious movement of the Progressive Era was the rise of the "Social Gospel", a disposition to apply the teachings of Christ to present-day social. economic, and political problems, and to urge activism on behalf of the disadvantaged as the ultimate test of true spirituality. It included both moderate Social Christians and more radical Christian Socialists. Among the most prominent exponents of the latter gospel was Walter Rauschenbusch (1861-1919), a theologian at the Rochester Theological Seminary who had been educated in Germany and served his apprenticeship in New York City's "Hell's Kitchen" district. His book Christianity and the Social Crisis, *(New York: Macmillan, 1907), is widely considered to be the "bible" of the Social Gospel. The following excerpt is taken from pp. 367-372.*

The spiritual force of Christianity should be turned against the materialism and mammonism of our industrial and social order. If a man sacrifices his human dignity and self-respect to increase his income, or stunts his intellectual growth and his human affections to swell his bank account, he is to that extent serving mammon and denying God. Likewise if he uses and injures the life of his fellow-men to make money himself, he serves mammon and denies God. But our industrial order does both. It makes property the end, and man the means to produce it.

Man is treated as a thing to produce more things. Men are hired as hands and not as men. They are paid only enough to maintain their working capacity and not enough to develop their manhood. When their working force is exhausted, they are flung aside without consideration of their human needs. Jesus asked, "Is not a man more than a sheep?" Our industry says "No." It is careful of its live stock and machinery, and careless of its human working force. It keeps its electrical engines immaculate in burnished cleanliness and lets its human dynamos sicken in dirt. In the 5th Assembly District in New York City, between 10th and 11th avenues, 1321 families in 1896 had three bathtubs between them. Our industrial establishments are institutions for the creation of dividends, and not for the fostering of human life. In all our public life the question of profit is put first. Pastor Stocker, in a speech on child and female labor in the German Reichstag, said: "We have put question the wrong way. We have asked: How much child and female labor does industry need in order to pay dividends, and to sell goods abroad? Whereas we ought to have asked: How ought industry to be organized in order to protect and foster the family, the human individual, and the Christian life?" That simple reversal of the question marks the difference between the Christian conception of life and property and the mammonistic.

"Life is more than food and raiment." More, too, than the apparatus which makes food and raiment. What is all the machinery of our industrial organization worth if it does not make human life healthful and happy? But is it doing that? Men are first of all men, folks, members of our human family. To view them first of all as labor force is civilized barbarism. It is the attitude of the exploiter. Yet unconsciously we have all been taught to take that attitude and talk of men as if they were horse-powers or volts. Our commercialism has tainted our sense of fundamental human verities and values. We measure our national prosperity by pig-iron and steel instead of by the welfare of the people. In city affairs the property owners have more influence than the family owners. For instance, the pall of coal smoke hanging over our industrial cities is injurious to the eyes; it predisposes to diseases of the respiratory organs; it depresses the joy of living; it multiplies the labor of housewives in cleaning and washing. But it continues because it would impose expense on business to install smoke consumers or pay skilled stokers. If an agitation is begun to abolish the smoke nuisance, the telling argument is not that it inflicts injury on the mass of human life, but that the smoke "hurts business," and that it really "pays" to consume the wasted carbon. In political life one can constantly see the cause of human life pleading long and vainly for redress, like the widow before the unjust judge. Then suddenly comes the bass voice of Property, and all men stand with hat in hand.

Our scientific political economy has long been an oracle of the false god. It has taught us to approach economic questions from the point of view of goods and not of man. It tells us how wealth is produced and divided and consumed by man, and not how man's life and development can best be fostered by material wealth. It is significant that the discussion of " Consumption" of wealth has been most neglected in political economy; yet that is humanly the most important of all. Theology must become christocentric; political economy must become anthropocentric. Man is Christianized when he puts God before self; political economy will be Christianized when it puts man before wealth. Socialistic political economy does that. It is materialistic in its theory of human life and history, but it is humane in its aims, and to that extent it is closer to Christianity than the orthodox science has been.

It is the function of religion to teach the individual to value his soul more than his body, and his moral integrity more than his income. In the same way it is the function of religion to teach society to value human life more than property, and to value property only in so far as it forms the material basis for the higher development of human life. When life and property are in apparent collision, life must take precedence. This is not only Christian, but prudent. When commercialism in its headlong greed deteriorates mass of human life, it defeats its own covetousness by killing the goose that lays the golden egg. Humanity is that goose—in more senses than one. It takes faith in the moral law to believe that this penny-wise craft is really suicidal folly and to assert that wealth which uses up the people paves the way to beggary. Religious men have been cowed by the prevailing materialism and arrogant selfishness of our business world. They should have the courage of religious faith and assert that "man liveth not by bread alone." but by doing the will of God and that the life of a nation "consisteth not in the abundance of things" which it produces, but in the way men live justly with one another and humbly with their God.

Professionalism and Social Activism

Strongly influenced by evangelical Protestantism and by his graduate studies in Germany, Richard T. Ely(1854-1943) was the primary founder of the American Economic Association and the chief exponent of its philosophy of "New Economics": the critical role of government as a vehicle for human progress, greater use of historical and empirical studies in place of the theories of classical economics, and amelioration of the conflict between capital and labor through the collaborative intervention of government, church, and other agencies. He was also an important pioneer of the Social Gospel, author of The Social Aspects of Christianity, *and teacher to hundreds of economists and social scientists who became community activists and government officials. In his autobiography* Ground Under Our Feet, *(New York: Macmillan, 1938),135-160, Ely describes the formation and principles of the American Economic Association.*

When it became evident that the "Society for the Study of National Economy" could not be established, I undertook to draw up a project for the formation of a society to be called "The American Economic Association," which should be broad enough to appeal to all the younger economists who, irrespective of their personal views, felt the stirring of the new life in economics and who wished to unite in order to secure complete liberty of thought and discussion, even if their thought led them to "unorthodox" conclusions. In the statement of our "objects" and "declaration of principles" I retained the central idea of the authors of the constitution of the "Society for the Study of National Economy," namely, that the dogma of "laissez faire" should be abandoned by our leaders. My "program," was a much simpler one and differed from theirs in two important particulars. In the first place, it emphasized historical and statistical study rather than deductive speculation, and, in the second place, it laid less stress on government intervention and, on the whole, was "toned down" in the direction of conservatism. It was designed to attract as many members as possible. The prospectus sent out read as follows:

American Economic Association

Objects of This Association

I.   The encouragement of economic research.
II. The publication of economic monographs.
III. The encouragement of perfect freedom in all economic discussion.
IV. The establishment of a bureau of information designed to aid all members with friendly counsels in their economic studies.

Platform

1. We regard the state as an educational and ethical agency whose positive aid is an indispensable condition of human progress. While we recognize the necessity of individual initiative in industrial life, we hold that the doctrine of laissez faire is unsafe in politics and unsound in morals; and that it suggests an inadequate explanation of the relations between the state and the citizens.

2. We do not accept the final statements which characterized the political economy of a past generation; for we believe that political economy is still in the first stages of its scientific development, and we look not so much to speculation as to an impartial study of actual conditions of economic life for the satisfactory accomplishment of that development. We seek the aid of statistics in the present, and of history in the past.

3. We hold that the conflict of labor and capital has brought to the front a vast number of social problems whose solution is impossible without the united efforts of church, state, and science.

4. In the study of the policy of government, especially with respect to restrictions on trade and to protection of domestic manufactures, we take no partisan attitude. We are convinced that one of the chief reasons why greater harmony has not been attained is because economists have been too ready to assert themselves as advocates. We believe in a progressive development of economic conditions which must be met by corresponding changes of policy.

The Gospel of Business Efficiency

Few Progressive Era organizations exerted more influence in practical government and politics than the National Municipal League, which was founded in 1894 by representatives of over 250 civic clubs. At its annual National Conference for Good City Government, the NML advocated various structural changes in urban government and politics, and developed a comprehensive model city charter designed to produce honesty, efficiency, and economy. Two of its most widely adopted innovations were the commission and city manager forms of governance. In the following excerpt, one of its leading authorities, Harry Aubrey Toulmin, The City Manager: A New Profession, *New York: Appleton,1915), 259-262, makes the case for professionalism in municipal government.*

Essentials: Three radical principles are essential to a modern municipal administration. First, candidates must be tested on the basis of efficiency, not political faithfulness; technical men must be selected for technical jobs and business men for policy-forming positions. Second, publicity and responsibility of a few well-known men are the necessary prerequisites for results. Third, business methods must be utilized in a business corporation.

These three vital objects were the ambition of the charter framers of the city manager plans. Efficiency, publicity, and concentrated responsibility stand the triple commandments of the new gospel of government.

Efficiency: Business of any complication demands trained men to guide it. Municipal officers are no exception to the rule. England, Germany and France have a body of municipal officials of long training who regard the work as a professional man would regard his own. Why should not we, being of practical genius, adopt so obvious a plan? We are adopting one. We have not done so sooner, for one excellent reason, because there has been until now no class of men of this type from which to draw competent municipal executives. We have a professional administrator now. The city manager plan secures efficiency through the employment of an expert municipal governor. His technical training, his business experience, and his knowledge of city needs are valuable adjuncts to executive ability. They are the highroad for the application of his personality. This insures efficiency.

Concentration: The civic system is simplified. The whole city is unified under one management; the municipality is vigorously controlled under one competent responsible head. A city, no more than an individual, can realize its fullest promise under an dual personality. The city manager plan provides, therefore, concentrated responsibility. The legislative function is left unimpaired. Men of sound business experience under this plan can feel free to accept, without detriment to their private interests, the position of commissioner. It is within the scope of their experience and they can bring to the position the valuable ideas of a ripe business judgment; and furthermore, this plan con- templates that this body of business men, styled the commission, who are trained in the selecting and fitting of men to their duties, shall select the manager. The selection of the chiefest personal factor is left to them. Two advantages result. On the one hand, there is no trust put in the dangerous method of allowing a selection of an expert by popular elections at short intervals; on the other hand, the people do not have the restriction im- posed on them in selecting commissioners, of electing at the same time in the same persons those who are capable of the twin duties of legislation and administration.

Publicity: Intelligent action of a voter can only be exercised. when he is thoroughly equipped with reliable information. Public hearings on the budget, readable and understandable publications as to the city's financial and physical condition, a public reason publicly stated for the transaction of a public affair, all constitute a great guardianship of civic interests. To know is to understand, to understand is to interest, to interest is to treat with success.

Questions

1. *To what extent do each of the Progressive Era activists seem to be motivated by their religious convictions? By the natural and social sciences? By the "languages" of social bonds and social efficiency?*
2. *Which of the interpretations given by the modern-day scholars comes closest to providing a comprehensive explanation that each of the Progressive Era activists might accept? Are there any interpretations that at least some of the contemporary activists would reject?*
3. *Imagine a discussion among the three modern-day scholars and Benjamin Parke DeWitt over the merits of his three "essential tendencies." What areas of agreement and disagreement would likely emerge?*
4. *Compare and contrast Howe's recommendations for urban reform with those of Toulmin and the National Municipal League. Which would the modern-day scholars regard as the more "progressive" of the two? Which one would each of the other activists most likely favor?*
5. *Based upon your analysis of both the primary and secondary sources contained in this module, write a paragraph explaining the essence of "progressivism."*

FURTHER READING

The historical literature on the Progressive Era is voluminous. The best gateway is through two reference works: John D. Buenker and Nicholas C. Burckel, eds., Progresssive Reform: A Guide to Information Sources *(Detroit, 1980) and John D. Buenker and Edward R. Kantowicz, eds.,* Historical Dictionary of the Progressive Era, 1890-1920, *(New York, 1988). Fuller exposition of some of the most influential interpretations by modern day scholars are Arthur Mann, ed.,* The Progressive Era: Major Issues of Interpretation, *(Hinsdale, IL, 1975), David M. Kennedy, ed.,* Progressivism: The Critical Issues, *(Boston, 1971), Arthur Mann, "The Progressive Tradition" in John Higham, ed.,* The Reconstruction of American History, *(New York, 1962, and Robert H. Wiebe, "The Progressive Years, 1900-1917," in William H. Cartwright and Richard L. Watson, eds.,* The Reinterpretation of American History and Culture, *(Washington, DC, 1973). An excellent topical anthology is Lewis L. Gould, ed.,* The Progressive Era, *(Syracuse, NY, 1974). The variety of municipal reform efforts is the theme of Michael H. Ebner and Eugene M. Tobin, eds.,* The Age of Urban Reform: New Perspectives on the Progressive Era, *(Port Washington, N.Y., 1977). More advanced students may be able to benefit from a reading of four specialized works: David B. Danbom,* The World of Hope: Progressives and the Struggle for an Ethical Public Life, *(Philadelphia, 1987); James T. Kloppenberg,* Uncertain Victory: Social Democracy and Progressivism in European and American Thought, 1870-1920, *(New York, 1986); Eldon J. Eisenach,* The Lost Promise of Progressivism, *(Lawrence, KS, 1994), and Daniel T. Rodgers,* Atlantic Crossings: Social Politics in a Progressive Age, *(Cambridge, MA, 1998).*

The Grueling Battle for Woman Suffrage

Susan M. Hartmann

INTRODUCTION

Women voiced their first formal demand for the ballot at the Seneca Falls convention in 1848. It took seventy-two years to win ratification of the Nineteenth Amendment to the Constitution granting women throughout the United States the right to vote in 1920. Not all women had to wait that long. By 1890 women in sixteen states had partial suffrage, that is, they could vote in school board or other local elections. Wyoming became the first state to grant women full suffrage in 1890, followed by Colorado, Utah, and Idaho in the next six years. These victories invigorated anti-suffrage forces, and thereafter the suffrage movement endured one defeat after another. Using a state-by-state approach, between 1896 and 1909 women attempted dozens of times to get legislatures to authorize popular referenda on suffrage. They obtained only six referenda, and lost every one. But after 1910, when the state of Washington enfranchised women, the momentum shifted to the suffrage forces.

Suffragists were overwhelmingly native born, white, and middle class, and they sometimes used nativist and racist arguments to advance their cause. The National American Woman Suffrage Association (NAWSA) distanced itself from black women eager to work for the ballot, but by 1910 some activists had begun to strengthen the crusade by mobilizing across class and ethnic lines. With an expanded constituency, suffragists continued to struggle state by state, but they increasingly focused on the national level and an amendment to the federal Constitution.

The effort gained momentum when a new group split off from NAWSA. First called the Congressional Union and then the National Woman's Party (NWP), it energized the movement with

Some of the opposition to the enfranchisement of women was obviously based on the prejudices of individuals. But the more closely one looks, the clearer it becomes that suffragists faced far more than mere conservative opinion; no distaste for women in new social roles, no feeling about the sanctity of motherhood or the sacredness of the home could account for the animus that expressed itself in highly organized and articulate form against women as voters, becoming increasingly intemperate as woman suffrage spread slowly from one state to another.

Where did the multitude of anti-suffrage organizations, male and female, that cropped up across the country come from? Who supplied the organizers and the witnesses at legislative and Congressional hearings, so often masculine in gender? Who paid the bills for the stream of newspaper articles and advertisements, the hoardings and handbills? Who bought the referendum votes that were stolen from the suffragists? . . . Who paid for the immigrant and saloon vote in city after city, state after state, in suffrage elections from the Dakotas to New Jersey? . . .

Inevitably the main source of opposition varied from one part of the country to the other. In the South the source of sentiment lay in fear of the Negro vote—in fear of strengthening any attempts to overthrow the system of Jim Crow restrictions (including the poll tax) which, in defiance of the Fourteenth and Fifteenth amendments, disfranchised the colored population. In the Middle West much of the opposition stemmed from the brewing interests; in the East from industrial and business sources.

The original "anti" leaders were women of irreproachable social position, like the wives of General Sherman and Admiral Dahlgren, who as early as 1872 headed one thousand signers to a petition to the United States Senate against granting woman suffrage. In 1882, in opposition to the campaign for the municipal vote for women in Massachusetts, two women "remonstrants" appeared at a legislative hearing on the bill, but preserved their modesty by presenting a written statement instead of verbal testimony against the proposed bill. . . .

In 1895 to combat the drive to put woman suffrage into the revised New York state constitution (an attempt which failed), anti-suffragists, men and women, organized in New York, and the Massachusetts group re-formed itself into the Massachusetts Association Opposed to the Further Extension of Suffrage to Women; it continued the most active and vocal, although similar organizations eventually appeared in some twenty states. In 1911 a National Association Opposed to Woman Suffrage was formed in New York, headed by Mrs. Arthur M. Dodge.

Almost without exception the women in these organizations were ladies of means and social position. The main burden of their argument was that woman suffrage placed an additional and unbearable burden on women, whose place was in the home; the fact that this argument came largely from women whose housework was done by an adequate force of servants and that they presumed to speak for women less fortunately placed, never seemed to disturb the "antis," who also argued that they did not need political suffrage since their menfolk represented them and cared for their interests.

No one in the suffrage camp credited the "antis" with great effectiveness. Their arguments seemed too puerile and roused more than one woman who eventually became a suffrage leader to thought and action. While the antis' appearance at hearings and in print, through a flood of pamphlets and letters to the newspapers, did furnish legislators with the excuse that a body of respectable women did not want the vote, their real role in the opinion of the women working with Mrs. Catt was to serve as a front for more potent forces working against woman suffrage, principally the liquor interests. Mrs. Catt declared categorically that "a trail led from the women's organizations into the liquor camp and it was traveled by the men the women antis employed. . . .["]

The anonymity in which the brewers preferred to carry on their opposition to woman suffrage was punctured in 1918 by a Senate Judiciary Committee investigating charges of propaganda carried on by them during the war in both Bolshevik and German interests. The complaints which had for years flooded suffrage headquarters after every referendum received unexpected authoritative documentation when the subpoenaing of the files of Percy Andreae, who masterminded much of the brewers' publicity, turned up such letters as one marked "confidential" to a Milwaukee brewing concern in 1914:

> In regard to the matter of woman suffrage, we are trying to keep from having any connection with it whatever. We

These suffragists picketing the White House in 1917 carry a banner exposing the contradiction between President Woodrow Wilson's wartime rhetoric about democracy and his refusal to support democracy at home by supporting woman suffrage. Their banner quotes his war message, "We shall fight for the things which we have always carried near our hearts, for Democracy, for the right of those who submit to authority to have a voice in their government." (Courtesy of The Library of Congress.)

are, however, in a position to establish channels of communication with the leaders of the anti-suffrage movement for our friends in any state where suffrage is an issue. I am under the impression that a new anti-suffrage association has been organized in Illinois and is a retail liquor dealers affair. I consider it most dangerous to have the retailers identified or active in any way in this fight, as it will be used against us everywhere.

A brewers' strategy conference on October 13, 1913, whose minutes unaccountably survived (since it was the practice of the brewers' organizations to keep neither minutes nor financial records), revealed their role in more than one woman suffrage referendum defeat. An organizer for the brewers declared that in Nebraska, woman suffrage was defeated in 1911 at tremendous expense. His report for Wisconsin stated: "We have had the usual bills, like every other state—county option (liquor selling), women's suffrage in about six different forms and we have had everything else, which were all defeated; and I say that can be done only by organization and by active work of the brewers being on the job all the time and not leaving it to somebody else." . . .

The means employed by the liquor groups to achieve their goal went beyond buying editorial support for their "educational campaigns" or open editorial opposition, or allocating quotas to saloon keepers and bartenders of the number of customers for whose appearance and "no" vote at the polls they would be held accountable. Their influence reached openly into the halls of legislation. The Lieutenant-Governor of Wisconsin, as one instance alone, told Mrs. Ben Hooper, one of Mrs. Catt's most active co-workers, that he had seen the Milwaukee lawyer who "lobbied" for the brewers "sit in the gallery of the Senate and tell his men with his hands how to vote." As late as 1918, with Prohibition staring them in the face, lobbyists for the brewers were still lobbying against the woman suffrage amendment in Washington.

It is more difficult to pinpoint some of the other elements in the opposition to woman suffrage. Easiest to identify, after the liquor groups, were the political machines, whose weight was invariably thrown against votes for women until Tammany Hall gave up in 1917. Machine men were plainly uncertain of their ability to control an addition to the electorate which seemed to them relatively unsusceptible to bribery, more militant, and bent on disturbing reforms ranging from better sewage control to the abolition of child labor and, worst of all, "cleaning up" politics. The arguments many suffragists used in their own behalf, such as the inherent interest of women in such improvements as better schools or protective legislation for women workers, sounded in the ears of the machine bosses like the trumpet of doom. . . .

Most difficult of all to link with the opposition to woman suffrage were the business interests. The proceedings of the annual conventions of the National Association of Manufacturers and the U. S. Chamber of Commerce, or the pages of the *Wall Street Journal,* do not contain a word of protest against granting women the vote. There was no nation-wide mobilization of Big Business against woman suffrage. Yet some business groups fought suffrage tenaciously and bitterly, albeit with the greatest circumspection. One suffrage organizer after another reported the presence and activity of railroad, oil, and general manufacturing lobbies, whenever suffrage was up for legislative action or referendum.

In March 1916 Mrs. Catt was in Iowa, with a state referendum scheduled for June and what looked like a good chance of victory. Yet already a cloud no bigger than one man's hand was visible:

> That man Maling is in Iowa doing dirty work. I had a talk with him myself, and . . . I have called on one and all to institute an investigation as to who or what is backing this man. He is saying that it is the business interests of Colorado. I half believe it. I am a bit fearful that the banks, mine owners and other big business are really sending along an official warning to the men of the other states to beware of this terrible menace of woman suffrage, but, if it is so, it is better to smoke our enemy out and know where he is.

There were other instances. In the course of a Congressional investigation into the affairs of Swift & Company, the meat packers were shown to have made secret contributions to the "antis"—secret because the company recognized that eventually woman suffrage was likely to "sweep the country." An appeal to Nebraska voters to vote against the woman suffrage referendum in that state in 1914 carried the signatures of nine railroad and municipal transit executives, seven bankers, and other assorted businessmen, leavened by those of two Episcopalian ministers. . . .

In Massachusetts, where the "antis" were so entrenched that defeat of the state referendum in 1915 left suffrage workers hopeless of progress by the state method, the *Woman's Journal* looked

Five thousand suffragists marched in the first suffrage parade in 1913 in Washington, D.C. The parade was scheduled to coincide with the inauguration of President Woodrow Wilson. (Courtesy of Brown Brothers, Sterling, PA.)

into the election expense reports which the law required be filed with the Secretary of State. Reports from three anti-suffrage organizations showed the majority of their contributions coming from individuals, four fifths of them from men. An amount of $31,695 was reported from 135 men, an average of $235 apiece. The outraged *Journal* asked, "What sort of man can afford to sign a check for $235 with which to fight the enfranchisement of women?" and answered its own question: "the powerful directors of the moneyed section of Boston."

It is not too difficult to see why such corporate interests as railroads, oil companies, and other manufacturers were opposed to giving women the vote. The Federal Income Tax, which had been authorized by the Sixteenth Amendment to the constitution in 1913, had been bitterly opposed as "communistic"; so had popular election of United States Senators, provided by the Seventeenth Amendment in the same year. Other elements of the "New Freedom," such as the institution of the Federal Reserve banking system, the Tariff Commission and the Federal Trade Commission, along with new anti-trust legislation and a widespread movement for the initiative and referendum, all appeared as cumulative threats to vested interests. In such circumstances, the addition of a large body of new voters, control of which appeared uncertain and many of whose leaders were vocal in the cause of further reform, presented a fresh menace. What might not such an infusion into the body politic do to the enormous advantages concealed in grants to railroads, franchises of various kinds, and rate schedules? . . .

There was also a strong feeling, particularly in some of the industries that would be most closely affected, that women would use the vote to improve the conditions of working women. The National Council of Women Voters, which had been organized in 1911 as an abortive attempt to gather together the voting strength of the enfranchised women in the West, had stated as its threefold purpose: extension of equal suffrage to other states; changing conditions in the suffrage states to improve conditions for women, children and the home; and "to claim justice for women in the political and economic world." The legislative record of some states which had enjoyed woman suffrage for a number of years could be used to substantiate such a view; so could innumerable speeches and articles by women like Florence Kelley, Margaret Dreier Robins, Leonora O'Reilly, and others, as well as publications issued by the National [Council of Women Voters] itself.

The men from northern states who led the fight against the suffrage amendment on the floor of the United States Senate were spokesmen for business interests, and the fact was spread out in their voting record on a score of measures. Senator Wadsworth of New York who did not alter by one jot his opposition to suffrage after his state gave its women the vote in 1917 also voted against the income tax, the direct primary, the taxation of war profits, and an investigation of Wall Street. Senator Weeks, leader of the Republican machine in Massachusetts, voted against the direct election of senators, the income tax, taxation of war profits, and the establishment of the Federal Trade Commission. . . . The reputation of Brandegee of Connecticut was such that even the impersonal Dictionary of American Biography noted that "his influence was largely negative, if not reactionary in effect"; he opposed the direct election of Senators, extension of parcel post, the Federal Reserve system, and the income tax.

These men alone would not have been able to delay the suffrage amendment as long as they did without the support of the large majority of southern Democrats. For decades the question of woman suffrage had carried, for politicians and the dominant interests in the South, some of the same explosive impact of desegregation today [1974], as a threat to established social, economic, and political patterns. . . .

This keynote sounded through most of the speeches in the Senate against the amendment in the closing battle, as in the words of Senator Smith of South Carolina, who was assailing the few southerners who supported woman suffrage by constitutional amendment:

> I warn every man here today that when the test comes, as it will come, when the clamor for Negro rights shall have come, that you Senators from the South voting for it have started it here this day. . . . If it was a crime to enfranchise the male half of this race, why is it not a crime to enfranchise the other half? . . . [A]nd when the time comes, as it will, when you meet the results of this act, you cannot charge that it was a crime to pass the 15th amendment. . . . By thus adding the word "sex" to the 15th amendment you have just amended it to liberate them all, when it was perfectly competent for the legislatures of the

several states to so frame their laws as to preserve our civilization without entangling legislation involving women of the black race.

Nor were the Southerners alone in voicing this point of view. Senators Wadsworth of New York and Reed of Missouri took the states' rights position to the point where they declared they would vote against a federal amendment *forbidding* woman suffrage! And Borah of Idaho, who always based his opposition on the states' rights issue, declared that he had no wish to add to the already heavy burden borne by the South. . . .

Borah was not the most striking example of the strange coalition which, despite everyday partisan alignments, faced the suffrage amendment down to the final vote. With regard to the tacit filibuster which prevented a vote on the amendment a whole year before the end, the *Woman Citizen,* in the person of Alice Stone Blackwell, commented acidly:

> It was clear that Senator Lodge (Rep.) of Massachusetts was the leader and general floor manager for the opposition, but the loving camaraderie between the "wilful few" Republicans and the "wilful few" Democrats who in normal relations do not waste time in each other's company, was an amazing sight to the galleries. Mr. Lodge of Massachusetts and Mr. Ellison Smith of South Carolina, Mr. Brandegee of Connecticut, Mr. Martin of Virginia, Mr. Wadsworth of New York, Mr. Underwood of Alabama, as divided as the Kaiser and the King of England in most matters, were as united as twin brothers in defending the nation against the "awful disaster to the nation should women be enfranchised by the Federal Amendment." . . . [B]ut it cannot record the pictures of Republicans and Democrats with arms around each other's necks, with Democrats slapping Republicans on the back in token of a common jubilation that they had scored a mighty victory in preventing the Senate from taking a vote!

"The unholy alliance," Mrs. Catt christened this combination after she and Mrs. Park, watching from the gallery, had once seen Lodge of Massachusetts and Martin of Virginia standing arm-in-arm at the back of the chamber, comparing notes. It did not in the end prevent women from getting the vote, but it caused far more delay and difficulty than one would ever imagine from reading the usual phrase in the history books, announcing that American women were enfranchised after World War I.

Ladies Against Women

Suffragists tended to dismiss their female opponents as members of an economic elite who feared losing their privileges and/or as dupes of the liquor interests. In the following account, however, historian Carl Degler argues that women played the crucial role in blocking the suffrage campaign and suggests reasons why some women would oppose their own emancipation. The account is taken from Carl N. Degler, At Odds: Women and the Family in America from the Revolution to the Present *(New York, 1980), 349–58, 360–61.*

[T]he active opposition of thousands of women was one of the most striking aspects of the struggle for the vote . . . Historians who favor woman suffrage have either ignored the anti-suffragists or dismissed them as women who were merely expressing the opposition of their husbands. But the size, persistence, and activities, not to mention the character of the leadership of the anti-suffrage groups, beginning in the 1890s, belie the argument that the opposition was male-directed. . . .

The reason why women, alone of all social groups, organized against their own political emancipation is that many women perceived in the suffrage a threat to the family, a threat so severe that the vote did not seem worth the possible cost. Although the anti-suffrage case comprised almost an infinite number of arguments and justifications—as the pro-suffrage case did, too—behind all the arguments and justifications loomed the fear that bestowing the ballot upon women would force an alteration in the traditional family. The argument runs all through the anti-suffrage literature from the 1880s right down to 1920.

Underlying the anti-suffrage arguments was the fundamental assumption that the natures of women and men were different. As an anti-suffrage document submitted to the Illinois legislature in 1897 phrased it, the pivotal question is that "of sex. We believe that men are ordained to govern in all forceful and material matters, *because they are men,* physically and intellectually strong, virile, aggressive; while women, by the same decree of God and nature, are equally fitted to bear rule in a higher and more spiritual realm, where the strong frame and the weighty brain count for less, but the finer fibre of the woman's body and the spiritual uplift of her affection and her soul are the indications of a power not less than that of a man, and even more necessary to the progress and elevation of the race." This was, of course, a biological justification of the old principle of the separate spheres. And though it denied the identity of the sexes, it asserted their equality, with perhaps a slight edge to women.

Some anti-suffragists were even more precise in equating the intellectual abilities of men and women, while asserting their basic difference in character. "You cannot dodge the fact women have work in the world that men cannot do, and it is equally true that men have work that women cannot do," contended Ann Watkins in 1912. "Neither man nor woman is superior or inferior to the other; the two are just different, positive and negative, two great manifestations of a still greater force." . . .

What differentiated the Antis from the Suffs was not their conceptions of the differences between men and women, but the Antis' denial of *individual* differences in women. The Antis thought and acted much as racists—they assumed that all people in a given biological category—in this case women—were alike and so much so that social policy—the suffrage—should be based on that assumption. "The Anti-Suffragists grant the equality of sexes," wrote a well-known Anti in 1909. "Men are no better than women and science assures us that they are no more intelligent. But the Anti insists that the *difference* between the sexes shall not be ignored." The work of the two sexes, wrote another anti-suffragist, was "not to be measured by the same standard of values." It was their differences that made "any home a symmetrical thing. . . . We do those things for which we are best fitted by physical and mental powers." The response of the Antis to the suffragists' contention that sex had nothing to do with work, she continued, was that *"sex happens to be the pivot upon which the whole question turns.* It has fixed our place in the home and in the world, and no matter how far astray we go mentally from our right appreciation of this truth, sex will inexorably drive us back to wifehood and motherhood until the world ends." It was the feminists' and suffragists' counter-assertion that some women could perform the work of men that fully exposed the quasi-racist, anti-individualist assumptions of the Antis. "That woman could develop better under masculine conditions of life," contended Margaret Robinson in 1916, "is a totally unsupported theory. Woman cannot become man—she can only become a poor imitation. She develops best along the lines of her aptitudes and instincts." . . .

Alice George thought the suffrage must disrupt the family because of its emphasis upon women's individuality. Should the vote be granted, she wrote, "the whole sweep of relations of the sexes must be revised, if the woman's vote is to mean anything more than two people doing what one does now." For if women simply duplicated the votes of men there would be no purpose in giving them the suffrage. Yet if women used the vote as individuals with interests different from those of their husbands, then we "reinforce those who clamor for individual rights" and "strike at the family as the self-governing unit upon which the state is built." . . . To Helen Johnson, the fundamental threat of the suffrage was that it brought "the possibility of civil war . . . to the door of every family."

If the suffragists worried about the lack of interest the mass of women showed in achieving the suffrage, the anti-suffragists made capital out of it. The more perceptive of them recognized the women's apathy or hostility toward the suffrage stemmed from the threat it posed to the family. Caroline Corbin, one of the leading anti-suffragists in Illinois, made the point in the form of a question as early as 1887. If women become politically and economically independent, she inquired, "what then becomes of marriage and the home? Is there any escape from the conviction that the industrial and political independence of women would be the wreck of our present domestic institutions? May it not be possible," she asked, "that an intuitive sense that woman suffrage is incompatible with the present relations of men and women in the home, has something to do with the fact that . . . an overwhelming majority of women do not desire the ballot?" She might have added that the refusal of most suffragists and feminists to acknowledge the conflict between the family and women's emancipation was in itself a sure sign that there was a threat. . . .

In the end, then, the conflict between the Suffs and the Antis was over whether women ought to be treated as individuals or as subordinates who served the family. . . . The Antis attacked Elizabeth Cady Stanton's *Woman's Bible* because it frankly emphasized women's thinking of themselves rather than of others—that is, acting as self-interested individuals. "What sort of a 'next generation' would evolve," asked the *Anti-Suffragist* in 1909, "if all women considered their 'first duty' to be themselves, and overlooked the fact that their strongest power and highest possibility is that of unselfish—and often unnoticed—service." This is also why many anti-suffragist women were among the leaders in the opposition to easier divorce laws, for they saw in divorce not only a sign of family instability but a heightened sense of self among women, which they could only deplore. Helen K. Johnson, the author of a major anti-suffrage book, for example, was also a leader in the opposition to any easing of the divorce laws. The Antis also asserted that divorce was easier in those states where woman suffrage prevailed. . . .

If a perceived threat to the family explains why women were reluctant to support the suffrage, we are still left with the question of how it was that the suffrage finally was accepted in 1920. Two kinds of reasons suggest themselves.

First of all, there was the powerful and well-organized campaign mounted by the suffragists, especially after 1910. Just about then a decision was made by the suffrage leadership to abandon the fifty-year-long campaign to win the suffrage state by state and to concentrate upon amending the federal Constitution. After all, as late as 1910 no more than four states, all of them small and western, had enacted full suffrage for women. Once the decision was made to fight for a federal amendment, the suffrage leaders moved to win over Congress and the President, much more concentrated targets than some forty state legislatures. Notable in this regard was the intense and often violent campaign of the radical wing of the suffragists in 1913–14, led by the indefatigable Alice Paul. Emulating the passive-resistance tactics of the contemporary English women's movement, suffragists picketed the White House, chained themselves to fences, and, when taken to jail, went on hunger strikes. There they resisted the brutality of forced feeding and, when freed, went back to jail immediately and eagerly. Meanwhile membership in the more conventional organizations swelled, and the propaganda and political pressure mounted. Although in 1915 referenda on woman suffrage were defeated in four eastern states, the proponents came close to winning. They captured 46 per cent of the total in Pennsylvania, 42 per cent in New York and New Jersey, and 35 per cent in Massachusetts. President Wilson himself supported suffrage when he voted that year in New Jersey. Membership in the National American Woman Suffrage Association reached almost two million members, with a gross income of three-quarters of a million dollars a year. In short, by 1915 the suffrage had been raised to a national political issue, causing the Progressive and Republican parties officially to endorse the suffrage in time for the election of 1916. . . .

The second reason why resistance to the suffrage was finally overcome has to do with a decline in the fear that the suffrage threatened the family. During the first decade or so of the 20th century it became increasingly clear that, whatever the suffrage might portend in theory, in fact it was not a threat to the family. By 1910 woman suffrage had been tried in four states for over a decade; yet there nothing much had changed, one way or another. . . .

The most important reason of all why many women could forget about their apprehension that the suffrage threatened the family was that the justifications for the suffrage shifted ground in the early 20th century. The original and most common argument on behalf of woman suffrage in the 19th century had been that which has been sketched in previous pages—namely, that votes for women symbolized their individuality, their sense of self-interest, their need to be able to speak politically as individuals. Feminists and suffragists like Elizabeth Cady Stanton pushed that argument hard, contending that no man could speak for a woman, any more than a white person could speak for a black. Suffrage was justified on the grounds that women were individual human beings, who must express their own preferences individually.

By the opening years of the 20th century, however, the original suffragist leaders had passed from the scene, and the old appeal to individual rights as the basis for the suffrage for women was gradually abandoned. The principal reason it was dropped was that it was not working. . . . At the same time, the advancement of women in education, business, professions, and in a great variety of social and reform organizations by the early 20th century suggested a more practical argument in support of the suffrage. The new justification was that women had a special contribution to make to society, something that men could not provide. This special contribution, so the argument went, came from their character as women—as wives and mothers, as homemakers. Jane Addams, for example, pointed out early in the 20th century that the problems of modern cities were those that women had long been familiar with: child labor, unsanitary housing, adulterated food, and so forth. "May we not say," she asked, "that city housekeeping has failed partly because women, the traditional housekeepers,

This poster presents a typical suffrage argument—that women should have the right to vote because of their role as mothers. (Courtesy of the North Carolina Museum of History.)

have not been consulted as to its multiform activities?" And in 1914 Alice Stone Blackwell urged woman suffrage on the ground that it would have a salutary effect on foreign policy because women were different from men. "Let us do our utmost to hasten the day when the wishes of the mothers shall have their due weight in public affairs, knowing that by so doing we hasten the day when wars shall be no more." In short, politics and voting were but an extension of the home, so they needed the special character of women to improve them. Suffrage now became a way of extending women's special sphere to society, rather than being a way of providing political expression for women's self-interest as individuals. Those suffragists who advanced such a defense of the suffrage were, in effect, arguing that women's character as a sex should be represented, but not a woman's interest as an individual. This new justification for the suffrage was thus very close to the Antis' assertion that women as a group were basically different from men. In the process, of course, that assertion played down, if it did not deny outright, a woman's individuality. It fitted in well, however, with the idea that woman's place in the family was as helper and nurturer of others, and thus supported, rather than threatened, the traditional relation between husband and wife in the family. . . .

. . . [T]he suffrage fight has been treated as a conservative reform, which is certainly the way it was defended in the last stages of the campaign. In fact, though, the suffrage was the political side of a drive for woman's individuality that was re-shaping the traditional family. The suffrage may have been only a first step in the achievement of women's equality, rather than the last one that the suffragists contended. Yet it was certainly an integral and necessary part of that long revolution concerning woman's place through which American society is still passing.

Questions

---

1. *Why would liquor interests devote funds to blocking woman suffrage instead of focusing their resources on preventing prohibition? Does Flexner's evidence convince you that other corporate interests worked against suffrage? According to Flexner, why did they do so? Why did the strongest opposition to woman suffrage come from the South?*
2. *To what extent can we say that women's opposition to suffrage represented a rational calculation of their self-interest?*
3. *Should the woman suffrage movement be characterized as conservative or radical? How great a change do you think its achievement brought to American society?*
4. *Do you find any parallels between the opponents of woman suffrage and the groups that oppose feminist goals today?*

Arguments and Actions

As befitted their views of women's appropriate roles, anti-suffrage women conducted their campaigns more quietly than their opponents. They testified before state legislatures and Congress, gave public speeches, and wrote profusely, as did the men on their side. Suffragists used words just as vigorously, but the elusiveness of their goal drove them to bolder, more innovative, and more extensive efforts. The following documents illustrate the arguments used by anti-suffragists and the strategies and tactics employed by suffragists.

The Threat to the Home

From 1911 to 1916, Mrs. Arthur M. Dodge, a Vassar-educated, wealthy widow and mother of six sons, led the National Association Opposed to Woman Suffrage. Dodge devoted her public life to the anti-suffrage cause and to the day nursery movement, whose goals were to provide care for children of employed mothers and inculcate American middle-class values into the children of immigrants. In this selection, Dodge's views on suffrage are quoted in Edward Marshall, "Our Suffrage Movement is Flirtation on a Big Scale," New York Times, May 25, 1913, Sec. V.

"Never has there been a propaganda so destructive of great values as that which women now are preaching, marching, dancing, dressing. While suffrage must inevitably lead to the destruction of the old home idea, it offers for it not the slightest substitute.

"Even the word 'home' is becoming a rare joke among the suffragists. From their platforms they continually ridicule us—the anti-suffragists—because we talk of it.

"That is a sad state of things isn't it? Home has been the woman's business and her love and life for centuries. It is the foundation of society, the basis of all morals. Without the home we should become unmoral and without morals society, in turn, must perish.

"No man ever made a home. It has been ever women's work. If she refuses to accomplish it, then it must remain undone; if it remains undone, what can ensue but something close related to a social reign of terror? . . .

"When women cease to strive to learn the art of home-making then will the world indeed go wrong. And all this agitation of the present day trends certainly in that direction.

"The tendencies toward feminism and toward socialism both find in home the chief object of attack, although only the Socialists are brave enough to make acknowledgment of this. One, not less than the other, means its loss.

"The old-time woman made herself the idol of the world not through stump speeches or mad 'hikes,' (leaving her little ones to hired nurses' care,) but through her sacrifices. Each of the great moral teachers has assured us and has proved by his own life that in sacrifice must lie the greatest of achievements. . . .

"To offset the suspicion in the public mind that suffrage means destruction to the home, the leaders of the movement are now bending every effort to prove otherwise. Watch the newspapers and periodicals of recent days and those of days immediately to come and you will find a flood of pictures showing suffrage leaders with their progressive cheeks pressed tight against the velvet faces of their babies. They doubtless have decided that this variation of the plan of their publicity is necessary as a means of proving to the public that a suffragist can be a mother.

"And in thinking of this matter men must not fail to take count of the link between the suffragists and Socialists. I have already spoken of it. It cannot too often be brought to the public mind. As suffrage grows in strength so socialism grows in strength, and vice versa. California, Oregon, Kansas—all these States were carried for the suffrage cause by Socialistic votes. . . .

Don't Know What They Are Doing.

"I don't want to seem discourteous toward my sisters in the suffrage movement. I believe the greater portion of them are not really aware of what they do. I am certain the majority of them do not desire to bring about destruction of the home, with all that must imply—of loose or no domestic life; I believe many of them to be good mothers, and that among their younger workers may be many girls who are not infected and who will not become infected with a horror of the highest function given to woman by her God, that of motherhood. . . .

"I am no advocate of retrogression among women. I believe in education, culture, full development. In these days woman, to do the best which in her lies for her own home, must get much for it from outside. My point is that she must get these outside things for the benefit of her home and not neglect her home so that she may go adventuring for them for her own benefit, amusement, and dissipation.

"I am not certain that in suffrage influences may not be found the causes which are making good homes fewer, families smaller, marriages later. Suffrage and the voluntary or forced entrance of woman into industrial life is the greatest threat against the home. In a nation's homes lies its strength. It would be a world-tragedy if woman, in her blind and mistaken efforts to uplift herself, should bring ruin on the Nation and with it destroy herself.

"And what does the vote amount to? Women do not need it to accomplish really good things. . . .

"A woman can do anything if she does not vote; she is likely to do little if she does. Only through constructive methods has any nation ever thrived. We women must be wives and mothers, and as wives and mothers, through increasingly good education, must build our children's character.

"We need more, not less, of the mother-daughter and mother-son influence. We must continue to build citizens through individual efforts: machinery can never do it.

"These things being true, is it not obvious that anything which takes woman from her home is dangerous? May I call attention to the fact that immigration of undesirable Europeans is coincident with our own decreasing birth-rate?

"Is not that inevitable? Our country will be stocked with human beings of one kind of another. Would it not be better business if our women ceased their thinking and their prating, their hiking and hurrahing about votes and took some thought of this condition?

"If they keep their eyes upon their homes and those within them, the ballot box will take care of itself; if they keep their eyes upon the ballot box, the homes will not."

The Threat to American Institutions

Many opponents of suffrage portrayed it as a radical threat to American values and institutions. Helen Kendrick Johnson, a prolific anti-suffrage writer, makes this case in a letter to the New York Times, *March 12, 1911.*

Woman suffrage, like Socialism, has been the enemy of sound government and of true republican progress since the days of the ancient republics, when Sparta, the commune, brought up its women like men, and progressive Athens builded homes. Socialism has given the Old World every particle of constitutional woman suffrage that exists there. There is no such woman suffrage in the Republics of Switzerland and France.

As to our own country, woman suffrage was introduced into it by Mormonism, when Utah was still a Territory. Populism and a ridiculous incident gave it to Wyoming; Populism and the free silver madness were its sponsors in Colorado, and to Mormonism it owes its entrance in Idaho. Its late success in Washington was a Socialistic triumph, which, according to a decision of the Court of Appeals in a case brought in Texas, is likely to be pronounced unconstitutional. In the past twelve years suffrage bills in various States have been defeated, on an average, oftener than once a month. The movement was originally the child of Communism, and that the mother has come to claim her child is evident from the present merging of suffrage and Socialism in our city. One Saturday evening recently I heard the Socialist pleaders for woman suffrage denounce the home, marriage, religion, and the Republic. If in these rests our hope of progress, then woman suffrage is an obstacle that will continue to be swept aside by sound legislation. There is evidence that many American women are beginning to realize that they must either rush into the destructive tide or renounce the delusion that has been fostered with a zeal that blinded their womanly vision. This is the hour when patriotic, progressive citizens must devote thought and energy to maintaining American institutions.

HELEN KENDRICK JOHNSON

Essential Differences between the Sexes

Female anti-suffragists offered abundant reasons why they did not want the ballot. But that did not stop men from claiming to speak for women, as did Lyman Abbott, a retired Congregational minister and editor of Outlook, *an influential journal espousing progressive Christianity. Abbott focuses on two popular arguments against woman suffrage in this selection from his article, "Why Women Do Not Wish the Suffrage,"* Atlantic Monthly *92 (September 1903): 289–93.*

Certainly few men or women will doubt that at the present time an overwhelming majority of women are either reluctant to accept the ballot or indifferent to it. Why this indifference, this reluctance? This is the question which in this article I seek to answer. Briefly, I believe it is because woman feels, if she does not clearly see, that the question of woman suffrage is more than merely political; that it concerns the nature and structure of society,—the home, the church, the industrial organism, the state, the social fabric. And to a change which involves a revolution in all of these she interposes an inflexible though generally a silent opposition. . . .

The first and most patent fact in the family is the difference in the sexes. Out of this difference the family is created: in this difference the family finds its sweet and sacred bond. This difference is not merely physical and incidental. It is also psychical and essential. It inheres in the temperament; it is inbred in the very fibre of the soul; it differentiates the functions; it determines the relation between man and woman; it fixes their mutual service and their mutual obligations. . . .

This difference in the sexes is the first and fundamental fact in the family; it is therefore the first and fundamental fact in society, which is but a large family. . . . And the fundamental fact, without which there could be no family, is the temperamental, inherent, and therefore functional difference between the sexes.

Because their functions are different, all talk of equality or non-equality is but idle words, without a meaning. Only things which have the same nature and fulfill the same function can be said to be superior to or equal with one another. . . . Man is not an inferior woman. Woman is not an inferior man. They are different in nature, in temperament, in function. We cannot destroy this difference if we would; we would not if we could. In preserving it lies the joy of the family; the peace, prosperity, and well-being of society. If man attempts woman's function, he will prove himself but an inferior woman. If woman attempts man's function, she will prove herself but an inferior man. Some masculine women there are; some feminine men there are. These are the monstrosities of Nature. . . .

[It] is not woman's function to fight against human foes who threaten the home. She is not called to be a soldier. She is not to be welcomed with the volunteers nor coerced into military service by the draft. It is in vain to recite the story of Joan of Arc; it is in vain to narrate the efforts of the Amazons. The instinct of humanity revolts against the employment of woman as a soldier on the battlefield. No civilized man would wish to lay this duty upon her; no civilized woman would wish to assume it. . . . For like reason society exempts woman from police functions. She is not called to be sheriff or constable or night watchman. . . .

. . . The question, "Shall woman vote?" is really, in the last analysis, the question, "Ought woman to assume the responsibility for protecting person and property which has in the past been assumed by man as his duty alone?" It is because women see . . . that the first and fundamental function of government is the protection of person and property, and because women do not think that they ought to assume this duty any more than they ought to assume that police and militia service which is involved in every act of legislature, that they do not wish to have the ballot thrust upon them.

Let us not here make any mistake. Nothing is law which has not *authority* behind it; and there is no real authority where there is not *power* to compel obedience. It is this power to compel which distinguishes law from advice. Behind every law stands the sheriff, and behind the sheriff the militia, and behind the militia the whole military power of the Federal government. No legislature ever ought to enact a statute unless it is ready to pledge all the power of government—local, state, and Federal—to its enforcement, if the statute is disregarded. A ballot is not a mere expression of opinion; it is an act of the will; and behind this act of the will must be power to compel obedience. Women do not wish authority to compel the obedience of their husbands, sons, and brothers to their will. . . .

. . . She is glad to counsel: she is loath to command. She does not wish to arm herself, and, as police or soldier, enforce her will on the community. Nor does she wish to register her will, and leave her son, her brother, or her husband to enforce it. If she can persuade them by womanly influence she will; but just in the measure in which she is womanly, she is unwilling to say to her son, to her brother, or to her husband, "I have decreed this; you must see that my decree is enforced on the reluctant or the resisting."

Suffrage Strategies in Ohio

Proponents of political change always have a harder time than those who want merely to preserve the status quo. This account of suffrage efforts in Ohio indicates the enormous amount of effort women expended, the succession of defeats they endured, their changing strategies, and their perceptions of their opponents. It is written by Mrs. Harriet Taylor Upton, president of the Ohio Woman Suffrage Association for the years 1899–1908 and 1911–1920, for The History of Woman Suffrage, *ed. Ida Husted Harper (New York, 1922), 6:508–17.*

The history of woman suffrage in Ohio is a long one, for the second woman's rights convention ever held took place at Salem, in April, 1850, and the work never entirely ceased. . . . Other States did more spectacular work and had larger organizations but none finished its tasks with a stronger spirit of loyalty and love for the work and the workers.

The State Woman Suffrage Association was organized in 1885 and held annual conventions for the next thirty-five years. . . .

From the first gathering of Ohio suffragists in 1850 until . . . 1920, few years passed when some suffrage measure was not asked for and few Legislatures went out of existence without having considered some legislation referring to women. In 1894 a law gave them the right to vote for members of the boards of education. In 1904 and 1905, the Legislature was asked to submit to the voters an amendment to the State constitution giving full suffrage to women but the resolution was not reported out of the committees. In 1908 it was reported but no vote was taken. In 1910 it was defeated on the floor. This was the experience for years.

Periodically attempts had been made to revise the State constitution of 1851 without success but the Legislature of 1910 provided for submitting to the voters the question of calling a convention, which was carried in the fall of that year. . . .

Interests, vicious and commercial, fought the suffrage amendment from every possible angle but on March 7 the convention adopted it by a vote of 76 to 34. If accepted by the voters it would eliminate the words "white male" from Section I, Article V, of the present constitution. The enemies secured the submission of a separate amendment eliminating the word "white." This was done to alienate the negro vote from the suffrage amendment and the negroes were told that it was a shame they should be "tied to the women's apron strings." . . .

. . . The constitution was ready on May 31 and the special election was set for Sept. 3, 1912. Three months of vigorous campaign for the amendment followed. The German-American Alliance and the Personal Liberty League, two associations representing the brewers' interests, fought it in the field as they had done in the convention. It was estimated that the suffragists spent $40,000 and it was learned that the liquor forces first appropriated $500,000 and later added $120,000 to defeat the suffrage amendment. The chief work of the suffragists was done in the cities, although women spoke at picnics, county fairs, family reunions, circuses, beaches, institutes, labor meetings, at country stores, school houses and cross roads. More than fifty workers came into Ohio from all directions to assist, the larger number from the eastern States. They received no financial recompense and gave splendid service. In August an impressive suffrage parade of 5,000 took place in Columbus.

The president of the German-American Alliance at a meeting in Youngstown boasted openly that it defeated the amendment. It advertised everywhere, by posters and in street cars, and had no voluntary workers. It was evident that huge sums were being spent. The amendment was lost by a majority of 87,455—ayes, 249,420; noes, 336,875. Only 24 out of 88 counties were carried and but one Congressional district, the Eighteenth.

There was never any state-wide anti-suffrage association of women but only small groups in Cleveland, Cincinnati, Dayton and Columbus. Most of them were rich, well situated, not familiar with organized reform work and not knowing the viciousness of their associates. The real foe was the associated liquor men, calling themselves at first the Personal Liberty League, later the Home Rule Association, appearing under different names in different campaigns and they had in their employ a few women who were connected with the Anti-Suffrage Association. The amendment was lost in 1912 because of the activity of the liquor interests and the indifference of the so-called good people. . . .

The amendment eliminating the word "white," left over from ante bellum days, also was defeated and the new constitution retained a clause which had been nullified by the 15th Amendment to the National Constitution forty years before! The initiative and referendum amendment was carried. The State Suffrage Association, therefore, early in 1913, decided to circulate a petition initiating a woman suffrage amendment to the constitution, as there was no hope that the Legislature would submit one. It required the signatures of ten per cent. of the voters at the last election, in this instance 130,000 names. . . .

Who but women fighting for their freedom could ever have had the courage to keep on? They had no money to pay circulators and all was volunteer work. Over 2,000 women circulated these petitions. To have more than 130,000 men write their names and addresses on a petition and the circulator see them do it and swear that she did was no light task but it was accomplished. On July 30 petitions bearing 131,271 names were filed with the Secretary of State. A petition was secured in every county, although the law requires them from a majority only, and each was presented by a worker from that county. The sight of scores of men and women with arms laden with petitions marching up to the State House to deposit them brought tears to the eyes of some of the onlookers.

The campaign opened in Toledo, April 14, 15, was hectic. Everything possible was done to bring the amendment to the attention of the voters. Cleveland suffragists put on a beautiful pageant, A Dream of Freedom. A pilgrimage was made to the Friends' Meeting House in Salem where the suffrage convention of 1850 was held and the resolutions of those pioneers were re-adopted by a large, enthusiastic audience. Women followed party speakers, taking their audiences before and after the political meeting. State conventions of all sorts were appealed to and many gave endorsement, those of the Republicans and the Democrats refusing. Groups of workers would visit a county, separate and canvass all the towns and then keep up their courage by returning to the county seat at night and comparing notes. Street meetings and noon meetings for working people were held. Everything which had been tried out in any campaign was done.

From the beginning of 1913 to the election in November, 1914, there was constant work done for the amendment. The total number of votes cast on it was 853,685; against, 518,295; for 335,390; lost by 182,905 votes. There were gains in every county but only 14 were carried, where there had been 24 in 1912.

That the liquor interests and the anti-suffragists worked together was clearly established. The Saturday preceding the election the president of the State Suffrage association saw in her own city of Warren a man distributing literature from door to door and accompanied by a witness she followed him and picked up several packages in different parts of the city. They contained two leaflets, one giving information on how to vote on the Home Rule or "wet" amendment, the other giving instructions how to vote against the suffrage amendment. The latter had a facsimile ballot marked against it and was signed by five women. . . .

After the defeats of 1912 and 1914 the suffragists abandoned the idea of carrying an amendment. The revised constitution provided for "home rule" for cities, which allowed them to adopt their own charters instead of going to the Legislature. Suffragists believed that these charters could provide for woman suffrage in municipal affairs. In 1916 East Cleveland decided to frame a charter and they saw a chance to make a test. This campaign was the work of the Woman Suffrage Party of Greater Cleveland. On June 6 a city charter was submitted to the voters and adopted including woman suffrage. . . .

In the fall of 1917 the women of Lakewood, a city adjoining Cleveland on the west, gave municipal suffrage to its women by charter after a vigorous campaign. Columbus undertook to put this in its charter and a bitter campaign took place. It was the house to house canvass and the courageous work of the Columbus women and State suffrage officers which brought the victory when it was voted on at the election in August, 1917. Sandusky was not successful.

A partial poll of the Legislature on the subject of Presidential suffrage for women in 1915 had shown that it would be futile to attempt it but after endorsements of woman suffrage by the national party conventions in 1916 it was determined to try. [The bill passed and the governor signed it on February 21, 1917.] . . .

Very soon the opponents opened headquarters in Columbus and circulated petitions to have the Presidential suffrage bill referred to the voters for repeal. The story of these petitions is a disgraceful one. Four-fifths of the signatures were gathered in saloons, the petitions kept on the back and front bars. Hundreds of names were certified to by men who declared they saw them signed, an impossibility unless they stood by the bar eighteen hours each day for some weeks and watched every signature. Some petitions, according to the dates they bore, were circulated by the same men in different counties on the same day. Some of them had whole pages of signatures written in the same hand and some had names only, no addresses. The suffragists copied some of these petitions after they were filed in Columbus and although the time was short brought suit to prove them fraudulent in six counties. . . .

The law made no provision to meet the expenses of petition suits and the suffragists had to bear the cost, no small undertaking. The election boards which were dominated by politicians who had been notorious for their opposition to suffrage, interposed every possible obstacle to the attempt of the suffragists to uncover fraud. In some counties it was impossible to bring cases. Women were absorbed in war work and thousands of them bitterly resented the fact that at such a time their right to vote should be questioned. The referendum was submitted with the proposal so worded on the ballot that it was extremely difficult to know whether to vote yes or no.

At the election in November, 1917, the majority voted in favor of taking away from women the Presidential suffrage. The vote for retaining it was 422,262; against 568,382; the law repealed by a majority of 146,120. . . .

Ohio suffragists now turned their attention entirely towards national work. It was apparent that while the liquor interests continued their fight, women with a few thousand dollars, working for principle, could never overcome men with hundreds of thousands of dollars working for their own political and financial interests. Intensive organized congressional work was carried on henceforth for the Federal Suffrage Amendment.

Suffrage Tactics in New York

New York suffragists waged a massive referendum campaign in 1915 for an amendment to the state constitution. This account of the effort in New York City reveals the detailed planning, imaginative tactics, and huge amounts of sheer legwork that went into the campaign. Written by Mrs. Oreola Williams Haskell, head of the Press Bureau of the New York City Woman Suffrage Party, the narrative is taken from The History of Woman Suffrage, *ed. Ida Husted Harper (New York, 1922), 6:460–64.*

The Woman Suffrage Party of Greater New York was launched . . . at Carnegie Hall, October 29, 1909, modelled after that of the two dominant political parties. Its first convention with 804 delegates and 200 alternates constituted the largest delegate suffrage body ever assembled in New York State. The new party announced that it would have a leader for each of the 63 assembly districts of the city and a captain for each of the 2,127 election districts, these and their assistant officers to be supervised by a borough chairman and other officers in each borough, the entire force to be directed by a city chairman assisted by city officers and a board of directors. Mrs. Catt, with whom the idea of the Party originated, and her co-workers believed that by reaching into every election district to influence its voters, they would bring suffrage close to the people and eventually influence parties and legislators through public opinion.

The population of Greater New York was 4,700,000 and the new party had a task of colossal proportions. It had to appeal to native Americans of all classes and conditions and to thousands of foreign born. It sent its forces to local political conventions; held mass meetings; issued thousands of leaflets in many languages; conducted street meetings, parades, plays, lectures, suffrage schools; gave entertainments and teas; sent appeals to churches and all kinds of organizations and to individual leaders; brought pressure on legislators through their constituents and obtained

"New York" by Mrs. Oreola Williams Haskell reprinted from *The History of Woman Suffrage*, Volume VI, 1900-1920, Ida Husted Harper, ed. Copyright ©1922 by the National American Woman Suffrage Association. Reprinted by permission of the League of Woman Voters.

Suffragists demonstrate in New York City in 1912; their banner refers to the fact that women in some western states, including Colorado, Utah, and Washington, had already won the right to vote. (Courtesy of Corbis-Bettmann.)

wide publicity in newspapers and magazines. It succeeded in all its efforts and increased its membership from 20,000 in 1910 to over 500,000 in 1917. . . .

The City Party began the intensive work of the campaign in January, 1915. . . . It was decided to canvass all of the 661,164 registered voters and hundreds of women spent long hours toiling up and down tenement stairs, going from shop to shop, visiting innumerable factories, calling at hundreds of city and suburban homes, covering the rural districts, the big department stores and the immense office buildings with their thousands of occupants. It was estimated that 60 per cent of the enrolled voters received these personal appeals. The membership of the party was increased by 60,535 women secured as members by canvassers. . . .

The spectacular activities of the campaign caught and held public attention. Various classes of men were complimented by giving them "suffrage days." The appeal to the firemen took the form of an automobile demonstration, open air speaking along the line of march of their annual parade and a ten dollar gold piece given to one of their number who made a daring rescue of a yellow-sashed dummy—a suffrage lady. A circular letter was sent to 800 firemen requesting their help for all suffragists. "Barbers' Day" produced ten columns of copy in leading New York dailies. Letters were sent in advance to 400 barbers informing them that on a certain day the suffragists would call upon them. The visits were made in autos decorated with barbers' poles and laden with maps and posters to hang up in the shops and then open air meetings were held out in front. Street cleaners on the day of the "White Wings" parade were given souvenirs of tiny brooms and suffrage leaflets and addressed from automobiles. . . .

Forty-five banks and trust companies were treated to a "raid" made by suffrage depositors, who gave out literature and held open meetings afterward. Brokers were reached through two days in Wall Street where the suffragists entered in triumphal style, flags flying, bugles playing. . . . [H]undreds of colored balloons were sent up to typify "the suffragists' hopes ascending." Workers in the subway excavations were visited with Irish banners and shamrock fliers; Turkish, Armenian, French, German and Italian restaurants were canvassed as were the laborers on the docks, in vessels and in public markets.

A conspicuous occasion was the Night of the Interurban Council Fires, when on high bluffs in the different boroughs huge bonfires were lighted, fireworks and balloons sent up, while music, speeches and transparencies emphasized the fact that woman's evolution from the campfire of the savage into a new era was commemorated. Twenty-eight parades were a feature of the open air demonstrations. There were besides numbers of torch-light rallies; street dances on the lower East Side; Irish, Syrian, Italian and Polish block parties; outdoor concerts, among them a big one in Madison Square, where a full orchestra played, opera singers sang and eminent orators spoke; open air religious services with the moral and religious aspects of suffrage discussed; a fête held in beautiful Dyckman Glen; flying squadrons of speakers whirling in autos from the Battery to the Bronx; an "interstate meet" on the streets where suffragists of Massachusetts, New Jersey and New York participated. . . . [T]he suffragists ended their campaign valiantly with sixty speakers talking continuously in Columbus Circle for twenty-six hours.

On the night of November 2, election day, officers, leaders, workers, members of the Party and many prominent men and women gathered at City headquarters in East 34th Street to receive the returns, Mrs. Catt and Miss Hay at either end of a long table. At first optimism prevailed as the early returns seemed to indicate victory but as adverse reports came in by the hundreds all hopes were destroyed. . . . [T]hough many workers wept openly, the gathering took on the character of an embattled host ready for the next conflict. After midnight many of the women joined a group from the State headquarters and in a public square held an outdoor rally which they called the beginning of the new campaign.

The vote was as follows: . . . Total opposed, 320,853; in favor, 238,098; adverse majority, 82,755.

Two days after the election the City Party united with the National Association in a mass meeting at Cooper Union, where speeches were made and $100,000 pledged for a new campaign fund. The spirit of the members was shown in the words of a leader who wrote: "We know that we have gained over half a million voters in the State, that we have many new workers, have learned valuable lessons and with the knowledge obtained and undiminished courage we are again in the field of action."

Questions

1. *How did anti-suffragists argue that suffrage would be bad for the nation? How did they argue that it would be bad for women?*
2. *What were the most compelling of anti-suffragist arguments?*
3. *To what extent do you think anti-suffragists' concerns about woman suffrage actually proved true once women had the ballot?*
4. *What different routes to suffrage did women attempt? What strategies or tactics might have proved more effective?*
5. *From what you have learned about other reform movements in American history, how was the woman suffrage movement similar to or different from them?*

FURTHER READING

Eleanor Flexner, Century of Struggle: The Woman's Rights Movement in the United States *(New York, 1974), remains the best overall history of the suffrage movement. Aileen S. Kraditor,* The Ideas of the Woman Suffrage Movement, 1890–1920 *(New York, 1965), provides a good analysis of the arguments on both sides. Rosalyn Terborg-Penn's article, "Discontented Black Feminists," in* Decades of Discontent, *ed. Lois Scharf and Joan M. Jensen (Boston, 1987), explores the suffrage experiences of African American women. For the broader context of American feminism before and after suffrage, see Nancy F. Cott,* The Grounding of Modern Feminism *(New Haven, 1987). For more on the militant suffragists, see Christine A. Lunardini,* From Equal Suffrage to Equal Rights: Alice Paul and the National Woman's Party *(New York, 1986).*

The Temperance and Prohibition Movement

K. Austin Kerr

INTRODUCTION

This unit raises three important questions. What was the temperance and prohibition movement? Why was there a temperance and prohibition movement? What did the temperance and prohibition movement accomplish?

A reform movement arose in American life in the 1830s that responded to drunkenness and the problems of what later generations called alcohol abuse. This reform movement preached temperance, urged Americans to "take the pledge" and abstain from consuming alcoholic beverages, and developed fraternal societies to provide social support for temperance behavior. The reform movement was remarkably successful, attracting thousands of followers and helping reduce drinking.

But it was not enough, some temperance reformers came to realize, simply to persuade individuals to abstain. Victory over the scourges of alcohol abuse seemed to require coercive measures, prohibition laws to make it illegal to manufacture and sell alcoholic beverages. In short, it seemed necessary to go beyond the individual and to change part of the social system in order to build a more perfect society of abstaining citizens. Between 1846 and 1855 every northern state, except Pennsylvania and New Jersey, enacted some form of prohibition.

The coercive aspect of this reform was always controversial, and the state prohibition laws generally fell into disfavor during and after the Civil War. The individual and social problems of alcohol abuse remained, however. The temperance and prohibition movement revived in 1869 when the Prohibition Party formed to offer candidates for president and other offices committed to enforcing prohibition. Then, in the winter of 1873-74 a mass move-

ment of women arose, the largest mass movement of American women yet, in a crusade to persuade drinkers to stop drinking and saloonkeepers to stop serving liquor. The women formed the Woman's Christian Temperance Union to keep the ideas of the crusade alive. The WCTU continued to press for prohibition, and a wide range of other reforms, including woman suffrage. During the 1880s the revived prohibition movement achieved a few local and state victories, but, overall, the results were disappointing. The businesses, especially breweries, that supplied liquor were expanding, and the problems associated with alcohol abuse seemed also to be enlarging.

The Anti-Saloon League organized in 1893 in a new attempt to bring reformers together and pass prohibition laws. The league, without too much success before 1900, worked to enact "local option" laws allowing neighborhoods to forbid "the liquor traffic" from plying its trades in specified communities. As more and more areas became "dry" under these measures, the league promoted state prohibition laws, winning initial victories in Oklahoma and Alabama in 1907. In 1913 the league announced its campaign to achieve national prohibition through a constitutional amendment. With the 1916 elections, and with much help from a revived WCTU, the drys elected the two-thirds majorities required in both houses of Congress to initiate their amendment. Congress submitted an amendment to the states in 1917, and by 6 January 1919, three-quarters of the states had ratified the eighteenth or prohibition amendment, to take effect one year hence.

Prohibition lasted nationally until 1933 when the twenty-first amendment repealed it. During those years—as well as the decades it took to pass prohibition—the reform was very controversial. Although prohibition received widespread support, with dry majorities in Congress peaking with the 1928 elections, and the consumption of alcoholic beverages dropped dramatically, many Americans complained that prohibition was an improper imposition on their personal liberty. Opposition centered in the cities, where many immigrant groups especially viewed prohibition as an attack on their cultural norms and religious practices. In New York City and Hollywood, important centers of the production *and dissemination of popular culture, and of the news, opponents of prohibition held sway.*

Wealthy Americans funded the repeal campaign, which carried the day after the onset of the Great Depression in 1929 changed American political attitudes. The wealthy hoped that taxes on liquor would replace taxes on their incomes, and other persons believed that the restoration of the liquor businesses would provide sorely needed employment opportunities. And newer immigrant groups, now more powerful politically than ever before, viewed repeal as an affirmation of the acceptance of their cultural traditions, which commonly included using drink in religious and other rituals.

In the end prohibition left little permanent mark on the American people. To be sure, the consumption of alcoholic beverages subsided, as did the individual and social problems associated with alcohol misuse. Drinking rates did not recover to pre-prohibition levels for about forty years, when Americans again saw the problems of alcohol abuse as widespread as to require renewed exhortations to refrain from overindulgence and government support for prevention and treatment programs for "problem" drinkers. Perhaps the most lasting impact of prohibition was the propagation of the myth that laws and public policy cannot change people's behaviors.

HISTORIANS VIEW PROHIBITION

Even before its repeal, prohibition attracted the attention of historians. Victors write history, and for several decades scholars essentially agreed with the propaganda of repeal advocates. Generations of history students learned about the "failure" of prohibition and read caricatures of dry advocates. As time passed, however, historians began to view the century-long debate over prohibition differently, and to understand the prohibition reformers as part of broader impulses for political change. When a new generation of Americans began to address the policy problems associated with alcohol misuse in the 1970s, historians also learned that prohibition sharply reduced beverage alcohol consumption. Some writers even saw prohibition in retrospect as a public health "success."

Prohibition and the American Progressive Reform Tradition

Historians have disagreed about what the prohibition movement was, and what and who it represented. Personal views toward the reform, and toward drink, sometimes color scholars' perceptions. Richard Hofstadter, whose book won a Pulitzer Prize and remains influential, took a dim view of the movement. Excerpted from Richard Hofstadter, The Age of Reform: From Bryan to F.D.R. *(New York, 1955), 287–91.*

Prohibition . . . *was* a major issue. . . . Prohibition, in the twenties, was the skeleton at the feast, a grim reminder of the moral frenzy [Progressive reform] that so many wished to forget,

Many Americans celebrated the end of prohibition. (Courtesy of AP/Wide World Photos.)

a ludicrous caricature of the reforming impulse, of the Yankee-Protestant notion that it is both possible and desirable to moralize private life through public action.

To hold the Progressives responsible for Prohibition would be to do them an injustice. Men of an urbane cast of mind, whether conservatives or Progressives in their politics, had been generally antagonistic, or at the very least suspicious, of the pre-war drive toward Prohibition; and on the other side there were many advocates of Prohibition who had nothing to do with other reforms.... Prohibition was a pseudo-reform, a pinched, parochial substitute for reform which had a widespread appeal to a certain type of crusading mind. It was linked not merely to an aversion to drunkenness and to the evils that accompanied it, but to the immigrant drinking masses, to the pleasures and amenities of city life, and to the well-to-do classes and cultivated men. It was carried about America by the rural-evangelical virus: the country Protestant frequently brought it with him to the city when the contraction of agriculture sent him there to seek his livelihood. Students of the Prohibition movement find it easy to believe that the majority

From *The Age of Reform: From Bryan to FDR* by Richard Hofstadter, Copyright © 1955 by Richard Hofstadter. Reprinted by permission of Alfred A. Knopf, Inc.

sentiment of the country stood in favor of Prohibition at the time the amendment was passed and for some years before; for even many drinking people were sufficiently persuaded by the note of moral uplift to concede that Prohibition might, after all, be a good thing. And even if the desire for Prohibition was a minority sentiment, it was the sentiment of a large minority, one whose intensity and insistency gave its members a power disproportionate to their numbers. Politicians, at any rate, catered to their demands, and there were among them some . . . who unquestionably believed that the conquest of the demon rum was one of the important tasks of political life.

. . . The demand for liquor reform, long familiar in American politics, seems to have quickened during the Progressive era, notably after about 1908, and the final victory of the amendment was the culmination of five years of heightened agitation by the Anti-Saloon League. The alcohol issue had been approached with the usual Populist-Progressive arguments: it was one of the means by which the interests, in this case the "whiskey ring," fattened on the toil of the people. Drinking was pre-eminently a vice of those classes—the plutocrats and corrupt politicians and ignorant immigrants—which the reformers most detested or feared. The saloon, as an institution pivotal to the life of vice on one side and of American urban politics on the other, fell under particular reprobation. . . .

George Kibbe Turner . . . probably went to the heart of the Prohibition sentiment when he wrote an article attacking the city saloon in which he pointed out that city people constituted each year a larger and larger portion of the whole population and insisted that the first thing to be done in the movement for city reform was "to remove the terrible and undisciplined commercial forces which, in America, are fighting to saturate the populations of cities with alcoholic liquor." During the war the alleged need to conserve materials and the Germanic names of the leading brewers added some force to the prohibitionist propaganda; but what stood the drys in the best stead was the same strong undercurrent of public self-castigation, the same reaction against personal and physical indulgence and material success that underlay the Progressive tirades against the plutocracy. . . . The sense that others were fighting battles and making sacrifices in which one somehow *ought* to share was greatly heightened by the war; and the dry agitation, with its demand for self-denial, struck an increasingly congenial note. . . . Of course this sort of thing could not last forever, but while it was at its pitch the dry lobbyists struck, and when they were finished the Prohibition mania was fixed in the Constitution; and there it remained for almost fifteen years, a symbol of the moral overstrain of the preceding era, the butt of jokes, a perennial source of irritation, a memento of the strange power of crusades for absolute morality to intensify the evils they mean to destroy.

But Prohibition was more than a symbol—it was a means by which the reforming energies of the country were transmuted into mere peevishness. All through the period . . . when the dry crusade spoke the language of social and humanitarian reform, leading Prohibitionists had often been leading reformers, and the churches that gave the strongest support to the Social Gospel movement in American Protestantism were all by the same token supporters of the dry cause. The victory of Prohibition, the transformation of the drinker from a victim of evil to a lawbreaker, the necessity of defending a law that was widely violated, drew many one-time reformers toward the camp of the conservatives, while the circumstances of American politics led them into Catholic-baiting and city-baiting in 1924 and 1928. Prohibition became a low grade substitute for the old Social Gospel enthusiasms.

The Popularity of Prohibition in the Progressive Tradition

Some historians disagree with Hofstadter. Based in part on research into popular political attitudes, they realized that prohibition reformers, and their opponents, expressed widely held cultural and religious outlooks. Prohibition was popular in every region and social class, in city and country alike. Taken from Jack S. Blocker, Jr., American Temperance Movements: Cycles of Reform *(Boston, 1989), xi–xv.*

During the years of national Prohibition . . . a stereotype grew up. . . . The stereotypical prohibitionist was a dour, cadaverous, puritanical fellow who was obviously not enjoying life very much because of his single-minded devotion to preventing other people from enjoying theirs. Misanthropy, not altruism, drove him; to his fellow human beings he offered a police club, not a helping hand. From his misguided efforts flowed violence and crime. The repeal of national Prohibition added to this stereotype the label of losers, a sour minority who tried but inevitably failed to deflect Americans from full enjoyment of the fruits of their abundant economy. For many years popular stereotype and historical perception coincided, as historians found inconceivable the notion that alcoholic damage could have any place in the causal chains they constructed to explain reform and reformers. Loss of status, loss of deference, loss of the certainty of sin, loss of traditional work habits, loss of order, virtually any lack but the lack of sobriety in the world around them was imaginable as motivation for reformers.

In truth, temperance folk have been such a varied lot that any attempt to put them into a single suit of clothes necessarily makes an awkward fit. Let us begin with the most basic of social distinctions. Although men led the reform in its early days, from the beginning women saw temperance as a woman's issue, one that allowed them to address important problems in their daily lives. In 1873 temperance crusaders launched the largest mass movement of women to that point in American history, and for the next quarter century women provided the reform's most creative and dynamic leadership. From Quaker women in the eighteenth century through the Woman's Christian Temperance Union (WCTU) of the nineteenth century to Mothers Against Drunk Driving (MADD). . . , women have entered temperance reform. . . .

Temperance was clearly a middle-class reform. . . . [I]t articulated most forcefully and forced upon the public most articulately the theme of self-control that lay at the core of middle-class identity in the nineteenth century. Even so, temperance reform has never been solely a mirror for the middle class. During much of the reform's long history . . . it received substantial infusions of support from working-class men and women. From an early point in temperance history manufacturers' desires for sober and therefore (they thought) productive workers brought powerful recruits to the cause, and during the Progressive period of the early twen-

From Author's Introduction to *American Temperance Movements: Cycles of Reform* by Jack S. Blocker, Jr. Copyright © 1989 by Jack S. Blocker, Jr. Excerpted with permission of Twayne Publishers an imprint of Simon & Schuster Macmillan.

tieth century a segment of the corporate elite provided crucial backing. . . .

Like other early-nineteenth-century reforms, the temperance ethos and organization originated in the Northeast. . . . By the late nineteenth century the Midwest became the prohibitionist heartland. Even during the years of northeastern hegemony a significant number of southerners gave their support to the cause, and the final wave of enthusiasm for statewide prohibition before the Eighteenth Amendment began in 1907 in Oklahoma and Alabama. That wave finally spread from the South through the West and Midwest to isolate the Northeast, which had changed in a hundred years from a temperance stronghold to the last redoubt of the antiprohibition forces.

Because rural states led the final march to national Prohibition, temperance has long been considered essentially an expression of rural values. We now know better. In the late eighteenth century the new ideology of temperance appeared first in Philadelphia, the metropolis of the infant Republic. . . .Voluntary associations . . . to promote the temperance ideology . . . found ready support in burgeoning industrial cities such as Worcester, Massachusetts, and Rochester, New York. Women's mass action against saloons later in the century sprang from small towns. Today . . . the temperance cause still flourishes in new forms in its cities and suburbs.

In the pages of the *Dictionary of American Temperance Biography* one finds few names that suggest other than English origins, and in this respect the leadership seems to have reflected faithfully the backgrounds of most temperance folk. Nevertheless, other groups have embraced temperance reform to control drinking within or outside their own group. During the antebellum period some blacks organized their own temperance societies while others joined white-dominated associations. Scandinavian-Americans during the late nineteenth and early twentieth centuries were overrepresented in the temperance ranks. Hibernian Total Abstinence Societies were not unknown, and Irish-Americans took the lead in organizing the Catholic Total Abstinence Union in 1872. . . . [T]emperance reform must shape its strategies to the reality of a multicultural nation.

A similar point might be made about religion. Evangelical Protestant lay people and clergy have usually provided the bulk of temperance leadership and grass-roots support. At times, however, nonevangelical Protestants have played key roles, and the existence of the Catholic Total Abstinence Union and other Roman Catholic temperance associations indicates the persistent presence of non-Protestant temperance folk. . . . [R]eformers learned that they would have to deploy more than biblical arguments if they were to succeed in a materialistic and pluralistic society. Accordingly, they pictured their reform as indispensable to individual health and social welfare as well as necessary to salvation and attainment of the millennium. By framing their arguments in secular terms temperance reformers helped to undermine the churches' claims for divine sanction as the basis for social action. Recognizing the threat, most churches maintained arm's length distance between themselves and the zealous drys. That temperance reformers were evangelical Protestants does not mean that their relations with their churches were either simple or stable.

Time, of course, changed the composition of temperance support along most of the dimensions we have considered. New generations of men and women came to the reform, bringing with them new experiences and ideas. Within a single generation the turnover in some organizations was massive. . . . Changes in movement policy, such as . . . the WCTU's alliance with the Prohibition party in the 1880s, drove out many. Experience, policy, and membership danced an intricate dance, to a tune called by none of the dancers alone, but improvised by all three together.

In pursuit of their reform, temperance reformers argued, pleaded, cajoled, confessed, denounced, and declaimed; they produced articles, stories, poetry, plays, songs, and novels; published books and pamphlets; and posted advertisements. They conducted surveys, prayed and sang, marched on saloons, marched in parades, marched in demonstrations, and attended meetings and conventions. They destroyed the contents of saloons with axes, hatchets, hammers, rocks, and metal bars. They formed associations at every level from the neighborhood to the nation; they appeared in courts as prosecutors, plaintiffs, informers, and defendants; they created pressure groups and political parties, petitioned, circularized candidates, canvassed, voted, and watched the polls. They served in lawmaking bodies from village councils to the U.S. Congress. They were harassed, mocked, beaten, hosed down, hung in effigy, shot at, and shot down.

Temperance advocates repeated the message that the saloon and drinking too often harmed families and the lives of children. (Courtesy of The New York Public Library.)

. . . The scale most commonly employed by historians of temperance reform . . . is a spectrum between persuasion and coercion. At one end lies the tactic known in the nineteenth century as "moral suasion," which assumes a symmetrical relationship between individuals of equal power and presumed rationality. Its essence is dialogue, in which the reformer appeals to the intellect and emotions of his or her listener in an attempt to convince the person of the rightness and goodness of the reformer's position. In contrast, coercion requires an asymmetrical relationship between individuals or groups of unequal power, involves only the crudest form of communication, and considers intellect and emotions peripheral to the outcome. The rightness and goodness of the reformer's position are not at issue; the only question is whether the reformer can mobilize enough force to compel acquiescence. Between these polar extremes lie many gradations encompassing many combinations of moral suasion and coercion. . . .

Temperance reform began . . . with methods more suasionist than coercive, but its history reveals no simple progression toward coercion. . . . [T]he Anti-Saloon League, among the most coercive of temperance organizations, made a strong commitment to "education," turning out from its presses at Westerville, Ohio, millions of pages of propaganda. Even after the passage of national Prohibition, the most coercive of temperance measures, a significant faction within the Anti-Saloon League argued for renewal of an educational campaign. Time and again frustration pushed temperance reformers toward coercion, but again and again moral suasion found ways to assert its claims.

The Saloon and Drinking

Students of the saloon, and of drinking customs, have concluded that the prohibition reformers were acting in response to very real human problems. Excerpted from Mark Edward Lender and James Kirby Martin, Drinking in America: A History, *rev. ed. (New York, 1987), 102-4, 106.*

The dramatic social changes inherent in rapid industrialization and urbanization placed traditional dry worries over alcohol and such civil maladies as poverty, vice, crime, disease, and violence in a new and more visible context. Poverty . . . was a major fact of urban life. Late nineteenth century economic fluctuations, language barriers among immigrants, and limited work skills kept thousands periodically unemployed or locked into poorly paid jobs. Equally worrisome, many people spent too much of what little they earned on liquor, and through drinking they often lost their jobs, thus impoverishing not only themselves but also their families. Even dispassionate studies of the matter—by urban reformers, municipal officials, and newly professionalized social workers—put alcohol at the root of a minimum of 20 percent of urban poverty cases. Such personal tragedy, of course, was not confined to the industrial poor; yet the relative novelty of seeing so many instances of drinking-related poverty made a distinct impression on the middle-class public. Indeed, by the turn of [the] century many students of urban affairs . . . and Progressive reformers . . . agreed that the liquor question must be tackled if the urban-industrial order were to be a fit, safe environment. . . .

Along with the skid row bum [popular stereotype of the alcoholic], the most ominous symbol of the dangers of drink became the urban saloon. Not that temperance workers liked rural or Western saloons any better, but the city version was more visibly associated with the ills of an industrializing society and thus seemed to be more immediately threatening. Most urban saloons were a far cry from . . . any of the elegant establishments . . . recalled so fondly. The majority were neighborhood bars, and too many were simply ginmills. The worst were dives serving as centers of drunkenness, crime, profanity, prostitution, gambling, and political corruption. Their patrons, frequently immigrants and unskilled industrial workers, held few values in common with those of the temperance movement.

In most major cities, political bosses used saloons as their headquarters and employed regular patrons to stuff ballot boxes (these same bars often served as polling places) or to terrorize opponents. Similarly, the rise of organized prostitution paralleled the growth of the urban ginmills. In Philadelphia, for instance, an 1876 canvass found 8,037 legal and illegal drinking establishments in the city: At least 3,782 of them had direct or indirect connections with "houses of ill fame." . . . The saloon, then, seemed to mock temperance conceptions of public virtue and stood starkly at odds with traditional American mores. . . .

But the [liquor] traffic did not worry very much about its image. In fact, it insolently faced down complaints. Large brewers owned most of the local saloons and used them as outlets for their beers. Breweries were highly competitive, and they openly encouraged heavy drinking. . . .

. . . Techniques kept liquor flowing. Many saloons lured customers with offers of a "free lunch"—usually well salted to inspire drinking (the saloon "bouncer" was generally on hand to discourage hearty appetites). New patrons also were given free drinks. As one Brewers' Association spokesman explained, this tactic extended even to children: A few cents spent on free drinks for boys was a good investment; the money would be amply recovered as these youths became habitual drinkers! At the time, many Americans, and by no means just temperance workers, regarded such practices much the same as our own generation would consider a modern drug-pusher giving children "free samples."

The saloons nevertheless scoffed at reform efforts. They had plenty of money for political wars and plenty of votes, which, as the *Liquor Man's Advocate* noted in 1874, they were ready to use. "Every saloon averages eighty regular customers," the paper observed, "and these eighty customers have eighty votes, and, if properly managed, every bartender might influence these eighty votes to a given point, decided by bartenders *en masse.*" The saloon thus accorded temperance workers a perfect target.

The Success and Failure of Prohibition

Conventional wisdom in the United States holds that prohibition was a failure. In this view, Americans did not stop drinking, organized crime mushroomed to slake thirsts, and a generation matured disrespectful of law in general. The selection that follows is a summary of this viewpoint. Taken from Samuel Eliot Morison, The Oxford History of the American People *(New York, 1965), 900-902.*

Orderly progress in temperance was rudely interrupted by the Volstead Act of 28 October 1919, . . . [which prohibited the manufacture, transportation, and sale of beverages] containing over one-half of one per cent alcohol; and by Amendment XVIII, which . . . went into effect in . . . 1920. The reasons for so precipitate an enlargement of the federal government's power over the citizenry were many. The dry states complained that they could not enforce Prohibition when adjacent states were wet; the war induced a "spirit of sacrifice," and the German-American Alliance . . . made drinking seem faintly treasonable. Wives of workingmen wanted their husbands to bring home their pay instead of spending half of it with "the boys" in a saloon; the liquor industry had been proved a major factor in political corruption and was tied in with prostitution, gambling, and other vices. Many business men and manufacturers favored Prohibition, hoping it would eliminate "blue Monday" absenteeism. The Anti-Saloon League printed some 100 million flyers, posters, and pamphlets, mostly to further the idea that alcohol was mainly responsible for poverty, disease, crime, insanity and degeneracy, and that national Prohibition would empty the jails, the asylums, and the poorhouses. . . .

Prohibition enforcement received much attention. Prohibition reformers sought to move beyond mere enforcement to education and persuasion. (Courtesy of Corbis-Bettmann.)

No sooner had national prohibition become law than the country seemed to regret it, and a new occupation, bootlegging, sprang up to quench the public thirst. The federal government in ten years made over half a million arrests for breaking the Volstead Act, and secured over 300,000 convictions; but smuggling increased. The Canadian and Mexican borders were full of "leaks." Small craft easily ran cargoes from Cuba into Florida and the Gulf states; mountain moonshiners multiplied; . . . carloads of grapes went to Italian- and Greek-Americans to be trodden out in a traditional winepress and allowed to ferment. Off every seaport from Maine to Miami, outside the three-mile limit, rode a fleet of ocean-going ships loaded with every variety of wine and liquor. Motor launches, too fast for coast guard or enforcement agents to catch, ran these cargoes ashore, where they were transferred to trucks and cars owned by bootleggers; but the truckloads often got "hijacked" by other criminals, and in any case the strong liquor was "cut" with water before being sold. Millions of gallons of industrial alcohol . . . were converted into bootleg whisky or gin, and bottled under counterfeit labels; poisonous wood alcohol, inexpertly "converted," caused numerous deaths. Liquor and wine imported under license for "medicinal purposes," easily found its way to the stomachs of healthy citizens. Every city became studded with "speakeasies" to replace the saloon, almost every urban family patronized a local bootlegger, and in defiant states like Rhode Island . . . one could buy a bottle of British gin right off the shelves of a grocery store for ten dollars. Those who did not care to patronize bootleggers and so contribute to crime and political corruption, made their own "bathtub" gin at home or got along with home-brewed beer and cider. Bravado induced numerous young people to drink who otherwise would not have done so; restaurants which refused to break the law themselves provided "set-ups" of ice, soda water, and ginger ale to be energized by whatever the patrons brought.

There were many social effects of Prohibition, apart from the encouragement of lawbreaking and the building up of a criminal class that turned to gambling and drugs [after the repeal of Prohibition in] . . . 1933. The high point in the Chicago gang war that was fed by bootlegging was the "St. Valentine's Day Massacre" of 1929. Al Capone ran one gang; George Bugs Moran, the other. In four years there had been 215 unsolved murders in the Windy City. The Capone hoods, disguised as policemen, machine-gunned six of the Moran gang in a garage where they were waiting to buy a truckload of liquor from hijackers. Nobody was punished for this multiple murder; it took the federal government to get the planner, Capone, for evasion of income taxes. . . .

Since beer and wine did not pay bootleggers like strong liquor, the country's drinking habits were changed from the one to the other. College students who before Prohibition would have in a keg of beer and sit around singing the "Dartmouth Stein Song," and "Under the Anheuser Busch," now got drunk quickly on bathtub gin and could manage no lyric more complicated than "How Dry I Am!" Woman . . . now helped her husband to spend on liquor the savings that formerly went to the saloon. Hip-flask drinking certainly helped the revolution in sexual standards. . . . And it encouraged hypocrisy in politics.

Both major parties successfully blinked the issue for a decade. The Republicans, strongest in the rural communities and the middle classes, in general stood behind what President Hoover called "an experiment noble in motive and far-reaching in purpose." The Democrats were torn between Southern constituencies which were immovably dry because Prohibition was supposed to help "keep the Negroes in order," and Northern cities, full of Irish-, German- and Italian-Americans who were incurably wet. This division almost split the party in 1924 when the drys supported McAdoo and the wets Alfred E. Smith. The wets, having gained the upper hand by 1928, then nominated Al Smith, who proposed to abandon national prohibition and return the alcohol problem to the States. This stand was partly responsible for his spectacular success in the urban centers of the North, as well as for his defeat in the solid South and West.

President Hoover, who really tried to enforce the Volstead Act, appointed a commission to investigate the question of law enforcement. This Wickersham Commission submitted, in January 1931, a confused report to the effect that federal prohibition was unenforceable but should be enforced, that it was a failure but should be retained! By 1932 the "noble experiment" was so palpable a failure that the Republican party favored a "revision" of Amendment XVIII: the Democrats demanded outright repeal.

Assessing Prohibition

Scholars who have studied the impact of prohibition carefully dispute the conventional wisdom that the policy was a failure. Theirs is a mixed assessment, with obedience to the law uneven across time and place. In any event, organized crime flourished prior to prohibition and thereafter, while drinking dropped dramatically under the policy, and consumption rates took about four decades to recover to pre-prohibition levels. Excerpted from Norman H. Clark, Deliver Us from Evil: An Interpretation of American Prohibition *(New York, 1976), 140-49.*

Some intriguing legends to the contrary, the beginnings of Prohibition did not seem so grim. Several states had been dry for six years, several others for more than a decade. . . . [T]he dry morning of January 17 [1920, the morning the Volstead Act took effect] brought no national trauma. In major cities not already dry,

Wealthy Americans championed the repeal of prohibition, which they hoped would shift their tax burden to beer drinkers. (Courtesy of AP/Wide World Photos.)

the barrooms of most larger hotels had closed weeks before, and there was no great guzzle at the final hour, no ultimate orgy of binges. . . . [C]ontemporary writers stressed that in hotels, clubs, and private homes they found people who wanted to obey the law and usually did. . . .

There were others, however, who were totally unprepared for even a delicate passage into a new era. John Allen Krout, then a young history instructor in New York City, observed that to many Americans, "prohibition came with something of a shock." Though they were vaguely aware that somewhere out in the tall grass of the Bible Belt were people called "drys," and that these people were interested in politics, "they had not realized that the reformers were so near the goal.". . . Their immediate response . . . was "to cry fraud, since it seemed impossible that the people of a great nation could be fairly persuaded to write into their fundamental law so radical a change in social custom." . . .

More than a few were not impressed, and their cries of *fraud* enlivened the early Volstead era. Their anguish was regularly enflamed by the more mindlessly impassioned nativists and Prohibitionists—both of which groups, in an age of frivolous journalism, were given inordinate newspaper publicity—whose sanctimonious platitudes and downright perversities did indeed darken the lives of men who shared the liberal persuasion. . . . [Some drys] applauded every raid of federal agents on private homes and every wiretapped telephone, demanded that the army patrol the Canadian border, asked the government to sterilize drinkers, and urged that violations . . . be made a capital offense. In this atmosphere it is no wonder that many broad-minded urbanites came to fear for their own security and that, in their anxiety, they began to explain their misfortunes in what became a legacy of conventional legends.

Such legends held that Puritans from the Corn Country and lady school teachers from the Rocky Mountains had deviously manipulated honest patriotism to force the 18th Amendment into the Constitution while the attention of all right-minded citizens was fixed on the war. . . . Then, suddenly, in . . . post war society . . . they discovered a grave crisis: The malignant repressions of the wicked Puritans were actually eroding the moral fiber of a free and creative America. Prohibition, by distorting the role of alcohol in civilized life, allegedly caused Americans to drink more rather than less, and to do so with increasing morbidity. . . .

There are today few reasons to believe that these legends [of prohibition's failure] . . . are more than an easy and sentimental hyperbole crafted by men whose assumptions about a democratic society had been deeply offended. To suppose, for example, that the principle of the 18th Amendment was generated by wartime hysterias . . . is . . . to ignore temperance legislation across a century of American history. To suppose, further, that the Volstead Act caused Americans to drink more rather than less is to defy an impressive body of statistics as well as common sense. The common sense is that a substantial number of people wanted to stop both their own and other people's drinking, and that the saloons where most people had done their drinking were closed. There is no reason to suppose that the speakeasy, given its illicit connotations, more lurid even than those of the saloon, ever . . . replaced the saloon. In fact, there is every reason to suppose that most Americans outside the larger cities never knew a bootlegger, never saw a speakeasy, and would not have known where to look for one.

The statistical evidence to support this takes more than a footnote. The most recent figures are those assembled by the task force of scholars from the Department of Health, Education and Welfare who prepared for Congress the special report entitled *Alcohol and Health* (1971). This report shows that the annual per capita consumption of alcoholic beverages in the United States—conveniently converted to gallons of absolute alcohol—stood at 2.60 for the period 1906-1910, which was the period before the state dry laws had any national impact and the period which must be regarded as "before Prohibition." After Prohibition, in 1934, the figure stood at 0.97. In 1940, by which time the effects of repeal had surely pervaded the national drinking habits, the figure was only 1.56. It would be difficult to overemphasize the significance of this change: Americans after Prohibition were drinking less than at any time since they had learned the technology of distillation, and the marked change had surely taken place during the 1920s. . . .

. . . Joseph Gusfield has . . . concluded that "Prohibition was effective in sharply reducing the rate of alcohol consumption in the United States. We may set the outer limit of this at about 50 percent and the inner limit at about one-third less alcohol consumed by the total population [than] that had been the case . . . [before Prohibition] in the United States." . . .

There is, furthermore, an abundance of evidence in social statistics from the 1920s indicating that Prohibition could not have encouraged drinking among most Americans. . . . [A]rrests for drunkenness fell off remarkably during the Volstead era, as did the public expenses for jailing drunks. There were marked decreases in the incidence of diseases associated with alcoholic psychoses, and for several years . . . articles on alcoholism simply disappeared from the periodicals of American medicine. . . .

. . . [There is] also a refutation of the "almost universal public belief" in a crime wave during the 1920s. The best studies in criminology . . . give no evidence of any "wave," though across the decade there probably was a slowly rising level of criminal activity. People believed the "wave" was real because of impressions left by journalists who saw a lot of crime, reported a lot, and—in the age of instant communication—were irresistibly tempted to romanticize it. Among competing newspapers, crime became the most welcome kind of "hot news," and it was eagerly fastened on the front pages. This is not to deny that there has always been a great deal of crime in the United States to see and to publicize; it is only to suggest that Prohibition did not make it any easier than it had been before to bribe a policeman, or commit a murder, or corrupt a friend of the President.

Questions

1. *What was the source of prohibitionists' actions? Were they responding to real or imagined problems?*
2. *Prohibition was about social values. Who were the prohibitionists? Who were their opponents?*
3. *Was prohibition a success or a failure? How does one decide? Is the question itself appropriate?*

THE LONG, GRUELING DISPUTE OVER THE LIQUOR TRAFFIC AND PROHIBITION

The use of beverage alcohol (liquor) has provoked disputes over private behavior, community norms, and public policy for most of the nineteenth and twentieth centuries. For much of the nineteenth century, dedicated, zealous "drys" fought to change behavior, affirm community norms of sobriety, and enforce public policies that denied the right to do business in the liquor trades. Dry sentiment and political power increased in the first quarter of the twentieth century, only to recede in the early 1930s. The prohibitionists always fought well-funded enemies who were zealous in their "wet" position.

The Woman's Crusade of 1873-74

The Woman's Crusade of 1873-74 culminated many years of women taking direct action against the saloon and the liquor traffic. Women in the United States then enjoyed no direct political power, and direct action—prayer vigils, petition campaigns, demonstrations, hymn-singing—were among the few means at their disposal for seeking change. The crusade sought to persuade saloonkeepers to destroy their beverages, close their doors, and enter some other line of business.

Eliza Daniel Stewart (she referred to herself as "Mother Stewart") was active during the Woman's Crusade and enjoyed a notable career as a temperance speaker thereafter. Taken from Mother Stewart, **Memories**

of the Crusade: A Thrilling Account . . . *(Columbus, Ohio, 1888),*
215-16.

I had just returned to the hotel . . . when I heard a great shout
in the street, and soon after all the bells in the city commenced
ringing. At the same time there arose a prolonged cheer from the
Granger's Convention just across the street from the hotel, and it
was evident that something unusual had happened.

Going out I saw crowds of people thronging towards
Whitman street, and heard on every hand in joyful accents, "The
Shades of Death [a saloon] has surrendered!" The good news
proved true, and I found Whitman street thronged with people. A
little before 3 o'clock, as it appeared from the general account, Mr.
Steve Phillips, of the "Shades of Death," invited the ladies to enter,
and announced that he gave up everything to them, and would
never sell anything intoxicating in Xenia again. Then the ladies,
joined by the spectators, sang "Praise God from whom all blessings flow," while the liquors were rolled into the street. A half-
barrel of blackberry brandy, the same of high-wines, a few kegs of
beer, and some bottles of ale and whisky were soon emptied into
the street, amid the shouts of the enthusiastic multitude. The
leading lady then announced that if Mr. Phillips went into any

This twentieth century artist captured some of the spirit of the woman's
crusade of 1873–74. (Courtesy of The Library of Congress.)

other business in Xenia, they should feel it a duty to support him. A dispatch was sent to the Grangers (the State Grange was in session in Xenia at the time,) eliciting three cheers, and all the bells were set ringing in honor of the first victory. When I arrived the liquor had mostly collected in one depression in the street, and such a stench went up—"a rank offense that smelt to heaven,"—as made me think it a very fortunate thing for somebody's stomach that the liquor had been poured out. Of the women around, some were crying, some were laughing, a few alternatly [alternately] singing and returning thanks. One elderly lady in the edge of the crowd was almost in hysterics, but still shouting in a hoarse whisper, such as one often hears at camp-meeting: "Bless the Lord! O, bless the Lord !" She had the appearance of a lady in good circumstances, and a citizen informed me that she is ordinarily one of the quietest, most placid of women. One of her sons died of intemperance, and another is much addicted to liquor.

On every side nothing was witnessed but smiles, laughter, prayers, hand-shaking, and congratulations. The "Shades of Death" was considered by the temperance people as the "backbone of the rebellion," and within twenty-four hours four more saloons surrendered. The movement continues with unabated vigor, and only twelve more saloons remain. Twenty-nine have been closed.

The Saloon Observed

The Anti-Saloon League, founded in 1893, proved the most successful of the dry political organizations. It focused attention on the saloon and "the liquor traffic"—the businesses that supplied and sold liquor. By choosing to focus on the evils of the saloon, the league was in the tradition expressed by the woman's crusade; it was also opposing an institution widely seen as undesirable.

The saloon won the attention of muckrakers, reform-minded journalists in the early twentieth century who exposed vice, corruption, and other social and political sores. Excerpted from George Kibbe Turner, "The City of Chicago: A Study of the Great Immoralities," McClure's Magazine 28 (April 1907): 576–79.

The sale of dissipation is . . . a great business . . . in Chicago. The leading branch . . . is the sale of alcoholic liquor. . . . [T]he liquor interests are vastly more extended in Chicago than any other. There are 7,300 licensed liquor sellers in Chicago, and . . . about a thousand places where liquor is sold illegally. The only business which approaches this in number of establishments . . . is the grocery trade, which has about 5,200. The city spends at least half as much for what it drinks as for what it eats. . . .

The great central power in the liquor business in America is the brewery. . . . [T]he breweries own or control the great majority of the saloons of American cities. They have a distinct policy:—If there are not as many saloons as there can be, supply them. This is what has been done in Chicago. Fully ninety per cent of the Chicago saloons are under some obligation to the brewery; with at least eighty per cent, this obligation is a serious one.

The business of the brewery is to sell beer. . . . The brewery, under present conditions . . . must sell beer at all cost, or promptly die. This is because the brewing business has been over-capitalized and overbuilt there for at least ten years. There has been furious competition. . . . [A]t the present time a full third of the capital invested in the forty companies and fifty plants is not earning dividends. Under these circumstances, the breweries of Chicago can have but one aim—to fill Chicago with beer to the point of saturation.

Each brewer disposes of his product by contracting with special saloon-keepers to sell his beer and no other. The more saloons he has, the better. . . . The brewers employ special agents to watch continually every nook and cranny in Chicago where it may be possible to pour in a little more beer. If a rival brewery's saloon-keeper is doing well, his best bartender is ravished from him and set up in business alongside. If a new colony of foreigners appears, some compatriot is set at once to selling them liquor. Italians, Greeks, Lithuanians, Poles . . . have their trade exploited to the utmost. . . . [N]o man with two hundred dollars [capital] . . . need go without a saloon in Chicago. . . . [T]he brewery sorts him out a set from its stock of saloon fixtures, pays his rent, pays his license, and supplies him with beer. He pays for everything in an extra price on each barrel of beer. . . .

Under this system . . . Chicago has four times as many saloons as it should have, from any standpoint whatever, except, of course, the brewers' and the wholesalers'. . . . There is . . . one retail liquor dealer to every two hundred and eighty-five people, disregarding, of course, the one thousand unlicensed dealers. In the laboring wards the licensed saloons run as many as one to every one hundred and fifty. Take the stock-yards. Around that long and dismal stockade, at every hole from which a human being can emerge, a shop or group of shops sits waiting. At the main entrance they lie massed in batteries. . . .

The Chicago market is thoroughly saturated with beer, and incidentally with other liquor. Reckoning it out by population, every man, woman, and child in Chicago drank, in 1906, two and one-quarter barrels of beer,—that is, seventy gallons,—three and one-half times the average consumption in the United States. . . .

Now, if the competition is red-handed among the breweries, it is simply ravenous among the saloon-keepers. There is a popular fallacy that there is great profit in the retail saloon business. The saloon-keepers themselves believe this when they go into it. . . .

All this means one thing—a premium on the irregular and criminal saloon-keeper. . . . A place is popular, or it is nothing. . . . There are two general business methods of attracting it [a good trade]: By giving unusually large measures and big bonuses of free lunch; or by carrying illegitimate and illegal side lines. The first . . . does not leave large margins of profit; the second does. A year ago the license fee was raised [to] . . . wipe out the criminal saloon. It did, of course, nothing of the sort. The poor, miserable little dives in the working-man's ward, each snatching a starvation living from the lips of the dwellers of the dozen smoke-befouled frame tenements about it, staggered down—a few hundred of them—and died. The man with the side-line of prostitution and gambling naturally survived and had the benefit of the others' failure.

Some Brewers Seek Saloon Reform

Some leaders in the brewing industry recognized that saloon conditions abetted the dry cause, and they sought to reform retail liquor businesses. One focus of the brewers' reform was to reduce the number of saloons to no more than one per five hundred people so that each establishment could operate profitably without resort to prostitution, gambling, and other vices. The following is an excerpt from a report done by brewers who sought to get the industry's house in order. Taken from "Summary of Replies to Inquiries Regarding the Causes of Opposition to Saloons," Brewing and Liquor Interests and German and Bolshevik Propaganda, Report and Hearings of the Subcommittee on the Judiciary, U.S. Senate, *65th Cong.,1919,1070.*

Replies were received from 118 representative brewers. . . . [T]heir replies do not constitute an indictment against all saloons, or even any considerable proportion of the saloons, but that the evils they speak of are found to exist in a sufficient number of cases to cast discredit upon the business as a whole.

Over half of the replies refer to the bad character of certain saloon-keepers and bartenders, and of the careless way in which some of the saloons are conducted. Special reference is made in a large number of the replies to the noise and profanity which takes place, not only inside the saloon, but in front of it. Over forty references are made to gambling in saloons, and fifty-five brewers speak of the use of the dive-saloon as a rendezvous for loafers, gangsters, prostitutes and criminals. No less than sixty-seven brewers state that the selling to known drunkards and intoxicated persons is one of the serious evils, while forty-eight brewers cite the selling of intoxicants to boys and girls.

Arguments For and Against Prohibition

The arguments for and against prohibition occurred all across the United States, in churches and political caucuses, town meetings and legislative sessions. Congress first debated the issue near the end of 1914. Each side advanced more than one argument; the four documents that follow represent core views.

For Prohibition

Richmond P. Hobson, a representative from Alabama, voiced his support for a prohibition amendment on the floor of the House of Repre-

sentatives on 22 December 1914. The proposed amendment received a majority of votes, but not the necessary two-thirds majority to proceed with the process. Excerpted from Richmond P. Hobson, "The Prohibition Amendment," in The Politics of Moral Behavior: Prohibition and Drug Abuse, *ed.* K. Austin Kerr *(Reading, Massachusetts, 1973), 97-100, 102.*

What is the object of this resolution? It is to destroy the agency that debauches the youth of the land and thereby perpetuates its hold upon the Nation. How does the resolution propose to destroy this agent? In the simplest manner. . . . It does not coerce any drinker. It simply says that barter and sale, matters that have been a public function from the semicivilized days of society, shall not continue the debauching of the youth. Now, the Liquor Trust are wise enough to know that they can not perpetuate their sway by depending on debauching grown people, so they go to an organic method of teaching the young to drink. Now we apply exactly the same method to destroy them. We do not try to force old drinkers to stop drinking, but we do effectively put an end to the systematic, organized debauching of our youth through thousands and tens of thousands of agencies throughout the land. Men here may try to escape the simplicity of this problem. They can not. Some are trying to defend alcohol by saying that its abuse only is bad and that its temperate use is all right. Science absolutely denies it, and proclaims that drunkenness does not produce one-tenth part of the harm to society that the widespread, temperate, moderate drinking does. Some say it is adulteration that harms. Some are trying to say that it is only distilled liquors that do harm. Science comes in now and says that all alcohol does harm; that the malt and fermented liquors produce vastly more harm than distilled liquors, and that it is the general public use of such drinks that has entailed the gradual decline and degeneracy of the nations of the past.

[The wets] have no foundation in scientific truth to stand upon, and so they resort to all kinds of devious methods.

Their favorite contention is that we can not reach the evil because of our institutions. This assumes that here is something very harmful and injurious to the public health and morals, that imperils our very institutions themselves and the perpetuity of the Nation, but the Nation has not within itself, because of its peculiar organization, the power to bring about the public good and end a great public wrong. They invoke the principle of State rights. As a matter of fact, we are fighting more consistently for State rights than they ever dreamed of. . . .

Neither can they take refuge about any assumed question of individual liberty. We do not say that a man shall not drink. . . . We do not say that a man shall not have or make liquor in his own home for his own use. . . . We only touch the sale. A man may feel he has a right to drink, but he certainly has no inherent right to sell liquor. A man's liberties are absolutely secure in this resolution. The liberties and sanctity of the home are protected. The liberties of the community are secure, the liberties of the county are secure, and the liberties of the State are secure. . . .

Little Less of a Man After Each Drink

Thus a man is little less of a man after each drink he takes. In this way continued drinking causes a progressive weakening of the will and a progressive growing of the craving, so that after a time, if persisted in, there must come a point where the will power can not control the craving and the victim is in the grip of the habit.

Slaves in Shackles

When the drinking begins young the power of the habit becomes overwhelming, and the victim might as well have shackles. It is estimated that there are 5,000,000 heavy drinkers and drunkards in America, and these men might as well have a ball and chain on their ankles, for they are more abject slaves than those black men who were driven by slave drivers.

Present-day Slave Owners

These victims are driven imperatively to procure their liquor, no matter at what cost. A few thousand brewers and distillers, making up the organizations composing the great Liquor Trust, have a monopoly of the supply, and they therefore own these 5,000,000 slaves and through them they are able to collect two and one-half billions of dollars cash from the American people every year. . . .

There can be but one verdict, and that is this great destroyer must be destroyed. The time is ripe for fulfillment. The present generation, the generation to which we belong, must cut this millstone of degeneracy from the neck of humanity. . . .

The Final Conclusion

To cure this organic disease we must have recourse to the organic law. The people themselves must act upon this question. A generation must be prevailed upon to place prohibition in their own constitutional law, and such a generation could be counted upon to keep it in the Constitution during its lifetime. The Liquor Trust of necessity would disintegrate. The youth would grow up sober. The final, scientific conclusion is that we must have constitutional prohibition, prohibiting only the sale, the manufacture for sale, and everything that pertains to the sale, and invoke the power of both Federal and State Governments for enforcement.

Against Prohibition

Richard Bartholdt, a Republican member from Missouri, was a principal speaker on the wet side. "There is, of course, no doubt about the final outcome," he told the House. "A nation which has thrown off the shackles of despotism will not, for any length of time, tyrannize over itself." Taken from Richard Bartholdt, "Ten Reasons Against Prohibition," in The Politics of Moral Behavior: Prohibition and Drug Abuse, *ed. K. Austin Kerr (Reading, Massachusetts, 1973), 112–13.*

Prohibition is a deathblow to the liberty of the individual because it prohibits what is not wrong in itself. No despot in history has ever dared to prohibit what is morally right, and the attempt to do so would have cost him his head. The exercise of rights which concern persons individually, and whose exercise does not injure the neighbor, is a basic condition of freedom which prohibition violates. The right to eat and drink what we please is an inalienable human right of which even a majority can not deprive us without at the same time robbing us of our liberty. But let us go to the bottom of this matter. It has ever been the aim of the friends of liberty to wrest the scepter of Government from the hands of individual rulers and place it in the hands of the people. Since this has been achieved in America the problem of liberty was believed to have been solved for all time, for no one dreamed that the Nation would ever need protection against its own will or would ever tyrannize over itself. The prohibition movement teaches us, however, that such tyranny after all is possible under self-government by the majority misusing its political liberty or its right to govern for the purpose of restricting personal liberty. In other words, we are dealing in this case with what John Stuart Mill called "the tyranny of the majority," an evil against which the Nation must protect itself if it desires to remain free; for individual liberty, the right of personal conduct, is an inalienable human right which should never be taken away either by majorities or by law or constitution. From this we can see how much larger than the mere drink problem this question really is, for if it were right in one respect to take away from the individual the privilege of self-control it would be right in all other respects, and the final outcome could be nothing less than a condition of complete slavery.

Our opponents say, "We do not propose to prohibit drinking, but merely the manufacture and sale of beverages," but remember that this hypocritical and insidious subterfuge is the very means by which despots always robbed the people of their liberties.

The Liquor Trade

The arguments for and against prohibition occupied hundreds of thousands of pamphlets, books, speeches, broadsides, and other publications. Percy Andreae was the liquor trade's most able political strategist before the First World War. He viewed the drys as simply intolerant, religious zealots. Excerpted from Percy Andreae, "A Glimpse behind the Mask of Prohibition," in The Prohibition Movement in its Broader Bearings upon Our Social, Commercial, and Religious Liberties *(Chicago, 1915), 9-19.*

It means that government by emotion is to be substituted for government by reason, and government by emotion . . . is, according to the testimony of all ages, the most dangerous and pernicious of all forms of government. It has already crept into the legislative assemblies of most of the States of the Union, and is being craftily fostered by those who know how easily it can be made available for their purposes—purposes to the furtherance of which cool reason would never lend itself. Prohibition is but one of its fruits, and the hand that is plucking this fruit is the same hand of intolerance that drove forth certain of our forefathers

Mr. POST. Why, it is obtainable, sir; the greater the attempts at enforcement the stronger the sentiment against it.

Senator REED of Missouri. Do bootleggers ply their trade among the students?

Mr. POST. Well, it is the reverse; the students go to the bootleggers.

Senator REED of Missouri. The students go to the bootleggers?

Mr. POST. Yes; they do not enter the university campus. . . .

Senator REED of Missouri. Is there any difficulty of any student of ordinary intelligence—and I presume they are all that at Yale University—getting all the whisky he wants to buy, or alleged whisky at least?

Mr. POST. No, sir.

Senator REED of Missouri. Is this liquor drunk on the campus or in the quarters of the students?

Mr. POST. Yes, sir.

Senator REED of Missouri. And is it drunk elsewhere?

Mr. POST. Yes, sir.

Senator REED of Missouri. That is all.

There were observations to the contrary. Taken from "The 'Old Days' and the New Among American Students," The International Student 26 *(November 1928): 21.*

Robert E. Reinow, dean of men [at the University of Iowa], "recalls the period before the saloons were outlawed when it was considered a collegiate accoutrement to be able to drink large quantities of liquor. . . . Now, despite some bootlegging, the problem of drinking is almost solved on the University of Iowa camps. . . ."

[Irving Fisher, a distinguished professor of economics at Yale University:] "The amount and evils of drinking among college students have been enormously exaggerated in the press. . . . There is certainly nothing like as much alcoholic liquor consumed by college students today as there was in pre-prohibition days."

A Mayor Speaks Out

Fiorello H. LaGuardia was a prominent New York City Republican politician who served several terms in the House of Representatives before being elected mayor. An outspoken critic of prohibition, he testi-

fied to the policy's failure. Taken from The National Prohibition Law, Hearings before the Subcommittee of the Committee on the Judiciary, *U.S. Senate, 69th Cong., 1st sess., 1926, 649–51.*

It is impossible to tell whether prohibition is a good thing or a bad thing. It has never been enforced in this country.

There may not be as much liquor in quantity consumed today as there was before prohibition; but there is just as much alcohol.

At least 1,000,000 quarts of liquor is consumed each day in the United States. In my opinion such an enormous traffic in liquor could not be carried on without the knowledge, if not the connivance of the officials entrusted with the enforcement of the law. . . .

I believe that the percentage of whisky drinkers in the United States now is greater than in any other country of the world. Prohibition is responsible for that. . . .

At least $1,000,000,000 a year is lost to the National Government and the several States and counties in excise taxes. The liquor traffic is going on just the same. This amount goes into the pockets of bootleggers and in the pockets of the public officials in the shape of graft. . . .

I will concede that the saloon was odious but now we have delicatessen stores, pool rooms, drug stores, millinery shops, private parlors, and 57 other varieties of speak-easies selling liquor and flourishing.

I have heard of $2,000 a year prohibition agents who run their own cars with liveried chauffeurs.

It is common talk in my part of the country that from $7.50 to $12 a case is paid in graft from the time the liquor leaves the 12-mile limit until it reaches the ultimate consumer. There seems to be a varying market price for this service created by the degree of vigilance or the degree of greed of the public officials in charge.

It is my calculation that at least a million dollars a day is paid in graft and corruption to Federal, State, and local officers. Such a condition is not only intolerable, but it is demoralizing and dangerous to organized government. . . .

The Government even goes to the trouble to facilitate the financing end of the bootlegging industry. In 1925, $286,950,000 more of $10,000 bills were issued than in 1920 and $25,000,000 more of $5,000 bills were issued. What honest business man deals in $10,000 bills? Surely these bills were not used to pay the salaries of ministers. The bootlegging industry has created a demand for bills of large denominations, and the Treasury Department accommodates them.

The drys seemingly are afraid of the truth. Why not take inventory and ascertain the true conditions. Let us not leave it to the charge of an antiprohibition organization, or to any other private association, let us have an official survey and let the American people know what is going on. A complete and honest and impartial survey would reveal incredible conditions, corruption, crime, and an organized system of illicit traffic such as the world has never seen.

Prohibition a Success

The widespread claims that prohibition was a failure prompted the National Federation of Settlements to commission a study, surveying social workers across the United States about the policy's effects. The following document is from the report of Estelle Jamison of the County and City Welfare Association. Excerpted from Martha Bensley Bruère, Does Prohibition Work?: A Study of the Operation . . . *(New York, 1927), 18-22, 273.*

In Sioux Falls there were two liquor cures doing a thriving business. Both cures went out of business for lack of patronage with the advent of prohibition. . . .

We have more crime now than in the days of the saloon, but much less disorder, due to the absence of drunken people on the streets and in public places. Police records show a tremendous falling off in the arrests for intoxication.

Since the advent of prohibition the red-light district and the disorderly houses have passed out of existence. The necessity for a red-light district seemed to pass away when the saloon went out of business.

. . . Since the closing of the saloons there has been very little trouble with the colored population. Prostitution and drunkenness among the colored people in this city have dropped to next to

nothing; at any rate, the police do not seem to have the trouble. . .
they used to have in the days of the saloon.

There is but very little bootlegging and illicit manufacture of
liquor. The majority of the people are in favor of enforcing the
liquor laws, and the sheriff and the chief of police are very active
in running down bootleggers and stills.

The poverty obtaining now can be ascribed wholly to the
industrial situation and other causes outside of the use of alcohol.

. . . The activity of the bootleggers in this city is so limited that
the amount of liquor sold does not appear to have any effect on
the community. Bootleggers do not remain in business very long,
however. There is not enough illicit liquor consumed in this city
to make any noticeable change in the general health of the
community.

Of 22 men who were formerly saloon keepers or bartenders in
Sioux Falls, 1 is dead, 1 has moved away, 1 is sick at home, 2 have
retired on their incomes, 2 are packing-house laborers, 3 are in the
real-estate business, and there is also a day laborer, a waiter in a
café, an auctioneer, a janitor of a church, a baker, an operator of a
lakeside resort, a truck farmer, a butcher, a grocer, a salesman of
electric apparatus, and a secretary of a club.

There is much complaint about the prevalence of drinking
among young people of high-school age, but an investigation of
such rumors always results in finding that such drinking is confined to a very few young people. In no instance has it been found
that the young people are acquiring the drink habit; even if they
should wish to, the source of supply is too limited. People will
start rumors that drinking is more common now among young
people than in the days of the saloon, that young women will not
go with a young fellow unless he carries something on his hip; but
the moment that the names of specific young women are demanded, at once comes the reply that, 'It is common talk; everyone knows the young people are drinking. I am only repeating
what everyone is talking about.' . . .

The bootleggers and moonshiners have no political pull in
this state whatever; not even the Democrats will get mixed up in
any way favoring the relaxing of our state liquor laws. Our city
and county officials, from the highest to the lowest, are all elected
on dry platforms.

There are some hold-over liquor addicts who insist on becoming intoxicated on canned heat, flavoring extracts and similar

impossible drinks, but these people are as a rule the derelicts left over from the days of the saloon. They are rapidly passing and leaving no successors.

Weeks pass by now in Sioux Falls without a single arrest for intoxication; while during the days of the saloons on Monday morning there would sometimes be as high as thirty cases of intoxication to be tried by the Municipal Court.

George W. Burnside, who was mayor of Sioux Falls twenty-one years, calls attention to the disappearance of the old-time saloon 'clean up.' Men who were down and out because of the drink habit, are no longer to be seen. . . .

Dean Woodruff of the Episcopal Church says that since the outlawing of the use of liquor there is not the squalid poverty in this city that obtained before prohibition.

The Hon. Mr. Gunderson, member of the legislature and candidate for United States Senator on the Democratic ticket, who lives at Vermilion, where the state university is located, says that there is not the drinking among the young people; you do not see any drunken people; you do not hear the boisterous and loud talk. . . .

The people to whom the social workers are neighbors throughout the great Atlantic port cities are not taking the prohibition law very seriously. Nowhere in their . . . history have they had any preparation for it. It is not a law which came upon them because they felt the need for it, but because another people . . . wanted it for them. Nothing could be more different than the way the fifth or sixth generation of Americans in the cities of the Northwest and the new citizens of the Atlantic ports are reacting to the law. But the fact remains that the social workers do see improved conditions even under this imperfect observance.

Questions

---

1. *What values were at the root of the disagreement over prohibition? What was the core of the disagreement between wets and drys before the enactment of national prohibition?*

2. *What conditions in the liquor trades fueled the prohibition movement? Why would women organize and march—lead a "crusade"—against the saloon?*

3. *What were the arguments that prohibition was a failure? What was the evidence that prohibition was a failure? a success?*

FURTHER READING

In addition to the books from which these readings were drawn, there are several important works. Jack S. Blocker, Jr. has written several books on the subject, including Retreat from Reform: The Prohibition Movement in the United States, 1890-1913 *(Westport, Connecticut, 1976). Ruth Bordin,* Woman and Temperance: The Quest for Power and Liberty, 1873-1900 *(Philadelphia, 1981) is important. Jed Dannenbaum,* Drink and Disorder: Temperance Reform in Cincinnati from the Washingtonian Revival to the WCTU *(Urbana, Illinois, 1984) and Robert Smith Bader,* Prohibition in Kansas: A History *(Lawrence, Kansas, 1986) are excellent local and state studies, respectively. Richard F. Hamm,* Shaping the Eighteenth Amendment: Temperance Reform, Legal Culture, and the Polity, 1880-1920 *(Chapel Hill, North Carolina, 1995) and K. Austin Kerr,* Organized for Prohibition: A New History of the Anti-Saloon League *(New Haven, Connecticut, 1985) explore the organization and politics of prohibition.*

Pictures and more texts are available on the World Wide Web at http:// www.history.ohio-state.edu/projects/prohibition

The First
Sexual Revolution

Leila J. Rupp

Introduction

In the decades before and after 1900, profound changes in American society constituted what historians have called a "sexual revolution." By this they mean a transformation of sexual behavior and attitudes, in particular an increase in sexual contact outside of both marriage and prostitution among some groups in society and a new openness about sexuality, especially women's sexuality. As more white working and middle-class women moved out of the home and into the factories, offices, department stores, and college classrooms of a rapidly industrializing society, the nineteenth-century separation of male and female spheres began to erode. As the economy shifted from the stage of heavy industrialization to the production of consumer goods, the societal emphasis on thrift gave way to the glorification of spending and pleasure. In the newly respectable world of commercialized entertainment— consisting of dance halls, amusement parks, and the movies— young men and women socialized freely with strangers, setting the stage for what commentators came to call the "revolution in manners and morals."

Urban areas served as the crucible for change. Here the massive wave of immigration from southern and eastern Europe and the northward trek of African Americans introduced different sexual attitudes and practices to the white native-born population. In addition, an influx of young, white, rural men and women contributed to the growth of urban working-class subcultures where changes in social and sexual behavior flourished. In traditional rural communities, young people socialized on the front porch or at church, under the watchful eyes of family or community, but in the cities "women adrift"—young women living apart from their families—mingled with strange men in public places. The automobile, too, for those who could afford one, provided privacy that facilitated greater intimacy. The phenomenon of dating, including various kinds of sexual activity, came to replace the more serious "courting" signified by the pairing off of a couple.

As social barriers between men and women crumbled, the nineteenth-century notion of women as "passionless" in contrast to men as inherently lustful came under attack. Women, too, were recognized as sexual beings, a perception underscored by their adoption of shorter skirts, bobbed hair, and makeup. Although a large gap remained between the sexual experience of men and women, both faced new societal demands for "sex appeal." Couples increasingly came to expect sexual satisfaction and fun in marriage. Sexuality separated from the demands of reproduction necessitated access to birth control, a battle originally fought by "emancipated" and radical women in the first decades of the century.

In accordance with the breakdown of social barriers between women and men, sexologists and psychologists emphasized the naturalness of heterosexuality, thereby stigmatizing the same-sex "romantic friendships" that had been widely accepted in the nineteenth century. The usage of the terms "heterosexual" and "homosexual" in the U.S. dates from the turn of the century, when the idea that sexual behavior defined categories of people first developed. Commentators began to notice subcultures of what they termed "inverts"—a description that associated "reversed" gender characteristics with same-sex sexual behavior—in American cities. The sexual revolution both sexualized relationships that had previously seemed non-sexual and categorized people by the sexual acts in which they engaged.

At the heart of all these transformations, then, lay a sexualizing of society. People talked more openly about sexuality, ironically spurred by the social hygiene movement that sought to fight the spread of venereal disease by controlling sexual behavior. People engaged more openly in sexual activity outside the confines of marriage and beyond the world of prostitution. Changes that began in the working-class urban subcultures attracted the attention of a bohemian vanguard in such places as Greenwich Village and Harlem, who then spread the word through their novels, paintings, and music. The "flapper" style of the 1910s and 1920s represented the acceptance by young middle-class women, particularly on college campuses, of styles of behavior pioneered by their working-class sisters. American society would never be the same again.

DATING AND PETTING

Historians often tend to assume that changes in behavior percolate down from the upper or middle classes. The sexual revolution of the early twentieth century first came to light in investigations of middle-class youth. But social historians investigating the working-class subcultures of cities such as New York and Chicago have discovered changes in sexual mores even before those that swept the middle class in the 1920s. Young single women and men, living in boarding houses or furnished rooms, pioneered many of the changes in sexual attitudes and behavior previously associated with college youth.

Paula Fass details the changing sexual norms among native-born, white, middle-class college students in the 1920s, a group that left readily accessible sources by which we can chart new attitudes and behavior. Certainly they played an important role in the transformation of modern American sexuality. But they were not as pioneering as we once thought, as Kathy Peiss's work makes clear. Her interpretation of working-class life in turn-of-the-century cities is based on a careful reading of the reports of middle-class observers—reformers, social workers, and journalists—who often reacted with alarm to what they saw as violations of decent morality. Peiss "reads against the grain" in order to try to understand, through the filter of middle-class minds, how working-class men and women viewed their own sexuality. Both Fass and Peiss are interested in the development of peer subcultures that challenged, to a lesser and greater extent, traditional understandings of morality.

upper
middle-class

Sexuality on Campus in the 1920s

Paula S. Fass, in a commentary on sexuality among white college youth, argues that young people "appeared suddenly, dramatically, even menacingly on the social scene" in the 1920s. By that she means that the stage of youth became increasingly significant for young people themselves and for the setting of trends in society as a whole. Excerpted from Paula S. Fass, The Damned and the Beautiful: American Youth in the 1920's *(New York, 1977), 260–68, 271–72.*

Students of modern sexual behavior have quite correctly described the twenties as a turning point, a critical juncture between the strict double standard of the age of Victoria and the permissive sexuality of the age of Freud. Too often, however, the sexual revolution of the twenties has been described exclusively in terms of scattered data suggesting an increase in premarital sexual intercourse on the part of women. One is tempted to picture investigators hunting for that special morning between 1919 and 1929 when 51% of the young unmarried women in America awoke to find that they were no longer virgins. Instead, of course, investigators are forced to deduce revolutionary changes from small, though important, increases in what remained a minority pattern of behavior. This kind of thinking, not unlike the Victorian concept of all or nothing, overlooks the fact that changes in sexual habits, as in most other areas of social relations, are evolutionary and take place through a gradual accretion of behavioral and value changes. These changes must be located not in sudden reversals of traditional beliefs and habits but in adaptations to new circumstances and in a reorientation to new social groups that set the standards and establish the patterns which most individuals imitate.

By concentrating so exclusively on the incidents of premarital coitus, analysts have overlooked the most fruitful area for understanding the changes in sexual patterns among the majority of the middle-class population. For it is to the behavior and attitudes of young men and women in the twenties, who had to deal with emerging sexual impulses and had the least vested interest in maintaining older norms, that one must look for the readjustments that underlay the process of change. From this perspective the post-war decade was indeed critical for the evolution of modern sexual patterns. The young, reared in a moral standard in which all sex was taboo, redefined that standard according to their own needs and laid the basis for a change in the standard itself. The college campus, especially, provided a fertile social environment for the new mores concerning the relationships between men and women. On the coeducational campuses of the 1920's (matrimonial bureaus, they were sometimes called), sex was a perpetual peer concern.

College youth of the 1920's redefined the relationship between men and women. In good part this resulted from a simple rediscovery—love is erotic. The remainder drew on an old assumption—that the goal of relations between men and women was marriage. Together the new insight and the old tradition resulted in a significant restructuring of premarital forms of sexual behavior as relationships were charged by a new sexual dynamism and a vigorous experimentalism. Sex for middle-class youths of the 1920's had become a significant premarital experience, but it continued to be distinctly marriage-oriented and confined by stringent etiquettes and sharply etched definitions. In the process of defining their future roles in the new society and within the context of already potent changes, the young helped to create the sexual manners of the twentieth century.

The norms established by college youths had a dual purpose. They provided room for the exploration of immediate sexual interests, and they facilitated mate selection for future marriage. The result was a sexual revolution: not, however, as often implied, a revolution erupting in a sudden and drastic increase in sexual intercourse among the unmarried young, but a revolution growing out of new patterns of sexual play. The young evolved a code of sexual behavior that was, in effect, a middle ground between the no-sex-at-all taboo officially prescribed by the adult world and inculcated by their families, and their own burgeoning sexual interests and marital aspirations. To this dual purpose, youths elaborated two basic rituals of sexual interaction—dating and petting. These behavior patterns accompanied and emphasized several important value changes: more tolerance for non-norma-

In the dance halls; painting by Thomas Hart Benton, "City Activities with Dance Hall." (Courtesy of The Equitable Life Assurance Soceity of the United States.)

tive sexual behavior, the recognition and approval of female sexuality, and a positive evaluation of emotional response and expression in relations between men and women. This nexus of behavior and value was the heart of the sexual revolution of the 1920's.

Dating was something definitely new in the ritual of sexual interaction. It was unlike the informal get-togethers that characterized youth socializing in the village or small town of the nineteenth century, for at such events there was no pairing early in an acquaintance. It was also unlike courting, which implied a commitment between two people. Dating permitted a paired relationship without implying a commitment to marriage and encouraged experimental relations with numerous partners. Dating emerged in response to a modern environment in which people met casually and irregularly, and in response to new kinds of recreations like movies, dance halls, and restaurants, where pairing was the most convenient form of boy-girl relation. . . . The lack of commitment permitted close and intimate associations and explorations of personality, and isolation and privacy laid the ground for sexual experimentation, both as a means for testing future compatibility and as an outlet for present sexual energies.

With the isolation of relations, the young were forced to rely on their own judgment in determining the degree and limits of permissible eroticism. It was this latitude for self-determination that produced the haunting fear of sexual promiscuity in the jeremiads of the twenties. The fear was unfounded. The young were thrown back on their own resources, but they were not free, either from the influence of childhood training or, more immediately, from the controls and sanctions of their peers. Basing their actions on an unyielding taboo against sexual intercourse and an elaborate network of peer norms and standards, they proceeded to open up the possibilities of sexual play without overstepping the bounds of family prohibition and peer propriety. . . .

"Petting" described a broad range of potentially erotic physical contacts, from a casual kiss to more intimate caresses and physical fondling. Even such limited eroticism would have automatically defined a woman as loose and disreputable in the nineteenth century. To the Victorians, who divided good women from bad, revered ideal purity, and were suspicious of female sexuality, all forms of eroticism on the part of women could be equated with total submission. Even in the twenties, it was not unknown for reformers to introduce legislation that would prohibit petting and define it along with fornication as illegal as well as immoral. But the young drew distinct boundaries between what was acceptable erotic behavior and what was not. Petting was the means to be safe and yet not sorry, and around this form of sexual activity they elaborated a code of permissible eroticism. As a result, while there remained two kinds of women among college students in the twenties, the difference was not between sexual women and non-sexual women but between sexual women who lived by the rules and those who did not. A Trinity College editor put it well when he asserted, "There are only two kinds of co-eds, those who have been kissed and those who are sorry they haven't been kissed." And he later added just the right note about the group norms that carefully tailored female behavior: "Although a girl will not always let you kiss her when you ask her, she usually appreciates your asking her, often so much that she has to tell her friends."
. . . [T]he youth of the twenties were incorporating dating and petting into a wholly new ritual of graded relationships. A casual first date might thus entail a good-night kiss, but greater intimacies and a certain amount of erotic play were permitted and expected of engaged couples. . . . The young first sanctioned

eroticism and then imposed degrees and standards of acceptability.

College youths were fully aware of, and highly sensitive to, the criticism that petting evoked from their elders. But the editors of college papers were quick to deny any widespread evil in the behavior or intentions of the young. They did not, however, deny the existence of petting or its importance in the social relations between the sexes. What they denied was the adult evaluation of such behavior as promiscuous or immoral, as in fact it was by an earlier standard. Peer norms, which deviated from adult attitudes, were now legitimate criteria for evaluating conduct. By the standards of the young, petting was not immoral. It was inappropriate when abused and when the rigid boundaries the young imposed on their own behavior were overstepped. In decrying the inordinate amount of attention that youth's morals were receiving from the public, the *Daily Illini,* for example, illustrated how out of touch older people were with the life of the young by referring to a recent questionnaire where the term "spooning" had been used. A sure way of antagonizing youth, the *Illini* noted, was to be so removed from the realities of their lives as to use an expression as archaic and wholly unreal as "spooning."

In view of the strength of peer-group influence, youth were unlikely to bypass the restrictions and staged ritual associated with sexual behavior. But neither was petting restricted to only a small minority of wildly experimental youths, for petting had become a convention and a necessary demonstration of conformity. One investigation of coed behavior found that 92% of all women admitted petting at one time or another. . . . One observed the restrictions on petting in order to remain respectable to peers, but given the occasion and the desire, one could and did pet because it was commonly accepted behavior. There was undoubtedly also considerable pressure to pet at least a little in order to remain in good standing in the eyes of peers and to assure that future dates would be forthcoming. One result of this peer compulsion was that experimental erotic exploration was often a group phenomenon. The petting party was probably the major contribution of the twenties to group sex, and it was in such groups that the first hesitant initiations into erotic play were often made. . . .

The rating system by which social connections were made and by which eligibility was established and maintained worked within a tight system of gossip, reference, bull-session discussions, and careful conformity to standards. A correspondent to the *Daily Illini* . . . asked pointedly, "At what fraternity house will you not find sooner or later just such a discussion of 'Girls Who Pet'?" If a woman could be criticized for the way she wore her hair, for excessive reliance on the paint box, or for overly suggestive dancing, and when it was generally known whether she was "a first-night petter," how much more would her reputation be affected by an imputation of officially and unofficially proscribed behavior? One study of undergraduate life noted, "Men are very dependent on one another's estimate of a girl. Some fraternities blacklist a girl for being obviously 'a speed,' too giddily dressed, or lacking sex attraction." There was a very clear differentiation between positive sex appeal and offensive behavior. For the majority, "a petting party is the right thing to do," but a really "fast woman" was disreputable. Sexual irregularity on the part of coeds, as one investigator of campus ethics discovered, was universally condemned by men and women as the worst of all possible offenses on the campus. Significantly, women still condemned such irregularities more consistently than men, and since it was women who usually regulated sexual behavior, there was still a tight lid on intercourse with campus women. Despite an easing of the double standard and an erosion of distinctions between virtuous women and sexual women, students still clung to a double standard in their own behavior and described illicit sexual behavior as far worse for women than for men. . . .

Dating and petting were, moreover, distinctly marriage-oriented in the twenties. Since mating was one of the chief aims of both rituals, immediate sexual satisfactions had to be carefully weighed in view of long-term goals. And while virginity in a bride was no longer an absolute prerequisite for most men, it was still considered desirable. For men, female chastity appears to have taken a back seat to considerations of compatibility, but there was still some ambiguity on this point, and the devaluation of virginity in the bride was probably related to a growing acceptance of intercourse among engaged couples rather than to a tolerance of casual promiscuity. Women too continued to display considerable anxiety about the consequences of lost virginity. These multiple ambivalences reinforced the sense of acceptable limitations on sexual indulgence. . . .

The controlled ritual of petting had opened up the possibilities of intimacy and response in the relationship between young men and women. At the same time, it also restricted complete spontaneity and laid the basis for the emotionally inhibiting cat-and-mouse game of staged seductions and "scoring" that continued to govern sexual relations among the young throughout the first half of the twentieth century. It was a first and necessary step toward modern patterns of sexual behavior, for the youths of the twenties redefined sexuality in erotic and emotional terms. But in ritualizing a process of personal and cultural experimentation, the youth of the twenties had also placed bonds on individual expression and behavior quite as real and determinate as those which ruled in the heyday of Victorian morals.

"Charity Girls" and City Pleasures

Beginning in the last decades of the nineteenth century, urban working-class youths created their own peer subculture that in many ways foreshadowed what would happen on campuses in the 1920s. Excerpted from Kathy Peiss, "'Charity Girls' and City Pleasures: Historical Notes on Working-Class Sexuality, 1880–1920" in Powers of Desire: The Politics of Sexuality, *ed. Ann Snitow, Christine Stansell, and Sharon Thompson (New York, 1983), 75–78, 81–84.*

My discussion focuses on one set of young, white working women in New York City in the years 1880 to 1920. Most of these women were single wage earners who toiled in the city's factories, shops, and department stores, while devoting their evenings to the lively entertainment of the streets, public dance halls, and other popular amusements. Born or educated in the United States, many adopted a cultural style meant to distance themselves from their immigrant roots and familial traditions. Such women dressed in the latest finery, negotiated city life with ease, and sought intrigue and adventure with male companions. For this group of working women, sexuality became a central dimension of their emergent culture, a dimension that is revealed in their daily life of work and leisure.

These New York working women frequented amusements in which familiarity and intermingling among strangers, not decorum, defined normal public behavior between the sexes. At movies and cheap theaters, crowds mingled during intermissions, shared picnic lunches, and commented volubly on performances. Strangers at Coney Island's amusement parks often involved each other in practical jokes and humorous escapades, while dance halls permitted close interaction between unfamiliar men and women. At one respectable Turnverein ball, for example, a vice investigator described closely the chaotic activity in the barroom between dances:

> Most of the younger couples were hugging and kissing, there was a general mingling of men and women at the different tables, almost everyone seemed to know one another and spoke to each other across the tables and joined couples at different tables, they were all singing and carrying on, they kept running around the room and acted like a mob of lunatics let lo[o]se.

As this observer suggests, an important aspect of social familiarity was the ease of sexual expression in language and behavior. Dances were advertised, for example, through the distribution of "pluggers," small printed cards announcing the particulars of the ball, along with snatches of popular songs or verse; the lyrics and pictures, noted one offended reformer, were often "so suggestive that they are absolutely indecent." . . .

Other forms of recreation frequented by working-class youth incorporated a free and easy sexuality into their attractions. Many social clubs and amusement societies permitted flirting, touching, and kissing games at their meetings. One East Side youth reported that "they have kissing all through pleasure time, and use slang language, while in some they don't behave nice between [sic] young ladies." Music halls and cheap vaudeville regularly worked sexual themes and suggestive humor into comedy routines and songs. At a Yiddish music hall popular with both men and women, one reformer found that "the songs are suggestive of everything but what is proper, the choruses are full of double

Luna Park—Coney Island Amusement Park, site of the working-class urban heterosocial subculture. (Courtesy of Culver Pictures, Inc.)

meanings, and the jokes have broad and unmistakable hints of things indecent." Similarly, Coney Island's Steeplechase amusement park, favored by working-class excursionists, carefully marketed sexual titillation and romance in attractions that threw patrons into each other, sent skirts flying, and evoked instant intimacy among strangers. . . .

The heterosocial orientation of these amusements made popularity a goal to be pursued through dancing ability, willingness to drink, and eye-catching finery. Women who would not drink at balls and social entertainments were often ostracized by men, while cocktails and ingenious mixtures replaced the five-cent beer and helped to make drinking an acceptable female activity. Many women used clothing as a means of drawing attention to themselves, wearing high-heeled shoes, fancy dresses, costume jewelry, elaborate pompadours, and cosmetics. As one working woman sharply explained, "If you want to get any notion took of you, you gotta have some style about you." The clothing that such women wore no longer served as an emblem of respectability. "The way women dress today they all look like prostitutes,"

The dance craze. (Courtesy of The Library of Congress.)

reported one rueful waiter to a dance hall investigator, "and the waiter can some times get in bad by going over and trying to put some one next to them, they may be respectable women and would jump on the waiter."

Underlying the relaxed sexual style and heterosocial interaction was the custom of "treating." Men often treated their female companions to drinks and refreshments, theater tickets, and other incidentals. Women might pay a dance hall's entrance fee or carfare out to an amusement park, but they relied on men's treats to see them through the evening's entertainment. Such treats were highly prized by young working women; as Belle Israels remarked, the announcement that "he treated" was "the acme of achievement in retailing experiences with the other sex."

Treating was not a one-way proposition, however, but entailed an exchange relationship. Financially unable to reciprocate in kind, women offered sexual favors of varying degrees, ranging from flirtatious companionship to sexual intercourse, in exchange for men's treats. "Pleasures don't cost girls so much as they do young men," asserted one saleswoman. "If they are agreeable they are invited out a good deal, and they are not allowed to pay anything." Reformer Lillian Betts concurred, observing that the working woman held herself responsible for failing to wangle men's invitations and believed that "it is not only her misfortune, but her fault; she should be more attractive." Gaining men's treats placed a high premium on allure and personality, and sometimes involved aggressive and frank "overtures to men whom they desire to attract," often with implicit sexual proposals. One investigator, commenting on women's dependency on men in their leisure time, aptly observed that "those who are unattractive, and those who have puritanic notions, fare but ill in the matter of enjoyments. On the other hand those who do become popular have to compromise with the best conventional usage." . . .

The extent of the sexual culture . . . is particularly difficult to establish, since the evidence is too meager to permit conclusions about specific groups of working women, their beliefs about sexuality, and their behavior. Scattered evidence does suggest a range of possible responses, the parameters within which most women would choose to act and define their behavior as socially acceptable. Within this range, there existed a subculture of working women who fully bought into the system of treating and sexual exchange, by trading sexual favors of varying degrees for gifts, treats, and a good time. These women were known in underworld slang as "charity girls," a term that differentiated them from prostitutes because they did not accept money in their sexual encounters with men. As vice reformer George Kneeland found, they "offer themselves to strangers, not for money, but for presents, attention, and pleasure, and most important, a yielding to sex desire." Only a thin line divided these women and "occasional prostitutes," women who slipped in and out of prostitution when unemployed or in need of extra income. Such behavior did not result in the stigma of the "fallen woman." Many working women apparently acted like Dottie: "When she needed a pair of shoes she had found it easy to 'earn' them in the way that other girls did." Dottie, the investigator reported, was now known as a respectable married woman. . . .

The charity girl's activities form only one response in a wide spectrum of social and sexual behavior. Many young women defined themselves sharply against the freer sexuality of their pleasure-seeking sisters, associating "respectability" firmly with premarital chastity and circumspect behavior. One working woman carefully explained her adherence to propriety: "I never go out in the evenings except to my relatives because if I did, I should lose my reputation and that is all I have left." Similarly, shop girls guarded against sexual advances from co-workers and male customers by spurning the temptations of popular amusements. "I keep myself to myself," said one saleswoman. "I don't make friends in the stores very easily because you can't be sure what any one is like." Settlement workers also noted that women who freely attended "dubious resorts" or bore illegitimate children were often stigmatized by neighbors and workmates. Lillian

Betts, for example, cites the case of working women who refused to labor until their employer dismissed a co-worker who had born a baby out of wedlock. To Betts, however, their adherence to the standard of virginity seemed instrumental, and not a reflection of moral absolutism: "The hardness with which even the suggestion of looseness is treated in any group of working girls is simply an expression of self-preservation."

Other observers noted an ambivalence in the attitudes of young working women toward sexual relations. Social workers reported that the critical stance toward premarital pregnancy was "not always unmixed with a certain degree of admiration for the success with the other sex which the difficulty implies." According to this study, many women increasingly found premarital intercourse acceptable in particular situations: "'A girl can have many friends,' explained one of them, 'but when she gets a "steady," there's only one way to have him and to keep him; I mean to keep him long.'" Such women shared with charity girls the assumption that respectability was not predicated solely on chastity.

Perhaps few women were charity girls or occasional prostitutes, but many more must have been conscious of the need to negotiate sexual encounters in the workplace or in their leisure time. Women would have had to weigh their desire for social participation against traditional sanctions regarding sexual behavior, and charity girls offered to some a model for resolving this conflict. This process is exemplified in Clara Laughlin's report of an attractive but "proper" working woman who could not understand why men friends dropped her after a few dates. Finally she receives the worldly advice of a co-worker that social participation involves an exchange relationship: "Don't yeh know there ain't no feller goin' t'spend coin on yeh fer nothin'?" . . .

For . . . young working women, respectability was not defined by the strict measurement of chastity employed by many middle-class observers and reformers. Instead, they adopted a more instrumental and flexible approach to sexual behavior. Premarital sex *could* be labeled respectable in particular social contexts. Thus charity girls distinguished their sexual activity from prostitution, a less acceptable practice, because they did not receive money from men. Other women, who might view charity girls as promiscuous, were untroubled by premarital intimacy with a steady boyfriend.

This fluid definition of sexual respectability was embedded within the social relation of class and gender, as experienced by women in their daily round of work, leisure, and family life. Women's wage labor and the demands of the working-class household offered daughters few resources for entertainment. At the same time, new commercial amusements offered a tempting world of pleasure and companionship beyond parental control. Within this context, some young women sought to exchange sexual goods for access to that world and its seeming independence, choosing not to defer sexual relations until marriage. Their notions of legitimate premarital behavior contrast markedly with the dominant middle-class view, which placed female sexuality within a dichotomous and rigid framework. Whether a hazard at work, fun and adventure at night, or an opportunity to be exploited, sexual expression and intimacy comprised an integral part of these working women's lives.

Questions

1. *How similar and how different were the definitions of acceptable sexual behavior shaped by the college culture in the 1920s and the working-class subculture in the period from 1890-1920?*
2. *What class differences in attitudes toward sexuality do you see in comparing working-class and middle-class Americans, including both middle-class college students and middle-class observers of the working-class subculture?*
3. *How "revolutionary" was the first sexual revolution?*
4. *In what ways might the changes described by Paula Fass and Kathy Peiss have set the stage for contemporary relations between the sexes?*

PERSPECTIVES ON SEXUALITY IN THE EARLY TWENTIETH-CENTURY UNITED STATES

Dating and petting among white, urban, working-class youth and college students represent an important sign of the first sexual revolution, but there were other manifestations of this important transformation in American society. Commentators from the 1910s on noticed the greater openness in discussions of sexuality, often linking them to public discourse about prostitution, venereal disease, and birth control. Perhaps nothing shocked the arbiters of traditional morality so much as young women—the "flappers" who revealed their boyish bodies, used cosmetics, and claimed the right to smoke and drink with men—who talked of "white slavery"—a term that implicitly contrasted involuntary prostitution to the enslavement of Africans and African Americans—without batting an eye. So, too, public discussion of birth control, pioneered by anarchist Emma Goldman and socialist Margaret Sanger, threatened the traditional order by validating sexuality apart from reproduction.

The changes associated with the sexual revolution also affected diverse groups of Americans. Alongside the cafes and dance halls catering to the heterosexual crowd, establishments for men (and to a far lesser extent women) attracted to members of the same sex grew up in urban areas. That the freer expression of sexuality—both heterosexual and same-sex—affected not just young white people is clear from the art, music, and social life that flowered during the Harlem Renaissance of the 1920s. Following the massive migration of African Americans from the rural South to the urban North, the vibrant mixed-class neighborhood of Harlem fostered both artistic and sexual experimentation. Novels, plays, poetry, and especially the blues celebrated sexuality and even fostered the recognition and grudging toleration of same-sex relationships. The fol-

lowing documents illustrate a range of perspectives on the widespread changes that comprised the sexual revolution.

"Sex O'Clock" in America

"Sex O'Clock in America," a much-cited article published in 1913, heralds the new openness about sexuality and discusses the views of a number of commentators who disagreed about what was going on and whether or not the new developments should be viewed as dangerous. This article appeared in Current Opinion, *55, no. 2 (August 1913): 113–14.*

A WAVE of sex hysteria and sex discussion seems to have invaded this country. Our former reticence on matters of sex is giving way to a frankness that would even startle Paris. Prostitution, as *Life* remarks, is the chief topic of polite conversation. It has struck "sex o'clock" in America, to use [journalist] William Marion Reedy's memorable phrase. The White Slave appears in the headlines of our newspapers. . . . [Journalist] Witter Bynner in *The Forum* exploits the White Slave in blank verse. *Leslie's Weekly* points out her lesson in short stories. *The Smart Set* makes her the subject of a novelette. In the theater, "Damaged Goods," a play of which the action springs from venereal disease, marks an epoch of new freedom in sex discussion. . . . Vice reports leap into print. Vice commissions meet and gravely attempt to rebuild in a fortnight the social structure of the world. Is this overemphasis of sex a symptom of a new moral awakening or is it a sign that the morbidity of the Old World is overtaking the New? Does it indicate a permanent change in our temper or is it merely the concomitant of the movement for the liberation of woman from the shackles of convention that will disappear when society has readjusted itself to the New Woman and the New Man? Has it struck sex o'clock permanently or will time soon point to another hour?

One writer in the St. Louis *Mirror*, James F. Clark, asserts that we must grant to-day to woman the same promiscuity that society tacitly grants to the male. This statement has aroused a storm of discussion and protest. Mr. Reedy himself, tho a radical, strongly dissents from the attitude of his aggressive contributor. . . .

"The laxity in sex matters in this and other countries cannot be said to be due to the broadening of women's views. The women who have entered upon the life of civic and social enlargement are not those who 'go astray.' The sexually loose women are not the so-called advanced women. They are the parasite women, the indulged women, the women who do not think. And I want to say that I don't believe in the theory that the woman has the same passions as a man. I, too, have been to Cyprus, and the woman of passion, from Sappho to Catherine of Russia, is a fake or a physio-psychological freak. Woman's passion is mostly a pretence. The idea that women in any great number would resort to promiscuity is absurd. The removal of the fear of consequences won't count for much with an intelligent womanhood. Not intelligence, but ignorance recruits the ranks of the social evil."

The brilliant Saint Louis editor has little use for the anti-vice crusades financed by Standard Oil money. There are, he says, and he speaks with the authority of a man of wide experience, plenty of women of evil life in all large cities. But these are not "White Slaves." The inmates of houses may be in debt to mistresses, but they are not held prisoners and cannot be. "But as young Rockefeller is putting up the money for the White Slave hunt, of course," Mr. Reedy goes on to say, somewhat cynically, "'White Slaves' have to be produced." Vice and crime, he insists, are the symptoms of poverty, which itself is a symptom of the disease known as privilege. We should strike at the root, not at the branches.

The vice crusade business in Chicago, New York, San Francisco, everywhere, thinks Reedy, is being overdone. There is too much sensationalism in its campaigns. There is too much censorship of songs and dances. . . .

"No one is particularly in favor of vice. But most thinking people are in favor of liberty and there cannot prevail much liberty when the raiding plan of reform is so generally adopted. I have an idea that people have a right to go to hell in their own way. And that a good way to drive them to hell is to begin to coerce and drive them towards other people's ideals of righteousness. Raids are going to produce more harm than good. If society is going to hell by way of the tango and the turkey trot and the cabaret show, who started it in that direction? Why, 'the best people.' It is 'the best people' that have exalted vaudeville and girl shows above the genuine drama. It is the best people who have made the cabaret show and demanded that it be ever more and more highly spiced. When the habits and customs of the best people broaden down to the common people, lo, there is a wild cry for reform. And it is all done now in the name of the working girl. Balderdash! The working girl is a working girl, not a bawd at large. The working girl doesn't keep the hot joints in the big town running. That is done mostly by folks who think themselves in the know and in the swim. The prevalent looseness in society is not to be checked by sensational raids or slumming expeditions by legislative committees of investigation. We must begin farther back than the patrol-wagon."

Reedy places the blame for the sex hysteria upon the hedonistic materialistic philosophy that pervades American life. The poor, he says, learn their worst vices from the rich. Everybody lives for a good time in the upper world, and the infection spreads downward. "Is there," he asks, "anything of the spiritual left in education in America, broadly speaking? There is not."

"Education is now directed to the end of enabling a man to get money. Our youths study what they think will enable them to get there quickest. No classics. No arts and no metaphysics. No religion. And science—well, science is fallen into the hands of those who pursue it not to *know*, but to *get*. Education is not to draw a man out of himself, but to draw material things to himself. No one is concerned with eternal things. All that interests us is the immediate gratification. And some few of us have the idea that, because we think we are better than other people, we have a right to say what they shall sing or dance and whom they shall marry and whether they shall marry at all. We want to make people good by science." . . .

Dr. Cecile L. Greil, a Socialist writer, welcomes the fact that society is drawing its head out of the sand of prudery where it had hidden it, ostrich-like. But she, too, fears the hysteria of sex discussion. She especially warns the members of her own sex. The pendulum with women swings more rapidly to extreme degrees, she asserts. This may be because of her highly sensitized nervous organism, which fastens with almost hysterical tenacity to anything which produces an emotional appeal. And surely nothing that has come to her for study or reflection in all the ages has been as important to her, and through her to posterity, as is this freedom of sex knowledge, which guards the citadel of society and makes for a better, finer race of citizens. "But one danger lurks in her midst. Sex freedom is frequently hysterically interpreted into meaning sex license. And the science which shall give her the right to freer, happier motherhood entails all the responsibilities that freedom in any other sense does." The modern social system, the writer continues in *The Call*, is a terrific endurance test against the forces within ourselves and the forces that attack us without. Vanity and love and sport she admits, quoting a Judge of one of the Night Courts, make more prostitutes than economic pressure and exploitation.

"Youth is extravagant to prodigality with itself. It is drunk with its own intoxicating perfume. It looks down into the glass of life as did Narcissus into the brook, and like Narcissus falls in love with its own beauty. And we surround that young, passionate, bursting blossom with every temptation to break down its resistant power, lure it into sentient, pulsating desire and eroticism by lurid literature, moving pictures, tango dances, suggestive songs, cabarets, noise, music, light, life, rhythm, everywhere, until the senses are throbbing with leashed-in physical passion—everything done to lure, but nothing to instruct. So one day the leash snaps, and another boy or girl is outside the pale. We do much for the developing of the intellect and for the use of our hands so that we may send our young people out into the big battle that lies beyond the home, but for the battle against the physical forces, the law, of the magnetic attraction of the sexes, at the dangerous period of puberty and adolescence, we do nothing. Education is the only thing that can save, rational libertarian education on the subjects pertaining to the laws of personal and social hygiene."

Society is apt to regard the fourteen-year-old adolescent as a little dreamy school-girl, ties pretty ribbons in her hair, and keeps her dresses well confined to knee length, forgetting that all the externals of the child mask the seething turbulent ocean underneath. In the child dwells a fully awakened woman. Nature goes through a vicarious process of sex awakening with all its stupendous morbid psychology and complexes. The position of the boy at puberty, contends Dr. Greil, is still worse. He has not even the hereditary instincts of inhibition that his little sister has.

"Society smiles on his acts, calls them 'sport,' sowing his wild oats, etc. He becomes a moral coward and sneak, conscious only of strong animal impulses that he need not curb, and these drive him early to secret vice, to the brothel, to dissipation and roguery. And the crop he reaps from the wild oats he sows fill our streets with prostitutes, fill our foundling asylums with nameless babies and give him a heritage of venereal disease to wreck his future usefulness and hand down as a sad legacy to his posterity. He fears no moral code! His mother and sisters live in a rarified atmosphere of imaginary purity that cuts him off from intimacy, and the understanding which his mother could impart to him if she were his friend instead of a transcendental ideal far up on a pedestal out of his reach. His father, perhaps the only human being who could save him at the crucial period, is his bitterest foe or at best a total stranger to him, shielding himself after exhausting all the phases of sex liberty for himself in an armor of virtue and respectability, which simply antagonizes the boy and widens the breach between himself and society.

"He becomes an alien in his own home, an outcast free to mingle with the world of vicious freedom that welcomes him with open arms, makes him the tool of lost souls and stains him with a smear of filth that ruins him utterly before he is old enough to learn that his much-prized sex freedom is a bondage that makes him pay exorbitant prices in loss of strength, ideals and health. Truly, life does teach as thoroly [thoroughly] as any academy, but how it makes us pay!"

The necessity of sex education is generally recognized. Yet there are also evidences of reaction. Thus the Chicago Board of Education rescinded the order issued by Mrs. Ella Flagg Young, in whose hands rests the school system of Chicago, providing for lectures on sex hygiene in the schools. *The Ecclesiastical Review,* a Roman Catholic publication, maintains that whatever warning and instruction may be necessary should be left in the hands of the priest. Nevertheless, the editor, tho grudgingly, prints a list of books on eugenics for the use of Roman Catholic teachers and priests to aid them in following intelligently the trend of public opinion. Another Roman Catholic publication, *America,* asks for the suppression of vice reports and of vice commissions, except for restricted particular investigations. The publication attacks Doctor Eliot's championship of the Society of Sanitary and Moral Prophylaxis. Eliot has no right, in the opinion of *America,* to declare that before the advent of the Society and its head, Dr. Morton, the policy of the world was "absolute silence" with regard to sex hygiene. "There is," we are told, "a world of difference between absolute silence and the wise and prudent discretion which bids father and mother and teacher refrain from handling the topic in public and without discriminating sense, whilst it at the same time inspires them to say at the fitting time the right word which shall safeguard their children, and to say it with a circumspection not likely to destroy the sense of shame, which is the best natural protection of the innocence of these little ones."

Radicals and conservatives, Free-thinkers and Catholics, all seem to believe in solving the sex problem by education, but as to the method that is to be followed there are abysmal differences of opinion.

The Flapper

This unsigned article written in 1915 by the renowned journalist and social critic H.L. Mencken caricatures the young upper- or middle-class woman who had embraced the flapper style and could discuss prostitution or venereal disease without blushing. Taken from H.L. Mencken, "The Flapper," in The Smart Set 45, no. 2 (February 1915): 1–2.

THE American language, curiously enough, has no name for her. In German she is *der Backfisch*, in French she is *l'Ingénue*, in English she is the Flapper. But in American, as I say, she is nameless, for Chicken will never, never do. Her mother, at her age, was a Young Miss; her grandmother was a Young Female. But she herself is no Young Miss, no Young Female. Oh, dear, no! . . .

Observe, then, this nameless one, this American Flapper. Her skirts have just reached her very trim and pretty ankles; her hair, newly coiled upon her skull,

Flapper fashions. (Courtesy of UPI/Corbis-Bettmann.)

149

has just exposed the ravishing whiteness of her neck. A charming creature! Graceful, vivacious, healthy, appetizing. It is a delight to see her bite into a chocolate with her pearly teeth. There is music in her laugh. There is poetry in her drive at tennis. She is an enchantment through the plate glass of a limousine. Youth is hers, and hope, and romance, and—

Well, well, let us be exact: let us not say innocence. This Flapper, to tell the truth, is far, far, far from a simpleton. An Ingénue to the Gaul, she is actually as devoid of ingenuousness as a newspaper reporter, a bartender or a midwife. The age she lives in is one of knowledge. She herself is educated. She is privy to dark secrets. The world bears to her no aspect of mystery. She has been taught how to take care of herself.

For example, she has a clear and detailed understanding of all the tricks of white slave traders, and knows how to circumvent them. She is on the lookout for them in matinée lobbies and railroad stations—benevolent-looking old women who pretend to be ill, plausible young men who begin business with "Beg pardon," bogus country girls who cry because their mythical brothers have failed to meet them. She has a keen eye for hypodermic needles, chloroform masks, closed carriages. She has seen all these sinister machines of the devil in operation on the screen. . . . She has followed the war upon them in the newspapers.

Life, indeed, is almost empty of surprises, mysteries, horrors to this Flapper of 1915. She knows the exact percentage of lunatics among the children of drunkards. . . . She knows exactly what the Wassermann reaction [a blood test for venereal disease] is, and has made up her mind that she will never marry a man who can't show an unmistakable negative. . . . She is opposed to the double standard of morality, and favors a law prohibiting it.

This Flapper has forgotten how to simper; she seldom blushes; it is impossible to shock her. She saw "Damaged Goods" without batting an eye, and went away wondering what the row over it was all about. The police of her city having prohibited "Mrs. Warren's Profession," [a novel about prostitution] she read it one rainy Sunday afternoon, and found it a mass of platitudes. . . . She slaved at French in her finishing school in order to read Anatole France. . . . She plans to read Havelock Ellis during the coming summer. . . .

As I have said, a charming young creature. There is something trim and trig and confident about her. She is easy in her manners.

She bears herself with dignity in all societies. She is graceful, rosy, healthy, appetizing. It is a delight to see her sink her pearly teeth into a chocolate, a macaroon, even a potato. There is music in her laugh. She is youth, she is hope, she is romance—she is wisdom!

Emma Goldman Lectures on Sex

Harry Kemp, a Bohemian writer known as the "Don Juan of Greenwich Village," relates part of the story of his life on the road as a tramp. Kemp, using the name "Johnnie," describes a lecture by the anarchist advocate of emancipation, Emma Goldman, here called "Emma Silverman." Goldman lectured widely on sex, birth control, and the emancipation of women. She was deported after the First World War for her radical views. Excerpted from Harry Kemp, Tramping on Life: An Autobiographical Narrative *(New York, 1922), 285–88. (Note: Kemp uses a modified form of ellipses in the text.)*

Emma Silverman, the great anarchist leader, came to Laurel, with her manager, Jack Leitman. I went to the Bellman House, the town's swellest hotel, to see her. I had never met her but had long admired her for her activities and bravery. . . .

Her first lecture was on Sex. The hall was jammed to the doors by a curiosity-moved crowd.

She began by assuming that she was not talking to idiots and cretins, but to men and women of mature minds—so she could speak as she

Emma Goldman, anarchist, birth control advocate, and apostle of sexual freedom. (Courtesy of UPI/Corbis-Bettmann.)

151

thought in a forthright manner. She inveighed against the double standard. When someone in the auditorium asked what she meant by the single standard she replied, she meant sexual expression and experience for man and woman on an equal footing . . the normal living of life without which no human being could be really decent—and that regardless of marriage and the conventions!

"The situation as it is, is odious . . all men, with but few exceptions, have sexual life before marriage, but they insist that their wives come to them in that state of absurd ignorance of their own bodily functions and consequent lack of exercise of them, which they denominate 'purity.' . . I doubt if there is a solitary man in this audience—a married man—who has not had premarital intercourse with women."

All the while I kept my eye on Professor Wilton, who sat near me, in the row ahead . . he was flushing furiously in angry, puritanic dissent . . and I knew him well enough to foresee a forthcoming outburst of protest.

"Yes, I think I can safely say that there is not one married man here who can honestly claim that he came to his wife with that same physical 'purity' which he required of her."

Wilton leaped to his feet in a fury . . the good, simple soul. He was so indignant that the few white hairs on his head worked up sizzling with his emotion. . .

"Here's one!" he shouted, forgetting in his earnest anger the assembled audience, most of whom knew him.

There followed such an uproar of merriment as I have never seen the like before nor since. The students, of course, howled with indescribable joy . . Emma Silverman choked with laughter. Jack Leitman rolled over the side table on which he had set the books to sell as the crowd passed out——

After the deafening cries, cat-calls and uproars, Emma grew serious.

"I don't know who you are," she cried to Professor Wilton, "but I'll take chances in telling you that you're a liar!"

Again Wilton was on his feet in angry protest.

"Shame on you, woman! have you no shame!" he shouted.

Excerpt from *Tramping on Life: An Autobiographical Narrative* by Harry Kemp, published by Boni and Liveright Publishers, New York, 1922. Copyright © 1922 by Boni and Liveright, Inc.

This sally brought the house down utterly. The boys hooted and cat-called and stamped again. . .

Emma Silverman laughed till the tears streamed down her face. . .

"I have something on my conscience," remarked Miss Silverman to me, "Johnnie, do you really think that old professor was speaking the truth?"

"I'm sure of it, Miss Silverman."

"Why, then, I'm heartily sorry . . and it was rough of me . . and will you tell the professor for me that I sincerely apologise for having hurt his feelings . . tell him I have so many jackasses attending my lectures all over the country, who rise and say foolish and insincere things, just to stand in well with the communities they live in—that sometimes it angers me, <u>their hypocrisy</u>— and then I blaze forth pretty strong and lay them flat!"

Same-Sex Subcultures

An excerpt from British sexologist <u>Havelock Ellis's</u> Sexual Inversion, *the second volume of a multi-volume work called* Studies in the Psychology of Sex, *describes the existence of same-sex sexual subcultures in U.S. cities. Most observers of such subcultures, like the middle-class reformers who described the heterosexual urban working-class world, expressed the kind of disapproval evident in Ellis's account. The term "invert," introduced by medical commentators at the turn of the century, reflected the assumption that men attracted to men were feminine and women attracted to women were masculine—their gender was "inverted." Taken from Havelock Ellis,* Studies in the Psychology of Sex, *vol. 2,* Sexual Inversion, *3d ed. (Philadelphia, 1933), 351–52, 299–300.*

As regards the prevalence of homosexuality in the United States, I may quote from a well-informed American correspondent:—

Excerpts from *Studies in the Psychology of Sex, Volume II, Sexual Inversion* by Havelock Ellis, published by F. A. Davis Company. Copyright © 1901, 1915 by F.A. Davis Company.

"The great prevalence of sexual inversion in American cities is shown by the wide knowledge of its existence. Ninety-nine normal men out of a hundred have been accosted on the streets by inverts, or have among their acquaintances men whom they know to be sexually inverted. Everyone has seen inverts and knows what they are. The public attitude toward them is generally a negative one—indifference, amusement, contempt.

"The world of sexual inverts is, indeed, a large one in any American city, and it is a community distinctly organized—words, customs, traditions of its own; and every city has its numerous meeting-places: certain churches where inverts congregate; certain cafés well known for the inverted character of their patrons; certain streets where, at night, every fifth man is an invert. The inverts have their own 'clubs,' with nightly meetings. These 'clubs' are, really, dance-halls, attached to *saloons*, and presided over by the proprietor of the saloon, himself almost invariably an invert, as are all the waiters and musicians. The frequenters of these places are male sexual inverts (usually ranging from 17 to 30 years of age); sightseers find no difficulty in gaining entrance; truly, they are welcomed for the drinks they buy for the company—and other reasons. Singing and dancing turns by certain favorite performers are the features of these gatherings, with much gossip and drinking at the small tables ranged along the four walls of the room. The habitués of these places are, generally, inverts of the most pronounced type, *i.e.*, the completely feminine in voice and manners, with the characteristic hip motion in their walk; though I have never seen any approach to feminine dress there, doubtless the desire for it is not wanting and only police regulations relegate it to other occasions and places. You will rightly infer that the police know of these places and endure their existence for a consideration; it is not unusual for the inquiring stranger to be directed there by a policeman." . . .

. . . [I]t is notable that of recent years there has been a fashion for a red tie to be adopted by inverts as their badge. This is especially marked among the "fairies" (as a *fellator* is there termed) in New York. "It is red," writes an American correspondent, himself inverted, "that has become almost a synonym for sexual inversion, not only in the minds of inverts themselves, but in the popular mind. To wear a red necktie on the street is to invite remarks from newsboys and others—remarks that have the practices of inverts for their theme. A friend told me once that when a group of street-boys caught sight of the red necktie he was wearing they sucked their fingers in imitation of *fellatio*. Male prostitutes who walk the streets of Philadelphia and New York almost invariably wear red neckties. It is the badge of all their tribe. The rooms of many of my inverted friends have red as the prevailing color in decorations. Among my classmates, at the medical school, few ever had the courage to wear a red tie; those who did never repeated the experiment."

"Prove It On Me Blues"

The blues played an important role as a cultural medium for the expression of sexuality, especially within African American culture. The lesbian lyrics of "Prove It On Me Blues," by bisexual blues singer Ma Rainey, is an example of the unconventional sexuality associated with the Harlem Renaissance. Written by Ma Rainey in 1928, the lyrics of this song are reprinted from Sandra R. Lieb, Mother of the Blues: A Study of Ma Rainey *(Amherst, 1981), 124.*

"Prove It On Me Blues"

Went out last night, had a great big fight,
Everything seemed to go on wrong;
I looked up, to my surprise,
The gal I was with was gone.

Where she went, I don't know,
I mean to follow everywhere she goes;
Folks said I'm crooked, I didn't know where she took it,
I want the whole world to know:

They say I do it, ain't nobody caught me,
Sure got to prove it on me;
Went out last night with a crowd of my friends,
They must've been women, 'cause I don't like no men.

Reprinted from *Mother of the Blues: A Study of Ma Rainey* by Sandra R. Lieb, published by the University of Massachusetts Press, 1981.

It's true I wear a collar and a tie,
Make the wind blow all the while;
They say I do it, ain't nobody caught me,
They sure got to prove it on me.

Say I do it, ain't nobody caught me,
Sure got to prove it on me;
I went out last night with a crowd of my friends,
They must've been women, 'cause I don't like no men.

Wear my clothes just like a fan,
Talk to the gals just like any old man;
'Cause they say I do it, ain't nobody caught me,
Sure got to prove it on me.

Questions

---

1. *What different perceptions of and attitudes about the sexualization of American society can you identify in these documents?*
2. *What different changes in sexual life can you identify from these documents?*
3. *Do you think the changes were greater for women or for men?*
4. *What evidence can you identify in these documents supporting the idea that urban life facilitated changes in sexual behavior?*

FURTHER READING

Intimate Matters: A History of Sexuality in America, *by John D'Emilio and Estelle B. Freedman (New York, 1988), provides a comprehensive overview of changes in sexual attitudes and behavior throughout the history of the U.S.* Kathy Peiss, Cheap Amusements: Working Women and Leisure in Turn-of-the-Century New York *(Philadelphia, 1986), and Joanne J. Meyerowitz,* Women Adrift: Independent Wage Earners in Chicago, 1880–1930 *(Chicago, 1988) discuss the lives of women in the urban working-class subcultures. Kevin White,* The First Sexual Revolution: The Emergence of Male Heterosexuality in Modern America *(New York, 1993), analyzes the impact of the sexual revolution on men.* Gay New York: Gender, Urban Culture, and the Making of the Gay Male World, 1890–1940, *by George Chauncey (New York, 1994), tells the story of changes in the male same-sex subculture of New York.*

Mexican Americans in the United States 1900–1940

Valerie Mendoza

INTRODUCTION

Since the Mexican American War and its settlement in 1848 with the Treaty of Guadalupe Hidalgo, people of Mexican heritage in the United States have endured a legacy of colonialism. Those living in the states once a part of Mexico (California, Arizona, New Mexico, Texas, and parts of Colorado, Utah, and Wyoming) became subordinate virtually overnight. Along with their new-found American citizenship, persons of Mexican descent were discriminated against socially, economically, and politically throughout the Southwest, consequently losing their landed wealth and social status. In order to survive, many resorted to poorly paid jobs, finding employment wherever they could and taking whatever pay was offered. In addition, Mexicans who had once been governors, mayors, law enforcement officers, judges, and the like no longer held their privileged political positions, and outright disfranchisement of Mexicans was the rule in some areas well into the twentieth century.

Despite these injustices, those who chose to remain in their homeland after it became part of the U.S. managed to carve out close-knit communities, maintain culture, and survive in this newly foreign and often unfriendly environment.

Disfranchisement and discrimination continued into the twentieth century, however, with the arrival of new immigrants. Massive migration from Mexico began in the first decade of the new era and continued unabated for thirty years. Mexicans poured over the border each year. The influx was so large that it forever changed the faces of both Mexico and the U.S. The period between 1900 and 1940 marks the first generation of Mexican migration. These migrants laid the foundation for future genera-

tions in terms of migration patterns, community formation, and cultural adaptation. These newcomers left behind political and economic turmoil due to the Mexican Revolution of 1910 and came in search of jobs and security. The policies of Porfirio Diaz, the dictator of Mexico from 1876–1911, caused inflation, decreased wages, and contributed to the loss of communal land. Employment was hard to find and the disruption caused by the fighting between the various revolutionary factions made life even more difficult. Many thought that their stay in the U.S. would be temporary and often traveled back and forth between Mexico and their American jobs in order to maintain ties with their families and communities south of the border.

American industries welcomed the Mexican immigrants, whom they considered desirable laborers. These companies reasoned that they could get away with paying the newcomers less and believed Mexicans to be tractable and not prone to union influence. In addition, they found Mexican laborers to be hard workers. Mexican immigrants, therefore, found ready work in agriculture, on the railroads, and eventually in the meat packing houses, automobile factories, and steel mills. Such jobs took many migrants beyond the border region to the Pacific northwest, the northern plains, the Midwest, and as far east as Pennsylvania.

Immigrants soon found that money did not go as far as they thought. Trips to Mexico became less frequent, and many eventually resigned themselves to making the U.S. their new home. Despite persistent discrimination, they worked hard to make a life for themselves and their children and created a uniquely Mexican American identity through the blending of two cultures.

MEXICAN MIGRATION: GENDER, WORK, CULTURE

Many scholars depict Mexican migration as a male phenomenon or as genderless—they concentrate on the experiences of male migrants. In addition, most focus exclusively on the Southwest, discounting the fact that Mexican migrants traveled in large numbers beyond this region since the early decades of the twentieth century. Finally, Mexican immigrants are often stereotyped as backwards and traditional, clinging to the "old ways" and as resistant to the influence of American culture—unlike their European counterparts. The following works show how scholars are rethinking different aspects of Mexican migration to the U.S. The first work discusses the importance of gender. The author focuses on female migrants and the special circumstances that they must face as women. The second selection discusses the importance of migration beyond the border region to the Midwest. This work contrasts the work experiences of men in the Midwest to that of the Southwest. The third reveals a complex negotiation of cultures and shows how Mexicans adapted to U.S. culture while at the same time retaining their own distinct culture and blending the two. While each of these selections depicts a specific piece of the migration puzzle, taken as a whole, they represent a nice cross-section of the Mexican migration experience.

"Women and the Border Journey"

Historian Vicki Ruiz demonstrates how the act of crossing the border differed for women traveling alone and how women built networks and coped with life in a new country. Excerpted from Vicki Ruiz, **From Out** of the Shadows: Mexican Women in Twentieth-Century America *(New York, 1998), 3–4, 6–9, 11–12, 15–16, 19, 24–32.*

Between 1910 and 1930, over one million Mexicanos (one-eighth to one-tenth of Mexico's population) migrated "al otro lado." Arriving in the United States, often with their dreams and little else, these immigrants settled into existing communities and created new ones in the Southwest and Midwest. In 1900, from 375,000 to perhaps as many as 500,000 Mexicans lived in the Southwest. . . .

Inheriting a legacy of colonialism wrought by Manifest Destiny, Mexicans . . . found themselves segmented into low-paying, low-status jobs with few opportunities for advancement. Living in segregated barrios, they formed neighborhood associations and church groups, and created a community life predicated on modes of production, economic and cultural.

This [article] surveys women's border journeys first in terms of migration and settlement followed by patterns of daily life. . . . Mexicanas claimed a space for themselves and their families building community through mutual assistance while struggling for some semblance of financial stability. . . . Mexican women nurtured families, worked for wages, built fictive kin networks, and participated in formal and informal community associations. . . .

Chain and circular migrations, of course, begin with the act of crossing the political border separating Mexico and the United States. In writing the history of Mexican immigration, scholars generally work within a "push/pull" model. What material conditions facilitated migration and what expectations did people carry with them as they journeyed north? Between 1875 and 1910, the Mexican birthrate soared, resulting in a 50 percent increase in population. Food prices also spiraled. . . . Mexican rural villagers . . . were displaced from their *ejidos* (communal land holdings) by commercial (often corporate American) agricultural interests. . . . By 1900, American-built and financed railroads offered mass transportation in Mexico. Since the major rail lines ran north and south (to make connections with lines on the U.S.

side), hopping a train to the border was a realistic and accessible option. . . .

Immigrants looked to the United States as a source of hope and employment. They soon discovered that material conditions did not match their expectations. . . .

Gender marked one's reception at the Stanton Street Bridge linking Ciudad Juárez and El Paso, especially if one ventured alone. . . . [I]mmigration inspectors routinely stopped those considered "likely to become a public charge"—in other words *solas* and single mothers. Agents scrutinized passport applications and conducted special hearings to determine women's eligibility for entrance into the United States.

Arriving in Ciudad Juárez with a nine-year-old daughter and a four-week-old infant, Pasquala Esparaza discovered she did not have the necessary funds to obtain the proper passports in El Paso so she stayed in Ciudad Juárez, finding a job as a housekeeper and a room in a boardinghouse. The landlady promised to look in on her daughters while Pasquala worked; however, it was nine-year-old Jesusita who shouldered the responsibility for herself and her sister. Jesusita remembered that as part of her daily routine she would carry Raquel a long distance to an affluent home where their mother worked. After preparing the noon meal for her employer, Pasquala would anxiously wait by the kitchen door. When her children arrived, she quickly and quietly ushered them into the kitchen. While nursing Raquel, she fed Jesusita a burrito of leftovers. Then Jesusita would take her baby sister into her arms and trek back to the boardinghouse to await their mother's return in the evening. One can only imagine her fears as she negotiated the streets of a strange city, a hungry child carrying a hungry baby. After six months, Pasquala had made enough money to complete the journey to California.

Immigration agents, however, still remained suspicious of a woman unaccompanied by a man. On their next attempt to cross, even with cash in hand, Pasquala and her family were denied a regular passport. Desperate, but not helpless, she secured a local passport generally reserved for Juárez residents who worked in El Paso and in that way she and her children crossed the border. . . .

After the grueling journey, Pasquala and her children resided with her sister's family in El Monte, California. Living under one roof with her tios and her cousins, Jesusita and her mother worked in the berry fields from February through June; then journeyed with the relatives to the San Joaquin Valley where they would first pick grapes, then cotton. By November, the extended family would return to El Monte. "We didn't work November . . . December . . . January. . . But we used to buy our sack of beans . . . and we'd get our flour and we'd get our coffee and we'd get our rice so that we could live on those three months we didn't work." . . .

While family and fictive kin may have eased the migrant journey and provided physical and emotional succor, human relationships are rarely perfect. . . . Bear in mind that the dynamics of power permeate the realm of decision-making whether one is situated at work or at home. . . .

Gender politics, however, is also enmeshed in economic and social stratification. Women like Jesusita Torres and her mother Pasquala lived and worked in extended family relationships often by necessity rather than choice. It was not until Pasquala secured employment at a walnut factory that she could save a portion of her wages and move her daughters and grandson out of her sister and brother-in-law's home. Although Señora Torres remembered that "when you live together, you think that they love you and you love them," she also revealed that her uncle's drinking took a toll on the family. "We couldn't sleep because they had to do their singing and their cussing . . . and we had a little corner in the kitchen where we slept." . . .

Just as women's work and family roles were intertwined, so too were the racial, economic, and patriarchal constraints they faced. Their legacies of resistance reveal their resiliency, determination, and strength.

A lifelong farm and nursery worker, Jesusita Torres stated simply:

> It's hard when you don't have an education. You go to work and you always have to do the hardest work. I used to think, "if I ever have children, I'm gonna work so hard my children will NEVER do this."

Migrant workers, both past and present, have occupied a vulnerable, precarious sector of the working class. Indeed, as an underclass of monopoly capitalism, frequently invisible in labor camps off the beaten track, farm workers have, in general, labored for low wages, under hazardous conditions, and with substandard housing and provisions. While individual qualities such as physical stamina and fortitude seem necessary for survival, a collective sense of family, neighborhood, and cultural bonds created thriving colonias among Mexican agricultural workers. . . .

Rural migrant women had few choices other than picking produce. Some became cooks in labor camps and others ran makeshift boardinghouses. In addition to picking produce, caring for her family, and serving as the local midwife, Irene Castañeda's mother took in laundry for which she earned $5 per week. Working as a housekeeper for local farm and merchant families offered another option, but domestic labor frequently contains the hidden psychological costs of prejudice, discrimination, and humiliation. . . .

Typical of working-class Mexican and Mexican-American households, the family served as the locus of production. Whether from a ranching or mining family, daughters were expected to perform a round of arduous chores. The labor of female kin, regardless of age, proved instrumental in ensuring the family's economic survival. Women preserved food for the winter, sold surplus commodities to neighbors, did laundry for Euro-American employers, and provided homes for lodgers. Like their pioneer foremothers, they also herded livestock, milked cows, built fences, and harvested crops. A strict division of labor according to gender became blurred. Yet this seemingly egalitarian assignment of tasks in no way subverted the traditional notion of "woman's place." . . .

With fortitude, faith, and unsung courage, single mothers relied on their domestic skills to feed their children. . . . Across . . . the Southwest, women participated in the informal economy in various ways—lodging single miners in Superior, Arizona, selling pan dulce door to door in San Bernardino, or swapping sex for food in El Paso. Some relied on their healing skills. As *curanderas* (healers) and *pateras* (midwives), Mexican women nurtured the networks essential for claiming a place in the United States. . . .

Women relied on one another and on their faith. Religious practices permeated everyday routines. . . . Church *jamaicas,* saints' days, and Mexican patriotic holidays constituted an integral part of . . . Mexican-American agrarian culture. . . . Mexicans . . . viewed their own interpretations of Catholicism as integral parts of their cultural life. Women also carved out a public cultural space in these community-based religious productions. . . .

Whether they lived in a camp, village, or city, Mexican women carved a place for themselves and their families based on shared experiences, cultural traditions, histories, and concerns. They relied on one another as family members and as neighbors whether they lived in a tightly knit rural colonia or a rolling boxcar barrio. Yet, as we have seen, patriarchy and even class distinctions existed; families could be source of strength or a source of trial. But the range of their lives and their struggles seemed lost on the American public. . . .

With the onset of the Great Depression, rhetoric exploded into action. Between 1931 to 1934, an estimated one-third of the Mexican population in the United States (over 500,000 people) were either deported or repatriated to Mexico even though the majority were native U.S. citizens. Mexicans were the only immigrants targeted for removal. Proximity to the Mexican border, the physical distinctiveness of mestizos, and easily identifiable barrios influenced immigration and social welfare officials to focus their efforts solely on the Mexican people, people whom they viewed as both foreign usurpers of American jobs and as unworthy burdens on relief rolls. . . .

Losing one child and struggling to support the other, Jesusita Torres held on to her place in the United States. She refused to apply for relief because she and her mother wanted to escape the notice of government authorities. "My mother said it was no use for us to [go] back . . . to what? We did not have anything out there." Describing the repatriation of two friends, she further remarked, "We were sorry that they left, because both of the ladies the husbands left them [in Mexico] with their children. It was pretty hard for them." Jesusita survived the Depression by picking berries and string beans around Los Angeles and following the crops in the San Joaquin Valley. From her wages, she raised a family and bought a house, one she purchased for seventeen dollars. . . .

The border journeys of Mexican women were fraught with unforeseen difficulties, but held out the promises of a better life. In the words of one Mexicana, "Here woman has come to have a place like a human being." Women built communities of resiliency, drawing strength from their comadres, their families, and their faith.

"Mexican Laborers in the Midwest"

In the following article historian Zaragosa Vargas reveals that Mexican laborers moved beyond the border region in search of work, better pay, and a less oppressive atmosphere than found in the Southwest. Migration from Mexico to the Midwest began in the first decade of the twentieth century and has continued ever since. Mexicans moved to new areas and formed communities where none had previously existed. He shows that Mexican immigrants also represent an important part of the history of the Midwest. Zaragosa Vargas, "Armies in the Fields and Factories: The Mexican Working Class in the Midwest in the 1920s," Mexican Studies/Estudios Mexicanos 7 (Winter 1991): 47–52, 57–60, 62, 71.

The fifteen-year period from the start of World War I to the end of the Great Depression marked the large scale immigration of Mexicans to the United States. Scholars estimate that by 1928 one tenth of Mexico's population resided in the United States. The great majority of the immigrants from Mexico settled in the Southwest where they worked in the agricultural, railroad, and mining sectors of the region. However, a steadily increasing number began to settle in the industrial Midwest. The entrance of Mexicans into factory work in the North represents an important moment in the history of Mexican workers for it marks their move from the fringes of the American working class to full participation in its expansion. . . .

The purpose of this essay is to provide a synthesis of the work experiences of the Mexican immigrant working class of the Midwest during its formation in the 1920s. . . . The essay examines the increasing migration of Mexicans into the Midwest; the internal migration patterns created by Mexican workers within this region; [and] the development of a northern Mexican working class. . . .

From "Armies in the Fields and Factories: The Mexican Working Class in the Midwest in the 1920's," by Zaragosa Vargas, in *Mexican Studies/Estudios Mexicanos* 7 (Winter 1991), copyright © 1991 by the Unversity of California Press, 47–52, 57–60, 62, 71.

Mexican Migration to the Midwest

At the end of World War I, one of the largest regional migrations of American workers was launched by the expansion of production in steel, automobile, rubber, and electrical manufacturing. The migrants traveled to industrial centers like Pittsburgh, Pennsylvania, Chicago, Illinois, and Detroit, Michigan, to fill unskilled jobs once held by southern and eastern European immigrants. Since the late nineteenth century the latter had constituted the greater part of America's work force but immigration laws enacted when the United States entered the war had substantially reduced their numbers. The continuing shortage of unskilled workers prompted industrial firms in the North to send labor agents to recruit Mexicans in Texas. This state received the largest number of immigrants from Mexico and it functioned as the great reservoir for Mexican labor throughout the 1920s. El Paso, Laredo, San Antonio, and Fort Worth, Texas, served as the staging areas for Mexicans migrating to the Midwest and as relay stations for immigrants returning to Mexico. The recruitment efforts of northern employers broke the virtual monopoly that Southwest farmers, railroads, and mining companies had held over Mexican labor for a quarter century. Lured north by the promise of higher wages, the immigrants bypassed work in Texas and came to know life and labor in the Midwest. . . .

Mexicans in the North labored among thousands of workers of different nationalities inside huge factories and were governed by new rules of work discipline which valued efficiency in machine tending. Their counterparts in the Southwest worked primarily among other Mexicans and were confined to repressive low-paying work like cotton picking and track maintenance and repair. Working conditions in Texas were especially notorious because they took place in the context of a system of racial segregation already firmly established by the turn of the century. . . .

The high-paying jobs in the North attracted Mexicans from a diverse range of backgrounds and work experiences. The arrivals included refugees who had fled the revolutionary upheaval in Mexico while others were journeying in search of adventure, to see firsthand the land they had heard so much about in their hometowns and villages. In 1923, Bureau of Immigration inspectors stationed at Laredo estimated that roughly 60 percent of the

Mexicans making the trek north consisted of displaced laborers from Mexico's overpopulated west central region. Like European immigrants, a large number of the Mexicans were familiar with different kinds of wage labor since they had already migrated temporarily from their hometowns to nearby cities within Mexico to seek wage work. For instance, Mexicans who went to Detroit had worked in shoe factories in Guadalajara, on railroad construction sites in northern Mexico, and in oil fields in Tampico on Mexico's gulf coast. The seasonal migrations of other Mexicans had furnished them with work in Texas for railroads, coal mining companies, and fruit and vegetable farms. These laborers recrossed the border for a second, third, and even fourth time to seek work.

The peregrinations of Mexican workers into the Midwest took them away from the familiar border region to an unknown part of *el norte* where few Mexicans lived prior to World War I. Those who could write sent letters to relatives and friends in Mexico and Texas telling them of the numerous opportunities for work in cities heretofore unheard of. . . .

Immigrants who returned to Mexico helped spread information about life in the Midwest. Their adventures were often exaggerated but the stories about the huge sums of money earned compelled many of their countrymen to make the trip north. The journey of Mexican immigrants to the Midwest was generally well-planned and corresponded with seasonal requirements of agricultural and industrial work in the spring. . . .

By 1927 the number of Mexicans in the Midwest had reached 63,700 and of these over 85 percent were unskilled and semi-skilled factory workers. The Mexican population increased to 80,000 during the summer months with the influx of migrant sugar beet workers into the farming regions. With the growth of the Mexican population in the Midwest, a discernible pattern of internal migration from city to city within the region developed. It coincided with and was timed to the cycles of employment on railroads and in the steel mills and automobile factories. . . .

Working for the Railroads

Large scale employment of Mexicans by the railroads during and after World War I was synchronized with this industry's seasonal requirements for common track laborers. . . . [T]he contracting of Mexicans coincided with the beginning of track bed maintenance and construction in the spring. Railroad companies diligently recruited Mexicans for common track work because Anglos, who enjoyed the privilege of extensive employment, refused to perform this physically demanding and low-paying labor.

Railroad companies contracted Mexicans as they made their way northward in Chicago and Omaha, Nebraska. Organized into extra gangs or floating gangs ranging in size from 50 to 200 men, Mexicans repaired and maintained passenger and freight rail lines, constructed new road beds, changed grades, laid new track, switches and spurs, and repaired washouts. . . .

> You see that poor devil out there lifting that heavy iron? He is as strong as an ox, but he can hardly lift it for the reason that it is so hot in the sun. Right now he has to have two pairs of gloves so as not to blister his calloused hands. Those are Mexicans. . . .
>
> The other rejoined: Yes, and what kind of a chance have they to enjoy their work? They are doing work that the average American would not and cannot think of doing. . . .

During World War I eastern railroad companies faced shortages of unskilled labor and began contracting Mexican workers in Texas where they had terminals. To reduce recruitment expenses, and to make additional contacts with prospective employees, the companies tapped their Mexican workers' networks of relatives and friends. The rail companies justified their large scale recruitment of Mexicans to the wary railroad unions, which feared the flood of cheap labor, by arguing that it aided America's war effort as food and munitions were carried by rail. Besides, the Department of Labor had sanctioned the use of Mexican contract labor by the railroads for the duration of the war. The Chicago, Rock Island and Pacific Railway was one company that expanded its recruitment of Mexicans for maintenance-of-way service in Chicago. In 1918, the Rock Island circulated the following announcement printed in Spanish among its Mexican workers so they could send it to their friends in Mexico. In this way the railroad circumvented the extra costs of direct recruitment,

Notice to Mexican Railroad Workmen Rock Island Lines

If any of you in your part of the country have a friend or a relative wishing to come to this country to work for a while . . . you can advise them by letter that . . . they can come with all assurances that they will . . . secure work at good wages and free return transportation on the Rock Island Lines.

. . . The most convenient place to cross from Mexico into the United States is through El Paso . . . at that point is where we have our representative who will . . . arrange to ship you to places on our lines where there is work. . . .

Eastern railroads brought thousands of Mexicans to Michigan, Ohio, Indiana, and Minnesota. They continuously replenished their supply of workers through recruitment and, along with the sugar companies, helped fix Mexican migration routes from Texas to the Midwest. The railroads helped increase the Mexican population of the region. And, as the rail lines began to recruit Mexicans from cities in the Midwest, they aided the dispersal of Mexicans throughout the region. The offer of free transportation, housing, and other incentives had lured Mexicans . . . to track work. . . .

Conclusion

The Mexicans who migrated to the industrial heartland of the Midwest in the 1920s had come to the region to seek work on the railroads, in the steel mills and foundries, and in the auto industry. Many signed contracts with sugar companies thus continuing to pursue seasonal agricultural labor as they had in Mexico and Texas. Mexican factory laborers in the North were influenced by the production cycles of industrial manufacturing and the kinds of work they performed directly shaped their work experiences. During boom years Mexicans enjoyed full employment, enabling them to participate in the overall prosperity of the period. They purchased automobiles, radios, and other consumer goods (on the installment plan) and sent money home to Mexico. . . .

Mexicans in the Midwest were integrated into the American labor force through cumulative factory work experiences. Settlement in predominantly ethnic working-class communities also exposed them to a life-style largely determined by the work rhythms of the nearby factories. Circumstances in the urban settings proved far from idyllic, however. Mexicans in Gary and Indiana Harbor lived in barracks-like company housing in an environment permeated by violence, while those in Chicago lived in factory districts with rampant overcrowding and pollution. The reality of alternating periods of hard work and joblessness was ever present and made community life undeniably unsettling. . . . Nevertheless, the communities Mexicans established in the industrial Midwest became home to them. The desire for economic betterment compensated for the hardships endured by Mexicans in the North. Through hard work, they successfully made the adjustment to an industrial working-class experience.

"Becoming Mexican American"

The following selection addresses the complex issues of culture, identity, and ethnicity. George Sanchez argues that culture is not static, but is constantly changing and that immigrants do not have a fixed identity that is attached to their homeland, but rather develop multiple ones. Excerpted from George Sanchez, Becoming Mexican American: Ethnicity, Culture, and Identity in Chicano Los Angeles, 1900–1945 *(New York, 1993), 3–4, 7–13.*

When Zeferino Ramírez stood up in front of his fellow residents of Belvedere, an unincorporated area east of the city of Los Angeles, on June 12, 1927, he had long since been recognized as a leader among the Mexican immigrants there. That Sunday night the meeting was to focus on a community crisis, and it was no surprise that Ramírez had been asked to preside over the discussion. At issue was a plan to incorporate the area into a full-fledged municipality, a move that would certainly make Mexican settlement more difficult in the district. At least three plans for incorporation had been submitted to Los Angeles County officials within the year by real estate and manufacturing interests in Belvedere. Their strategy was to increase the taxes of local residents to pay for city services, thereby forcing the largely working-class community to sell their property in a depressed market. The area in dispute could thereby be resold to middle-class Anglo Americans, forcing up the estate values in neighboring communities and making a tidy profit for real estate companies. . . .

Yet this story was more complicated than one of ethnic leadership against conniving Americans out to deprive Mexican residents of their land. The tensions endured by many Mexican immigrant families were exhibited in Ramírez's as well. Part of the reason he had been so active in establishing a school was that he had begun to worry when his own sons spoke English at home. Although his daughters had attended an American school and were now music teachers, he continued to prohibit them from going out alone, attending dances, or viewing American movies. His oldest daughter, however, controlled the business finances and "didn't leave much money within his reach." Ramírez himself had undergone a Protestant conversion after reaching Los Angeles, and he served as a lay preacher of a Methodist church on Brooklyn Avenue. The family's clothes and meals were largely American-style, yet they tended to decorate their home with both pictures of American subjects and patriotic Mexican portraits. Later, Ramírez would visit Mexico City with the intent of moving his business, only to conclude that "everything there [was] still very backward and very disorganized."

Despite these obvious signs of cultural adaptation, when some Anglo American supporters at the meeting counseled Belvedere's Mexicans to apply for naturalization, Ramírez was among the first to balk at the suggestion. These officials, among them municipal judges in the Belvedere area, argued that those Mexican immigrants without first papers would be unable to vote against incorporation, if the issue ever appeared in an election. But Ramírez joined *La Opinión* and the Mexican consulate representative in warning against this advice. To him, the negation of Mexican citizenship would have been a larger crime than that being perpetrated on the residents of Belvedere.

How does one make sense of the contradictory aspects of this story? What does Zeferino Ramírez's life, and his reaction to the

From *Becoming Mexican American: Ethnicity, Culture, and Identity in Chicano Los Angeles 1900–1945*, by George Sanchez, (New York, 1993), copyright © 1993 by Oxford University Press, 3–4, 7–13.

prospect of changing his citizenship, tell us about the cultural adaptation of Mexican immigrants to the United States in the early twentieth century? . . .

Though noting the severity of racial and class discrimination, some Chicano historians have . . . highlighted cultural change in the Mexican origin population, particularly among the children of immigrants and within the middle class. But these changes continue to be placed within a bipolar model of opposing cultures. . . .

Mexican American culture remained a tenuous site of cultural exchange, always a prelude to the attractions of a "purely" Mexican or "purely" American stance. . . .

Recently, however, new perspectives offered by scholars working in the field of cultural studies force us to reexamine such static assumptions. . . . In particular, any notion that individuals have occupied one undifferentiated cultural position—such as "Mexican," "American," or "Chicano"—has been abandoned in favor of the possibility of multiple identities and contradictory positions. . . .

It is not surprising that issues in Chicano culture should have such resonance for scholars reexamining our understanding of how culture and ethnicity work in the post-industrial age. . . . Since Mexican migrants move between two countries—one highly industrialized and the other severely impoverished—they have been among the first to experience what some have called the "postmodern condition." At least one anthropologist has recently suggested that we look toward the life experiences of these transnationals to understand our "confusing world, a world of crisscrossed economies, intersecting systems of meaning, and fragmented identities.

The movement between Mexican and American cultures is not so much a world of confusion, but rather a place of opportunity and innovation. In Los Angeles, living in this cultural "borderlands" can also lend itself to adaptations drawn from African American or other ethnic peoples, depending on the time period, the local community and the level and nature of contact. . . . Mexicans, long accustomed to cultural blending and creation, continue this custom in the United States, now incorporating aspects of the "others" they find in a multicultural setting like Los Angeles. . . .

Yet, is there still a "there" there? For earlier scholars, the comforting presence of Mexico was all that was needed in order to project a unified cultural concept to which Chicanos could turn.

Yet "Mexico," maybe even more so than other nations, was a national community that had to be "imagined" to exist, particularly given its racial and regional diversity. Not only was culture never static in Mexico, nor U.S. influence ever far removed in shaping its contours, but the construction of a Mexican national identity was never more ferociously pursued than in the aftermath of the Mexican Revolution—at the very moment thousands of Mexicans were making their way north.

Thus, my own study necessarily begins with an examination of the rural villages and burgeoning towns of Mexico. Mexico during the early twentieth century was undergoing fundamental socioeconomic upheaval. Partly because of this tumult, hundreds of thousands of Mexicans crossed the border into the United States, usually seeking temporary residence and better wages in order to help their families survive through difficult times. Yet the very meaning of crossing the border was undergoing a transformation during this period; moving north signified a momentous occasion. Though back-and-forth migration continued, increasingly durable settlement north of the border was a result of tightening immigration restriction. Los Angeles attracted an ever larger number of these migratory sojourners, drawn to the city because of its employment opportunities and vibrant Mexican community.

In the United States, new "traditions" had to be invented and older customs discarded or radically transformed at the same time that Mexicans in Mexico were creating "traditions" to cement national identity. . . .

Mexicans in the United States not only had to draw for their new traditions upon their memories of a Mexico now irreversibly transformed, but they also had to make sense of a new world north of the border that was undergoing rapid transformation. Nowhere was this more evident than in Los Angeles, where demographic upheaval meant that most residents were newcomers little versed in the culture of the region they now inhabited. Political and social power, however, was concentrated in the hands of a small group of Anglo American newcomers. This power enabled them to mold dominant "traditions" onto the cultural landscape of California. The growth of the Chicano community in Los Angeles created a "problem" for Anglo American residents, one which resulted in public efforts to alter cultural loyalties among Mexican immigrants. American officials launched programs to teach these newcomers idealized versions of American practices, customs, and values. The Mexican government, for its part, worked through its consulate office to instill loyalty to Mexico, trying to persuade citizens to return to their native country. Neither of these efforts had their intended effect, but both ironically served to stimulate the process of self-recognition as ethnic Americans among the immigrant population. . . .

But Mexican immigrants played their own part in this drama. Constrained by their lack of economic and political stature, they drew strength from the networks of family members and fellow countrymen who lived nearby. Through the daily struggle to survive in an oftentimes hostile environment, these newcomers constructed a world for themselves, shaped both by their memories of their past lives and by the reality of their present situation. During the 1920s, many Mexican immigrants gradually changed their orientation from that of temporary sojourner to permanent resident. Much of this process occurred within the family context, as individual migrants married and raised families in Los Angeles. Cultural adaptations marked the transition to a Mexican American lifestyle. Catholic religious practice, for example, increasingly narrowed to the province of women, and became less a community function and more a set of rituals performed at home. The secular entertainment industry of Los Angeles reshaped Mexican musical traditions, as immigrants made Los Angeles a center for Chicano cultural life in the United States. The search for stability encouraged Mexican immigrants to settle in particular barrios and assume new roles within their families, at work, and as American consumers.

Ethnicity, therefore, was not a fixed set of customs surviving from life in Mexico, but rather a collective identity that emerged from daily experience in the United States. As such, ethnicity arose not only from interaction with fellow Mexicans and Mexican Americans but also through dialogue and debate with the larger cultural world encountered in Los Angeles. Whether accommodation, resistance, or indifference marked an individual's stance toward American culture, everyone reacted to living in the United States. For those who chose to stay, their cultural adaptations would have lifelong implications. For over time, as Mexican immigrants acclimated themselves to life north of the border, they did not remain Mexicans simply living in the United States, they became Mexican Americans. They assumed a new ethnic identity, a cultural orientation which accepted the possibilities of a future in their new land. . . .

The struggle which forged a Mexican American identity was powerfully rooted in the decade of the 1930s. The onset of the Great Depression forced many Chicano residents to reconsider their decision to remain in the United States. Moreover, the deportation and repatriation campaigns launched against Mexicans in Los Angeles profoundly disrupted the cultural centeredness of the community. Los Angeles lost one-third of its Mexican residents, and those who remained were made keenly aware of the fragility of their social position. . . .

The repatriation campaign provided a symbolic break with the past for those who remained, while participation in American unions and other struggles for civic equality in the late 1930s and early 1940s created the context for a new identity. Rather than culture serving as a substitute for politics, it became a way to enter the political arena. . . . Ironically, it was not the search for Mexican nationalism which engendered political radicalism for large numbers of Mexicans and Mexican Americans in the 1930s, but the forging of a new identity as ethnic Americans. . . .

This new cultural identity was forged within the context of a hostile, racist environment which sought to deny Mexican Americans a claim to being "Americans." The so-called "Zoot Suit Riots" in Los Angeles in 1943 were only the most outward manifestation of the racism they experienced. As a result, parents and children alike forged an ambivalent Americanism. . . .

. . . [T]he emphasis in Chicano history on bipolar models that have stressed either cultural continuity or gradual acculturation has short-circuited a full exploration of the complex process of cultural adaptation. This problem is particularly regrettable when one realizes that Mexicans have been among the most numerous and significant of immigrant groups in the United States during the twentieth century. They number well over half of the total current Latino population of 30 million—a population destined to become America's largest minority group within the next thirty years. . . .

Questions

1. *How can we describe or characterize the Mexican immigrant experience beginning with the act of migration and continuing with the types of jobs and living conditions Mexicans faced once in the U.S.?*
2. *How did migration provide a unique experience for women that differed from that of men?*
3. *In what ways did migration to the Midwest, a region away from the border, differ from migration to the Southwest?*

MEXICAN MIGRATION:
ADAPTATIONS AND ATTITUDES

Mexican immigrants had great expectations for their lives in the United States. They left a war-torn country in the midst of political, economic, and social chaos in hopes of finding stability. Instead, they met countless obstacles—a foreign language, need for a job, and mistreatment at nearly every turn. Employers who hired Mexican laborers did so mostly out of a desire for greater profit. They justified their actions of paying the Mexican substandard wages because he was viewed as inferior to the American and "would not mind." As a result of so many migrants arriving in the U.S. during the first three decades of the century, the public began to perceive a "Mexican Problem." Most Americans believed that there were simply too many of them. Companies encouraged the large migrant flow, however, because Mexicans provided surplus labor, which in turn kept wages low.

Mexican immigrants themselves became disillusioned at their lives in the U.S. Many wondered if they had made a mistake coming to this country. They were aware of their lower salaries, substandard housing, inferior education, and the general discrimination and segregation they faced at the hands of their Anglo employers and neighbors. Despite the added burdens, or perhaps because of them, many Mexicans decided to fight for justice and their rights. They knew that returning to Mexico was at best improbable and that settlement in this country necessitated that they work to change their plight and the negative attitudes of Americans toward them.

A Long Hard Journey

The following is an excerpt of an interview conducted during the 1970s with Lucia Martinez who immigrated to the U.S. during the 1910s as a child. She describes the hardships of crossing the border and the relief at finally reaching her destination. From Margaret Beeson, Marjorie Adams, Rosalie King, Memories For Tomorrow: Mexican-American Recollection of Yesteryear *(Detroit, 1983), 65–66.*

On the twenty-fifth of June, 1916, we left Aguascalientes, Mexico. Our passenger train was stopped and we were told that we couldn't stay in the coaches but had to climb on top of the roofs of the cars. Since it was during the Revolution, soldiers took the coach seats whenever they wanted them.

Many people climbed on top of the train. But, we knew that often little babies and even grown women had fallen off and been killed. My mother was afraid and was determined not to climb up there. It was a bad situation.

Weeping, my mother said, "How am I going to get up there? I just cannot do that."

My father, seeing that my mother was very upset and wouldn't stop crying, asked the conductor, "Sir, will you please let my family get into that flatcar? It has a layer of dirt in it but that makes no difference. Let my family in so they won't fall from up there."

Then we all got onto the flatcar. I was eleven and my brothers were five and sixteen. As soon as they saw us climbing up, the people on top began to climb down. Immediately the flatcar was filled with children and adults—as many as it would hold. We were on that flatcar until we got to Zacatecas. . . .

[M]y mother had brought along a large sack of bread. It was all that we had to eat. The others had nothing—nothing at all. When we got hungry, we asked her for something to eat. She took a cup and filled it because now the fat little loaves were in pieces. As soon as the [other] women and children saw the food, they all began to ask for some too. In a moment the whole sack of bread

From *Memories For Tomorrow: Mexican-American Recollections of Yesteryear,* by Lucia Martinez, ed. Margaret Beeson, Marjorie Adams, Rosalie King, (Detroit, 1983) 65–66.

was gone. From there to El Paso we had nothing to eat. They didn't sell anything on the train. Everyone had to bear up. The only thing we had was water.

The soldiers stayed in Zacatecas so we were able to get into the coaches.

We arrived in Juarez where an aunt of mine took us across the border. We only paid a penny. First, the U.S. officials bathed us in foul water from head to toe. They took off our clothes and also washed them in that smelly water. We were really stinking when we entered the United States.

A labor contractor sent us to a small Texas town. On that trip we only had sardines and crackers to eat. Throughout the three months that we were in that town, my father never was paid more than fifty cents at a time. My sixteen year old brother, who worked on the railroad tracks, only received twenty-five cents. The bosses kept a list of what people bought to eat. When a check came, they gave us no money because they said that it had all gone for food. We only had potatoes, beans, flour, coffee, and sugar.

One day the commissary agent got mad at my older brother and said he was going to kill him.

"We can't stay here any longer," my father announced. "Any day that man might attack Elidoro. Let's leave."

We didn't have a cent. Absolutely nothing. We left at one in the morning so no one would see us. We packed some suitcases with bedclothes and a little clothing. My mother fixed some biscuits and beans. My cousin, his wife, his brother, and their two children who were three and one, fled with us. We walked along the track for eighteen miles until we came to another town. At five in the afternoon we arrived. Some Mexicans who lived in houses made of railroad ties let us stay outside.

The next day, my father and my brother went in search of a labor contractor. We were then put on a train and sent to Abilene, Kansas, where we remained for nine months. Then my sister and her husband, who were already in Hutchinson, Kansas, lent my father money so that we could come to Hutchinson. We arrived in December, 1916. We have lived here ever since.

First Contacts

During the 1920s Mexican anthropologist Manuel Gamio received a grant to conduct interviews with recent Mexican immigrants in order to document the effects of migration. These are excerpts from two interviews. In the first Jesus Garza describes the migration and job seeking process. In the second, Señora Concha Gutiérrez del Río discusses the loneliness and isolation associated with coming to a new country. From Manuel Gamio, The Mexican Immigrant: His Life-Story *(New York, 1969), 14–18, 165–66.*

Jesús Garza

This man is a native of Aguascalientes, *mestizo*, markedly Indian, twenty-four years of age.

"I have been in this country for three years and a half, for even though I went to Aguascalientes to see my parents about a year and a half ago I didn't stay more than a month. It had been my purpose to stay at home and work there but I found everything changed and dull, in other words different from this country, and now I like it better here and if I were to go back to Mexico it is only to visit a while and then return.

"Since I was very small I had the idea of going out to know the world, to go about a lot in every direction. As I had heard a lot about the United States it was my dream to come here. My father, however, wouldn't let me leave home because I was too small. He was very strict. . . . [W]hen I was about twenty I decided to leave home and come here. I waited one day until my father went out and then I took money out of the strong box, gold coins especially. I took out enough to take me to San Antonio and took the train for Nuevo Laredo. I crossed the border there. I had no trouble, although it was the first time I had come. I paid my $8.00, passed my examination, then changed my Mexican coins for American money and went to San Antonio, Texas. When I arrived there I looked for work but couldn't find any so that I went to the agency of *renganches* and contracted to work. They said that it was to go and work on the *traque.* I didn't know what that was but I contracted to work because my money was giving out. I only had three dollars left. I gave one to the *renganchista,* and he then took me with a lot of Mexicans to a railroad camp. I worked all day, but as I wasn't used to such a heavy kind of work I thought of leaving. I could hardly finish out working that first day, I thought that I was going to die because the work was so hard. At night I asked the boys slyly where Dallas, Texas, was or some other large city and they told me down the tracks and said that if I wanted to go I should catch a freight train and go as a tramp. But I didn't let them suspect anything but told them I was only fooling. . . . On the next day, without their noticing it, I left on foot, and went down the tracks. I left at about seven in the morning and reached the outskirts of Dallas at about six in the evening. It was already getting dark and I only had a dollar with me as I hadn't even gotten my day's pay. On reaching the outskirts of Dallas I saw a man who seemed to me to be a negro and at the same time a Mexican and I thought of speaking to him. As I didn't know English I said to myself, if he is a negro he isn't going to pay any attention to me. Finally I spoke to him in Spanish and it turned out that he was Mexican, although to tell the truth he looked like a negro. I told him how I had come and he said that I could spend the night there in his house. He gave me something to eat and a mattress on which to sleep. On the next day the same man took me to the house of an old man who rented rooms. This old man received me very kindly into his home and gave me a room. When I told him that I didn't have either money or a job he said that I shouldn't worry. I could pay him when I had some. I was there about a month without working and the man and his wife, both of them quite old, took as good care of me as though I was paying them. They gave me food, my room, and even cleaned my clothes. . . . Finally I managed to get work laying pipes and I was working for two weeks earning $2.50 a day. Then they laid me off because they said that I wasn't strong enough for that hard work. I returned to be without work and then a Mexican advised me to look for work in the hotels and restaurants because that fitted me, but I couldn't find that, because it is necessary to speak English for those jobs. Then I got a job with an electric company. I thought that it was some office work or some decent job of engineering but it turned out that they wanted me to go down into a well with a pick to make it deeper. I think that it was 20 meters deep and I also had to wheel stones. This work was so hard that I could hardly finish the day, for at about four o'clock in the afternoon the foreman wanted me to lift a rock so big that I couldn't even move it much less lift it. He then said that if I couldn't do that it was better that I quit so that I asked for my time, and they gave me $2.50. I kept on looking for work and in about three days I found one in a restaurant as "vegetable-man" (peeling vegetables). I stayed there about two months and on account of a Mexican who went to tell the manager that I couldn't do that work they fired me. Then I went to another restaurant and hotel and there they gave me a job as dishwasher. I was then learning a little English. When they needed a new "vegetable-man" I told the foreman that I could do that work and he gave it to me with an increase in pay. I think that they paid me $45.00 a month and my food. That boss was an American but very good and he told me that he was going to teach me how to do everything so that when anyone was missing I could take their place. He taught me to be a cook and to do all the work of the kitchen, bake, etc. He even increased my pay until I was getting $75.00 a month and my food. By that time I stopped living at the house of the old man of whom I have told you. . . .

Sra. Concha Gutiérrez Del Río

Sra. Concha Gutiérrez del Río, wife of the Nivardo del Rio, is a *mestiza,* markedly Indian, a native of Durango and educated in Chihuahua. . . .

Since I have been in this country I have lived very uncomfortably, for I don't like anything that they have here. It is all very different from that which there is in Mexico. Even one's own countrymen change a lot. The first months, almost for eight months, I lived here without friends of any kind. But in the end one begins to get used to things, because one has to. Although at times I even cried when alone, seeing myself living here without friends of any kind in such an ugly place and with such different customs. . . . Here there is hardly anything to do to entertain oneself. My husband didn't want me to dance or go out. He was very jealous, but little by little he is getting over that, and even better, he now lets me go to the dances once in a while. I like to do that a lot. I don't like the movies, for the films are in English and although I can read that a little it isn't as though they were in

Spanish, Anyway, I never liked the movies and here I hardly ever go except when they have Mexican vaudeville acts which come now and then. I like the Mexican music the best. For that reason I always have a lot of Mexican pieces for my Victrola. Here nothing is good. The food stuffs, besides costing a lot, are no good for making good Mexican food. One can't get the things that one needs, so that it might be said that the food is half-Mexican and half-American, being neither the one nor the other. It is impossible for the Mexicans and the Mexican-Americans to get along very well together here, because the latter are always speaking badly of Mexico. They say that one came from over there because one didn't even have anything to eat, and they are always finding a lot of faults with everything that is from Mexico. Some things that they say are true, but it hurts one to have them say them about one's country.

Anglo Attitudes Toward Mexicans

Paul Taylor is another scholar who received money during the 1920s to conduct research on Mexican migration. His primary focus was the economic consequences of border crossings, but his research took him in many directions. In the following excerpts, he shows the reception Mexicans received in the Winter Garden district of Dimmit County, Texas. Examples from the political, economic, and educational realm are given. Taylor also found distinct differences within the Mexican community— tensions between recent immigrants and American-born Texans of Mexican heritage. Paul S. Taylor, Mexican Labor in the United States *(Berkeley, 1930), 1, 336, 372–74, 378, 386–87, 396–97, 410–13.*

While the California anti-restrictionists have generally denied before Congress that Mexican labor is "cheap labor," the Congressman representing south Texas asserted what his constituents . . . told me, viz., that they want and need cheap labor:

> Mr. Chairman, here is the whole situation in a nutshell. Farming is not a profitable industry in this country, and in order to make money out of this, you have to have cheap labor. You can not take it like any other industry and pay

$5 or $6 or $7 a day and make a success of it. In order to allow landowners now to make a profit on their farms, they want to get the cheapest labor they can find, and if they get the Mexican labor it enables them to make a profit. If they have to pay a higher price for labor, there is a loss instead of a profit. That is the way it is along the border and I imagine that is the way it is anywhere else.

The advantage, and even necessity for cheap labor is the dominant economic philosophy in the Winter Garden district. . . .

Education

The educational system in the United States has provided one of the most important means by which individuals have ascended the socio-economic ladder. To what extent is the status of the Mexicans of Dimmit County affected by education? The answer is: very little. Probably at no time during the school year are more than 25 per cent of the Mexican scholastics, i.e., children aged 7 to 17 inclusive, in school; the average number in attendance is undoubtedly much less.

For those Mexican children who do attend school, the facilities in most respects are obviously below those provided for American children. This is true with respect to buildings and equipment, crowding, adequacy of instructional opportunity, frequently with respect to salary scale of their teachers, and frequently, though by no means always, with respect to the qualifications of their teachers. Besides, Mexicans who do advance through the grades are kept away from the American schools as long as possible.

The situation in one of the better schools for Mexicans was described by an informed American as follows:

There were no screens, no water, no maps for a long time. I know that for three years recently they taught geography without a map. The American school gives their old books which they don't want to the Mexicans. One

From *Mexican Labor in the United States,* by Paul Taylor, (Berkeley, 1930), copyright © by the University of California Press, 1, 336, 372–374, 378, 386–387, 396–397, 410–413.

teacher handles the primary, first, second, and third grades; another handles the fourth, fifth, seventh, and eighth grades. People think if there are few pupils there is less need of teachers, but it takes just as much time as if there were more to teach. Salaries of the American teachers in the Mexican school are from $10 to $35 a month below the minimum paid in the American school.

Similar conditions were found in other Mexican schools of the county. . . .

The attitude of Americans toward education of Mexicans within their midst exhibits a wide range. The dominant view is the one expressed by an onion grower:

The little education they get in the schools here spoils them, and makes them trifling. They become peddlers or bootleggers, or seek some easy way of making a living. They don't want to do this [onion-clipping] or other work. Some of them are bright, and get a good education at San Marcos [colleges] or some other institution, and are fine people. They should be taught something, yes. But the more ignorant they are, the better laborers they are. The law which keeps them out if they can't read [literacy test] keeps out the best laborers and lets in the worst. If these get educated, we'll have to get more from Mexico.

Another observed,

The white children are in school and the Mexicans in the fields. The whole community wants to make a living and get rich out of Mexican labor. . . .

The main reason for wishing the Mexicans to remain uneducated, then, is belief in the desirability of cheap laborers who will remain laborers. Besides, so long as the present method of apportioning state financial aid continues, there is an immediate financial advantage to the dominant group in discouraging others from attending school. . . .

The Mexican pupils old enough to answer my questions expressed desire for education. The reasons they wanted education were those which the farmers who preferred that they remain uneducated also gave, viz, different work or more pay, or both. J. says,

"My father wants me to be a teacher so I won't have to work in onions." Y. is in the seventh grade and expects to continue. He wants "to go to school and learn English (*sic*) "Why? " Easy job and more pay." He wants to work in stores or somewhere in town. . . . Their desires for a higher standard of living attained in a non-manual occupation conform to typical American ideals fostered, and to a large extent satisfied by our school system. . . .

At the present time, then, educational opportunities for Mexicans and Americans are not equal. . . . The State revenues apportioned on the basis of scholastics in the county are spent largely for the education of the American children, at the expense of the education of the Mexican children. The number of Mexicans which rises by the educational ladder is therefore inconsequentially small.

The dominant American view is that it is undesirable to educate the Mexicans. . . .

In south Texas each town is two towns—American and Mexican. Sometimes, as at Kingsville, it is three towns—white, colored, and Mexican. . . .

The towns of Dimmit County are typical in their separation of the residences of Mexicans from Americans. . . .

The basis of separation of domicile is the gregariousness of two distinct groups, differing in race, class, language, and culture. In some towns in California and at least one town in northeastern Colorado, there are deed restrictions; in Dimmit County there are none, based on race, but the social pressure of Americans resists any breaking down of the residential isolation.

. . . A leading citizen of another town, reported to have been a leader of the Ku Klux Klan, said,

People here won't sell real estate to the Mexicans in our part of town. I believe if some one did sell to a Mexican and he tried to move in, they would run him out. . . .

Americans seldom distinguish between Mexicans of Texan birth and those from Mexico. Unless they know the history of the individual Mexican they do not know whether he is Texan or Mexican. They see them intermingled and intermarrying, living, working, and playing together, looking alike, speaking the same language. They class them together under the inclusive term

"Mexican"; and characteristically, the term means an alien, not a citizen. The Texas-Mexicans are regarded as citizens neither in a political nor a social sense. The occasions upon which their citizenship was mentioned were with reference to disbarment from voting in the county white man's primary, their questioning by the immigration officers, or their standard of conduct; in the latter case, the word "citizen" had no reference to country of birth. . . .

A few Texas-Mexicans were conscious of a difference between themselves and the Mexicans. One Texas-Mexican asserted superiority but the comparison drawn was with Mexicans *in Mexico,* and, interestingly, when comparison shifted to Old Mexicans in the Winter Garden, the higher standard of living of a particular immigrant group was cited, and the lesser thrift of the Texas-Mexicans excused:

> We feel a little better than the Mexicans [from Old Mexico]. Over there they wear different clothes and never take pains about their persons. They don't have the same idea about schools. In X- they are not forced to go to school (*sic*). The Texas-Mexicans have a better standard of living. We have lumber houses and floors. There they have dirt floors, and in X- they have a dirty food market.
>
> Some of the Mexicans here save and buy good houses and trucks and feel above the Texas-Mexicans. But they know even if we don't save we have a good time. We can remember when they came with nothing and begged for food. They stay on the ranches and don't spend as much as the Texas-Mexicans [most of whom live in] town. . . .

Some Texas-Mexicans favored curtailment of immigration of Mexicans, and when work is scarce they blame the immigrants, and accuse them of not knowing or not adhering to standard prices of work.

Some Mexicans, on the contrary, advanced the idea of their superiority over the Texas-Mexicans. Said one of them.

> The Mexicans are more interested in education than the Texas-Mexicans.

but a Texas-Mexican present at the time was unwilling to admit this. Their usual attitude, however, was that there is no difference between Mexicans and Texas-Mexicans except the accident of birthplace.

Texas-Mexicans expressed some pride in their American citizenship, one of them who had served in the army during the war saying,

> The Mexicans born here are worth more because they are United States citizens. . . .

Assumption of superiority by the Texas-Mexicans was resented by the Mexicans.

> The *Texanos* think they are the same [*iguales*] as the Americans, but they can't be because of blood,

said a Mexican.

How to Handle Mexican Labor

In this article, a railroad foreman in California dispenses advice to other foremen on how to "handle" Mexican labor. The author offers tips on how to get the most work out of the Mexican and in doing so passes on many stereotypes and racist judgments.

Excerpted from James P. Craig, "How to Handle Mexican Labor," Railway Age, *November 1914.*

In handling Mexicans the first and most important thing is to establish a reputation as being a man of your word, one who will do what he says, who will not promise anything unless he can do it, who has courage enough to apologize if at fault, and who does not lack either physical or moral courage.

Of these the most important is moral courage, for the reason that the average Mexican has a superabundance of physical but very little moral courage. They invariably travel in pairs, trios or groups, consisting of relatives, neighbors or *compadres*. The different members of these groups will stick together through thick and thin, right or wrong. The boss generally will find that it pays to keep track of these groups, as any trouble with one is likely to be followed by demonstrations from his friends. . . .

You never will be able to control your men until you first can control yourself absolutely at all times. If a Mexican can see that he is succeeding in worrying or aggravating you he will in many cases do his best to make your life a burden. Many a good man has been worried off the job in just that way.

It is poor policy to make a practice of bullying these laborers, who are in no position to defend themselves. If this is done the company will have to pay more money to hold a gang or will get only inefficient workers. Men cannot work to the best advantage if continually afraid that their superior will "fly off the handle" because of some little misunderstanding. They are quick to resent and to "work out" a spite on a grouchy boss. This penchant is by no means confined exclusively to Mexicans. If the boss is in the habit of getting piqued he does himself more harm than anyone else. . . . Keep your temper and remember that verbal chastisement will only slide off the Mexicans like water off a duck's back. This may explain their appellation of "greaser." If you are grouchy all the time the Mexicans soon become accustomed to it, and it ceases to have any effect on them other than to make them dislike you. . . .

To get along with your subordinates you must have at least a liking for the men under you. If you hate Mexicans, or despise them, you will not be able to hide the fact from them for a single day. Nothing will cause dislike as quickly as dislike. Men certainly will not work well for a man they dislike—especially the average Mexican will not.

A knowledge of the Spanish language, or at least enough of it to be able to explain work, carry on a common conversation and tell what the men are talking about, is absolutely essential in your efforts to avoid friction. If you don't understand Spanish they pass their time ridiculing you to your face. This has a tendency to destroy their respect for you, if you are unable to detect and stop it. You never will get the best results through a head man or an interpreter. You are always at his mercy. Should he become angry at you or any of the men, you and the company lose. I have never known a Mexican straw boss or foreman who would not work out his personal spites on the men. Mexicans as a rule would rather work under an American than for their own countrymen. This is one distinct advantage that the American foreman has over his Mexican competitor.

The average Mexican is slow of comprehension and it requires a great deal of explanation for him to grasp an idea. After he gets it he holds it fairly well. He would rather listen to the boss explain than to work. If you are not on the alert he will take advantage of you by pretending he does not understand. If you will let him, he will lead you into an argument simply to take your attention from the work in hand. Never allow them to argue with you. A great many men make the mistake of thinking them stupid. In some ways they are. In dodging work, however, they are pastmasters and will tax the ability of anyone who tries to keep them at their tasks. On the other hand, when they become convinced that you are up to all their tricks, they will work very well, provided you treat them justly.

Constant reiteration of rules and orders is absolutely necessary in handling Mexicans. Like children, they soon forget. It is useless to become vexed about this failing. Just get the habit of reminding them. A peon's mind is very much like that of a nine or ten year old child, with the difference that the child's mind matures and the Mexican's never does. Take him all in all he is not a bad fellow. You must be able to see things as he sees them and divine which way he is going to jump. The man who doesn't study him will never make a success of handling him. When properly handled they are willing to do a great deal for a man, often working for ridiculously low wages or giving the very best of service for common wages.

To get the best results be an absolutely impartial judge. Reward by kind words and good treatment all men who try to do what is asked of them. Be patient and never reproach a man until it is a certainty that he is at fault. Never reproach a Mexican severely in the presence of others. The Mexicans are sensitive people and cannot stand being humiliated continually in the presence of their fellow workmen. If you make a practice of doing this you will never have a loyal crew of men. Some day when you are in trouble they will throw you down. . . .

No man ever will be able to secure very good results with a crew of men whose personnel is continually changing. If you cannot hold a good percentage of your men, you had better find the cause, because it takes several months to train a man and to learn what he can do well. This is decidedly bothersome and expensive.

If your men are changing all the time there is something wrong with your methods or those of your commissary clerk or with camp conditions. Possibly you have some valiant or would-be bad man who is running them off. Whatever the trouble may be, you will not get good results with a crew of green men.

Mexicans often will leave a job for fear of some other Mexicans, and pride keeps them from confessing the true reason. They will always give a false instead of a true reason for everything. Secretiveness is a national trait and they are very clever about hiding their motives. They more often quit because of some wrong, real or imaginary, than on account of the wages they are receiving. Even though they often say they are leaving on account of poor wages, Mexicans are not affected half as much by wages as by treatment.

Many Mexicans, after working several months in one place, become restless and want to move. Instead of quitting outright, they ask for more money and commence to "lay down" on the job and get impudent. In these cases there is only one thing to do and that is quietly to let them out. They may come back penitently in a week or so and become good workers. Do not hesitate to take a man back if you are convinced that he is penitent and that he intends to reform. It does not pay to hold spite against Mexicans; neither does it pay to remember faults or failings. All men have their shortcomings, but some do not interfere with their working ability. Always overlook such faults.

You cannot always get a full gang of remarkably good men, but you can gradually eliminate the poor ones. The best laborers are generally those who are most anxious to get money. For that very reason the best men are often heavy drinkers and gamblers. Those who spend their money on clothes, phonographs and other innocent luxuries are of course preferable. A good worker is usually a good spender, but a good spender is not always a good saver. Mexicans can live on very little and many would prefer to work half time and live on short ration rather than eat and dress well and work steady to do so. These are the kind of hands to let work for the other fellow.

Certain diseases are very common among Mexican laborers. They contract them and then do nothing to rid themselves of the strength-draining "leeches." After waiting a long time before going to a physician, they finally patronize a quack. Of course maximum laboring efficiency is impossible under such circumstances. I venture to say that over 50 percent of the company's Mexicans have been permanently injured by contracting these diseases and then neglecting to get medical aid. It would pay employers to make some arrangement whereby all such cases would immediately be taken care of for a small fee.

The Mexicans are born and raised under the padrone system. They must have someone in whom they have confidence to go to for advice. It will pay any man to act as a padrone to his Mexicans. Therefore, always try to avoid the appearance of bossing.

In working a gang of Mexicans personally allow them to talk and jest as long as it doesn't interfere with their work. Never stand very close to them unless one of them is "soldiering." In that case stand alongside the guilty one rather than call him down. If they work diligently stand farther away from them. It is hard for a man to work with the boss "looking down his collar." At all times endeavor to keep your voice low and pleasant. Speak sharply only on rare occasions; then, when you do, your words will have the desired effect. Another thing: Set a good example. If the boss relaxes, sits down or leans up against something to rest, the men ease up in their work.

Your men's inventory of you never is closed. They eventually will know you, and you will have to be a man in the full sense of the word to meet their acid test. If you are broadminded, energetic and capable, you will have little trouble in getting and holding a good gang of men. Your workers are usually a reflection of yourself. When you have convinced them that they will have to work hard and when they do so they will be well treated, then most of your troubles are over.

Mexican Disillusionment

Once Mexican immigrants became aware of the reality of life for them in the U.S., they became disillusioned and bitter, as this corrido or folk song shows. The composer laments his move to the U.S. and ultimately decides that he is better off in Mexico. Paul S. Taylor, Mexican Labor in the United States *(Berkeley, 1932), v–vii, 7.*

This corrido surveys from the immigrant's point of view the clashes which arise from his contact with American industrialism and American customs. The reaction is characteristically that of the male Mexican laborer in his gloomier mood of disillusionment. A handicraftsman at home, his skill is rendered useless by the machine. With patriotism accentuated by expatriation, he excoriates those of his countrymen who yield to American prejudices of nationality or color. The young men come in for criticism on their style of dress. The children, alas, dance and speak like Americans. Aspersion is cast on the substitution of Mexicanized English for good Spanish. But the chief castigation is reserved for the girls and women who follow freer standards of dress and conduct. Here is a glimpse into the Mexican's skepticism over *la libertad de las mujeres.* In disgust, and alone, he turns again to his Michoacán.

El Enganchado
(Literally, the hooked one, or more freely, the contract laborer.)

Desde Morelia vine enganchado
ganar los dólars fué mi ilusión
compré zapatos, compré sombrero,
y hasta me puse de pantalón.

> I came under contract from Morelia
> To earn dollars was my dream,
> I bought shoes and I bought a hat
> Even put on trousers.

Pues me decían que aquí los dólars
se pepenaban y de a montón
que las muchachas y que los teatros
y que aquí todo era vacilón.

> For they told me that here the dollars
> Were scattered about in heaps
> That there were girls and theaters
> And that here everything was good fun.

Y ahora me encuentro ya sin resuello
soy zapatero de profesión
Pero aquí dicen que soy camello
y a pura pala y puro azadón.

> And now I'm overwhelmed—
> I am a shoemaker by trade
> By here they say I'm a camel
> And good only for pick and shovel.

De qué me sirve saber mi ofcio
si fabricantes hay de a montón.
y en tanto que hago yo doe botines
ellos avientan más de un millón.

> What good is it to know my trade
> If there are manufacturers by the score,
> And while I make two little shoes
> They turn out more than a million.

Hablar no quieren muchos paieanos
lo qua su mamá lea enseñó
y andan diciendo qua son hispanos
y renegando del pabellón.

> Many Mexicans don't care to speak
> The language their mothers taught them
> And go about saying they are Spanish
> And denying their country's flag.

Los hay mss prietos qua el chapote
pero presumen de ser sajón
andan polveados hasta el cogote
y usan enaguas por pantalón.

> Some are darker than *chapote* [black tar]
> But they pretend to be Saxon;
> They go about powdered to the back of the neck
> And wear skirts for trousers.

Van las muehachas casi encueradas
y a la tienda llaman estor
llevan las piernas rete chorreades
pero con medial de esas chifón.

The girls go about almost naked
And call *la tienda* "estor" [store]
They go around with dirt-streaked legs
But with those stockings of chiffon.

Hasta mi vieja me la ban cambiado
viste de seda rete rabón
anda pintada como piñata
y va en las noches al dancing jol.

Even my old woman has changed on me—
She wears a bob-tailed dress of silk,
Goes about painted like a *piñata*¶
And goes at night to the dancing hall.

Mis chilpallates hablan puro "inglís"
ya no les cuadra nuestro español
me llamas fader y no trabajan
y son reguënos pa'l chárleston.

My kids speak perfect English
And have no use for our Spanish
They call me "fader" and don't work
And are crazy about the Charleston.

Ya estoy cansado de esta tonteada
yo me devuëlvo para Michoacán
hay de recuerdo dejo a la vieja
a ver si alguno se la quiere axmar.

I am tired of all this nonsense
I'm going back to Michoacán;
As a parting memory I leave the old woman
To see if someone else wants to burden himself.

Mexicans Fight Back

Through this letter to the editor, Mexican immigrant José Garcia dispels many myths. The letter shows Mexicans as assertive rather than docile, literate and articulate rather than uneducated. It also shows that discrimination was pervasive wherever Mexicans settled and that immi-

grants were willing to do something to change their situation. Topeka (Kansas) Daily Capital, *February 9, 1927.*

To the Editor of the Capital:
Some time ago I read in the Capital an editorial under the title "Cheap Labor or Better Citizens." Naturally, it deals with Mexicans and their incompetency: but it does not state why and how they are brought into this country.

To the American public, there are many questions that usually come to the mind when thinking about the Mexicans: some of these questions are: "Why do not Mexicans become citizens?" "Should we treat them as whites?" and so on. And it is usually taken for granted that all Mexicans are of the type of bandits and thieves we see in the "movies": yet, perhaps they would think that there are just few very few who will work like "those in the section gang." Their search usually stops there and never they try to understand the longings of these people, his wants or his needs and consequently he is condemned without a chance. . . .

There are many Mexicans in the United States who would gladly become citizens of his country, but there are a few of the reasons that prevent them doing so. In this city of Topeka there are some theaters where a Mexican can go and some where he can't. Last summer I went to the swimming pool at Ripley Park and was informed that Mexicans could not swim there. I took the matter to the Park Commissioner and he told me this: "I know it is not right, but right or wrong, you can't do it."

What an answer: besides there is no other place where they can [swim] except in the river . . . [T]here are two lunch stands on Fourth avenue where they will not let Mexicans sit at the counter. This is what holds them back. But the younger generation must be treated better as they are Americans in birth and makeup; they must have a chance. They are human and have ambitions like anybody else.

We need friends who will understand, and not mock and jeer at those who have been lured by the heartless moneymakers who are always looking for cheap labor. Some big concerns have men who go to the border and talk to those poor people and get them shipped in the box cars like sheep and are carried far into the unknown to suffer and waste their lives. Just think how much these unfortunate people have to stand. They are taken into the very heart of this country to the North, to the East, to every place where there is need of cheap work. When they go North they suffer from the cold because the stores that are run by the different supply companies will not let them have but one dollar's worth of trade for every day they have worked. Their health decays and sooner or later they will cease working and then what?

Who is to blame? The Mexican government has done all that is within its power to check the outgoing of the Mexican youth for that is what comes into this country. But whoever it be, I want to ask the good people of Topeka to be more friendly to them and make them feel that this is the Land of Liberty.

José M. Garcia
Topeka

Questions

---

1. *Describe the Mexican expectations of life in the U.S. Were these desires fulfilled?*
2. *What special circumstances did men face? Women? Children?*
3. *Describe American attitudes toward Mexicans.*
4. *How did Mexicans attempt to dispel the prejudices against them?*
5. *Do you see any similarities between Mexican migration then and now?*

FURTHER READING

For treatments of Mexican women migrants see Vicki Ruiz, *Cannery Women, Cannery Lives: Mexican Women, Unionization, and the California Food Processing Industry, 1930–1950* (Albuquerque, 1987) and Vicki Ruiz, *From Out of the Shadows: Mexican Women in Twentieth Century America* (Oxford, 1998). Zaragosa Vargas, *Proleterians of the North* (Berkeley, 1993) describes Mexican laborers in industry in the Midwest. Dennis Valdés, *Al Norte: Agricultural Workers in the Great Lakes Region, 1917–1970* (Austin, 1991) also discusses laborers in the Midwest in agricultural work. For a work that examines agricultural laborers and unionization in California, see Devra Weber, *Dark Sweat, White Gold: California Farm Workers, Cotton, and the New Deal* (Berkeley, 1994). For an excellent analysis of the change wrought to the Southwest due to the Mexican American war see Albert Camarillo, *Chicanos in a Changing Society: From Mexican Pueblos to American Barrios in Santa Barbara and Southern California, 1848–1930* (Cambridge, 1979). Mario Garcia, *Desert Immigrants* (New Haven, 1981) and David Montejano, *Anglos and Mexicans in the Making of Texas* (Austin, 1987). For Mexican repatriation during the 1930s Francisco Balderrama and Raymond Rodríguez, *Decade of Betrayal: Mexican Repatriation in the 1930s* (Albuquerque, 1995) is a good source.

Advertising and Marketing in American Society During the 1920s and 1930s

Albert J. Churella

INTRODUCTION

The years between 1880 and 1920 marked a period of profound change in the United States. Millions of immigrants entered the country, while millions of rural Americans moved to cities—both groups adjusting to the rapid pace of urban life. Railroads and telegraph lines knit the country together, allowing for rapid and reliable transportation and communication. In many industries, business firms grew to a massive size, producing vast quantities of steel, oil, chemicals, and agricultural products.

All of these developments helped to set the stage for an advertising and marketing revolution during the 1920s and 1930s. Although advertising and marketing are often seen as identical to one another, the two concepts are actually quite different. Marketing, the more inclusive term, refers to the efforts of a seller to exchange goods or services for money by developing new or improved products, implementing price structures, packaging these products, distributing them to the consumer, and making consumers aware of the products' existence through advertising. Advertising, only one component of marketing, uses print, radio, or other media to deliver simple repetitive messages emphasizing certain virtues of a particular product.

Before the American Industrial Revolution of the late 1800s, advertising had been primarily descriptive in nature. Ads simply stated that certain items were available at a particular price, and rarely mentioned whether or not these products would produce any benefits for the consumer. Patent medicine advertisements were considerably different, however. Around the turn of the century, many firms concocted patent "medicines" that usually *did little more than provide temporary pain relief—probably because most contained potent combinations of alcohol and narcotics. Manufacturers, however, issued lavish color ads, claiming that these medicines cured virtually every disease. Such obviously fraudulent claims discredited advertising in general, since the public assumed that only worthless products needed to be advertised.*

The First World War redeemed the power of advertising. President Wilson established the Committee on Public Information (CPI), a federal government agency responsible for encouraging popular support for the war effort. CPI ads, often prepared by commercial advertising agencies, blanketed the country and proved quite effective at whipping up anti-German feelings. The success of these ads persuaded many manufacturers to take another look at the advertising issue.

Other factors contributed to the rapid growth of advertising during the 1920s. The rise of American big business created a large group of managers, engineers, and scientists, and this new middle class possessed both the money and the leisure time necessary to enjoy consumer products. Many companies, having saturated the market for producers' goods (such as steel and oil), began to manufacture a truly incredible variety of consumer goods. Technological and manufacturing advances brought refrigerators, automobiles, radios, and other consumer goods within the reach of middle-class and working-class buyers. Trains allowed identical consumer products to be placed on store shelves throughout the United States. National circulation magazines, such as the Ladies' Home Journal, McCall's, *and the* Saturday Evening Post, *enabled manufacturers to reach an enormous audience. Advances in color printing technology enabled many ads to appear in color—far more effective than a black-and-white ad. As chain stores (smaller versions of modern supermarkets) like A&P replaced "mom and pop" groceries, consumers could no longer rely on the clerk behind the counter to provide advice on which products best suited their needs. Instead, shoppers frequently relied on labels, on national brand names, and on the advertisements they had just seen in a magazine or heard on the radio.*

The advertising and consumer goods explosion that character-ized the 1920s gave enormous power to advertising and marketing executives—the power to shape, or at least to influence, public opinion. Advertising and marketing executives tended to be young, well-educated, upper-middle class, and almost always male—this despite the fact that women made 75 percent of all consumer purchases. Ads reflected the demographic characteris-tics of ad writers, and most ads depicted middle-class, white, young professionals and their children. African Americans and other minorities rarely appeared, and even then were often por-trayed in subservient roles—as a janitor or railroad sleeping car porter, for example. Even though working-class Americans out-numbered middle-class Americans, the former group rarely ap-peared in ads.

Advertisers, it seems, exhibited both contempt and compas-sion for the American people. Ad writers often felt that the average American consumer was ignorant, badly dressed, unschooled in even the most basic social graces, and unaware of the vast and wonderful possibilities of consumerism. On the other hand, ad writers often exhibited compassion for these same prospective consumers, believing that all of their problems could be solved if they purchased the proper consumer goods. Advertisers insisted that they were not simply selling products, they were making consumers healthier, happier, and more successful. Advertisers even attempted to reconcile a basic tension between capitalism (which invariably concentrates wealth in the hands of a few) and democracy (which emphasizes the fundamental concept that "all men are created equal"). Ad writers did so through the idea of the "democracy of goods," which stressed that all people were essen-tially made equal through the products (goods) that they con-sumed, regardless of their level of income. At a time when some Americans—and even more Europeans—felt that socialism or communism constituted viable alternatives to capitalism, the de-mocracy of goods offered the promise of a peaceful and harmonious reconciliation between America's democratic ideals and the unde-niable class stratification of 1920s society. The poor need not envy the rich (nor challenge their elite economic, political, and social status) because rich and poor alike could enjoy the same mass-produced benefits of capitalism. A bit naïve, perhaps, but at least indicative of the advertisers' desire to help create what they perceived as a better society.

The Role of Advertising in American Society

Almost everyone agrees that advertising has had a significant impact on the American consumer culture. Considerable debate has emerged, however, over the exact nature of advertising's influence. Some historians argue that advertising executives and business leaders engaged in a near conspiracy designed to force Americans to buy consumer products. These scholars feel that advertising has warped American society by downplaying such important issues as class conflict (the rich vs. the poor, or managers vs. workers); that advertising has forced Americans to work long and hard simply to purchase items that they do not need. They further assert that advertisers are able to transform wants into needs and luxuries into necessities, in the process wasting natural resources, polluting the environment, and widening the gap between the "haves" and the "have-nots."

Other scholars regard advertising as much less pervasive and threatening. They argue that advertising merely reflects long-term changes in American society; in other words, advertisers see no value in writing ads unless people have already demonstrated a desire to own a new product. Ads may cause consumers to buy car "A" rather than car "B" but still have no impact on the consumers' initial decision to purchase some type of car. Exploitation of natural resources and rampant consumerism may indeed exist, they explain, but these often unfortunate trends are part of a natural human desire to acquire more "stuff" and are not the responsibility of advertisements or of advertisers.

The Crisco Story

Crisco is not only a familiar product found in grocery stores throughout the world; it also provides an example of a stunningly successful market-ing campaign, one that set the pattern for others during the 1920s, 1930s, and later. This excerpt shows that Procter and Gamble did not develop Crisco to meet a consumer need (actual or anticipated), but rather to increase the efficiency and profitability of their other manufac-turing enterprises. Once Procter and Gamble had developed Crisco, the challenge became to convince consumers that they actually needed a product that they had always done without and had never known they wanted. Excerpted from Susan Strasser, Satisfaction Guaranteed: The Making of the American Mass Market *(New York, 1989), 3-5, 9-15.*

In January of 1912, the Procter and Gamble Company of Cincinnati, Ohio, introduced Crisco, a solid vegetable shortening that it described to the readers of the *Ladies' Home Journal* and at least four other popular national magazines as "An Absolutely New Product, A Scientific Discovery Which will Affect Every Kitchen in America." . . .

. . . The experiments that produced Crisco had begun in 1905, supported by capital from Procter and Gamble's several success-ful brands of soap, including the well-known Ivory. In part, the research was an attempt to generate a product that would assure P & G its supply of cottonseed oil, which it was already using to make soap. . . . By creating and marketing new products that used large quantities of cottonseed oil, Procter and Gamble could achieve not only financial growth but a more powerful position in purchasing its raw materials. For five years, under top-secret conditions, the laboratories worked to solve the technical difficul-ties of producing an all-vegetable solid fat in commercial quanti-ties. In 1910, they achieved a patentable product. . . .

At the end of April 1911, the company's executive committee met in William Procter's office to vote on the name and the label

---

design. They approved a package incorporating the company's moon-and-stars logo and substituted "Crisco" for "Krispo," a name they had adopted the month before, but on which a Chicago cracker manufacturer had a prior claim. They then turned the product over to Stanley Resor, who had left Procter and Collier, the company's own advertising agency, to establish a Cincinnati office for J. Walter Thompson. Resor assigned copywriting responsibility to Helen Lansdowne, the woman he was later to marry and with whom he would acquire both financial and administrative control of this major New York advertising firm; Lansdowne would become the first woman in the Advertising Hall of Fame. Procter and Gamble was so concerned about marketing Crisco that the board of directors for the first time opened its meetings to a woman. Five times during 1911, Lansdowne took the train from New York to Cincinnati to represent the agency and "answer questions from the woman's point of view."

Product testing continued, now outside the company laboratories. University-based food researchers received samples for testing and recipe development; the company later quoted these scientists and home economists, testifying to Crisco's purity and goodness. The product made its first public appearance at a summer party for P & G employees. Like the Cincinnati clubwomen who soon began attending "Crisco teas," the workers carried home full-sized (one-and-a-half-pound) samples of the product. In October, Cincinnati's Burnet House Hotel and Queen City Club adopted the shortening; they were eventually followed by Chesapeake and Ohio Railway dining cars and New York City's Lüchow's Restaurant. During these tests, the company continued to refine the product, altering the formula in response to complaints that it went rancid.

Meanwhile, Resor and Lansdowne tested seven or eight different sales-promotion plans simultaneously. In one city, they tried newspaper advertising; in another, nothing but streetcar ads or outdoor posters or store demonstrations. In some cities, house-to-house canvassers sold the product; in others, salesmen courted retailers in conjunction with a house-to-house campaign. A specially hired staff worked on a more general analysis of the shortening market, investigating the competition and the uses of various products.

In December of 1911, a month before the first national advertising, the company sent packages containing three to six full-sized cans to every grocer in the United States, with a letter describing the forthcoming campaign. "We want you to have Crisco in stock, so that you can supply the first demand this advertising will create among your customers," one such letter read. "Sell the six cans, and then order what further supply you need from your jobber." "Crisco is being placed in the grocery stores as rapidly as possible," the January magazine ad told the grocers' customers. "If your own grocer does not yet keep it, you probably will find it in one of the other stores in your neighborhood." For the first few months, shoppers who failed to obtain Crisco through the stores could buy a package (but only one) direct from Procter and Gamble, for twenty-five cents and the name of the offending grocer. By the end of 1915, the company could report in a *Saturday Evening Post* advertisement that "through the length and breadth of the country, in big stores and little, Crisco is now a staple."

During those first four years, the company promoted Crisco extensively and continuously, not only advertising in national magazines but enlisting grocer support. Cooperating storekeepers wrote letters to their charge customers, enclosing booklets about the shortening and offering to add Crisco to the delivery order. "Just let us send you a small package today on our recommendation," a Dallas form letter read. "Then see if it doesn't change completely your ideas of fried foods." A Rochester, New York merchant sent his letter on a printed folder supplied by the company, picturing a black cook displaying a plateful of biscuits. "We have seldom had anything that has met with such immediate success," he wrote.

For several years, six Crisco demonstrators toured cities throughout the country from September through June, conducting week-long cooking schools. The schools were paid for by Procter and Gamble, arranged for by a P & G advance man, and cosponsored by local newspapers, which lent their names to the schools—the "*Herald* Cooking School"—and their columns to the new product. A pseudonymous writer for the Fort Smith, Arkansas *Southwest American*, for example, was much taken by demonstrator Mrs. Kate B. Vaughn, "a perfect dear" and a "woman's woman" who served her audience peas, lamb chops, potato nests, white cake, marshmallow pudding, and baking-powder biscuits. "Mrs. Vaughn used a new shortening for these biscuits and told why she used it," the writer declared, "all of which caused me to stop in at my grocer's and purchase a can of the stuff, which I tried with great success last night."

In its 1913 prospectus for newspaper publishers, the company asserted that the demonstrators downplayed product promotion. Although they did discuss Crisco, their lectures covered other topics as well. "For, if women believed the lecture was there merely to promote or advertise a trademarked article, they would not be so apt to come a second time," the company told the publishers. "The audience may or may not, however, believe that the manufacturer of Crisco remunerates the lecturer in some way for the endorsement she gives the product." Given that the endorsement involved handing out full-sized samples and Crisco recipe pamphlets, only the credulous would believe otherwise.

These pamphlets, illustrated with pictures of the demonstrators, published the results of a continuous process of recipe development that also enabled Procter and Gamble to furnish cookbooks through the mail. By June 1912, consumers could write for *Tested Crisco Recipes*, a free paperback with a hundred recipes and "the interesting story of Crisco's discovery and manufacture." Late in 1913, a new book appeared: *The Story of Crisco*, in a complimentary version with 250 recipes, and in a clothbound "quality edition" available for five 2-cent stamps. The latter, *A Calendar of Dinners*, suggesting 365 menus with 615 recipes, went through at least twenty-six editions by 1925. These books supplemented the company's other cooking instructions. Recipes appeared in Crisco advertising as early as April 1912, and an eight-page, circle-shaped recipe booklet was packed inside the lid of every can.

Other packaging innovations aimed the product at particular markets. Soon after a special ten-pound container was created for their compact dining-car kitchens, twenty-two railroads adopted Crisco. Another special package, advertised in the Yiddish media and sold in Jewish neighborhoods, bore the seals of Rabbi Lifsitz of Cincinnati and Rabbi Margolies of New York, who pronounced the contents kosher. Margolies, according to *The Story of Crisco*, "said that the Hebrew Race had been waiting 4,000 years for Crisco." By enabling immigrant cooks to bake American pie without lard, Crisco joined the forces of Americanization, a movement that enlisted many home economists and social workers who hoped to transform foreigners through their eating habits.

At the end of the first year of Crisco marketing, J. George Frederick, former editor of the widely read advertising industry weekly *Printers' Ink*, wrote that the campaign had established a new standard for modern marketing. In a *Printers' Ink* article entitled "Efficient Planning Before Advertising," he described the testing procedures, infusing his prose with the popular jargon of efficiency and scientific management. "Instead of filling the earth and the sky and all that therein is with flashes of publicity and grand hurrah," he maintained, Procter and Gamble "has in a final and authoritative manner indicated the maximum efficiency method of marketing and finding distribution for a new product."

The methods were not quite final; over the next seventy-five years, marketers developed more sophisticated techniques that employed technologies and systems undreamed of in 1912. Nonetheless, both the Crisco publicity and the campaign planning look strikingly modern. Today's marketers employ many of the same general planning principles and promotional techniques, although they apply them to television commercials and rely on computer-analyzed statistics. The testing and refining of the product formula, label, and marketing strategy continue, for Crisco and for other successful consumer products. The kosher packages and the dining-car marketing provide evidence of what is now called market segmentation and product positioning, with special packages, product formulas, and marketing campaigns aimed at particular groups of potential buyers. Late-twentieth-century consumers still receive free samples and read recipe suggestions in magazine advertising. And although little record remains of the Crisco teas, they probably sounded much like the focus groups that contemporary marketers convene.

Does Advertising Reflect Society or Distort It?

Advertisers frequently argue that their ads merely reflect existing social values and needs; that they only promote products and services that people know they want. While historian Roland Marchand does not believe that advertisers conspiratorially manipulate society, he does suggest that ads have selected and sorted; in other words, that advertisers chose a very narrow range of lifestyles and portrayed these as representative of the experiences of all Americans, regardless of gender, race, class, or occupation. Excerpted from Roland Marchand, Advertising the American Dream: Making Way for Modernity, 1920-1940 *(Berkeley, 1985), xvi-xvii, xxi, 1-2, 4, 359, 87, 264, 116, 217-18, 220, 285, 318, 300, 288, 290-91, 337.*

I cannot prove conclusively that the American people absorbed the values and ideas of the ads, nor that consumers wielded the power to ensure that the ads would mirror their lives. In fact, as advertisers quickly perceived, people did not usually want ads to reflect themselves, their immediate social relationships, or their broader society exactly. They wanted not a true mirror but a Zerrspiegel, a distorting mirror that would enhance certain images. Even the term Zerrspiegel, denoting a fun-house mirror, fails to suggest fully the scope of advertising distortions of reality. Such a mirror distorts the shapes of the objects it reflects, but it nevertheless provides some image of everything within its field of vision. Advertising's mirror not only distorted, it also selected. Some social realities hardly appeared at all. One has to search diligently in the ads of the 1920s and 1930s to find even fleeting glimpses of such common scenes as religious services, factory workers on the job, sports fans enjoying a boxing match or baseball game, or working-class families at home.

The angle of refraction, and hence the degree of distortion of these advertising images, was determined not only by the efforts of advertisers to respond to consumers' desires for fantasy and wish-fulfillment but also by a variety of other factors. The most obvious source of distortion in advertising's mirror was the presumption by advertisers that the public preferred an image of "life as it ought to be, life in the millennium" to an image of literal reality. "The people are seeking to escape from themselves," concluded a writer in *Advertising and Selling* in 1926. "They want to live in a more exciting world." Working under this assumption, ad creators tried to reflect public aspirations rather than contemporary circumstances, to mirror popular fantasies rather than social realities. Advertisers recognized that consumers would rather identify with scenes of higher status than ponder reflections of their actual lives. In response, they often sought to give products a "class image" by placing them in what recent advertising jargon would call "upscale" settings.

Even apart from such upscale strategies, advertisements of the 1920s and 1930s were likely to convey unrepresentative class images. Most advertisers defined the market for their products as a relatively select audience of upper-class and upper-middle-class Americans. Even had they sought to depict the lives of these consumers with absolute fidelity, their ads would have mirrored only this select audience rather than society as a whole. . . .

One significant bias of advertisers deserves particular attention; and it is a bias that, paradoxically, offers us the prospect of using the advertisements of the 1920s and 1930s more confidently as a key to understanding certain realities of American culture. The ad creators of that era proudly proclaimed themselves missionaries of modernity. Constantly and unabashedly, they championed the new against the old, the modern against the old-fashioned. This bias, inherent in their economic function, ensured that advertisements would emphasize disproportionately those styles, classes, behaviors, and social circumstances that were new and changing. . . .

At the same time, advertisers came to recognize certain vacuums of advice in modern society. They had always offered advice in a narrow, prescriptive sense: use our product. Now they discovered a market for broader counsel and reassurance. In response, they gave advice that promoted the product while offering expertise and solace in the face of those modern complexities and impersonal judgments that made the individual feel incompetent and insecure. Advertisers, then as now, recognized a much larger stake in reflecting people's needs and anxieties than in depicting their actual circumstances and behavior. It was in their efforts to promote the mystique of modernity in styles and technology, while simultaneously assuaging the anxieties of consumers about losses of community and individual control, that they most closely mirrored historical reality—the reality of a cultural dilemma. . . .

Other professional elites—scientists, engineers, and industrial designers—also claimed to epitomize the dynamic forces of modernization, but advertising agents insisted that they played a crucial role. Scientific inventions and technological advances fostered the expectation of change and the organization for continuous innovation that characterized modern society. But inventions and their technological applications made a dynamic impact only when the great mass of people learned of their benefits, integrated them into their lives, and came to lust for more new products. Modern technologies needed their heralds, advertising men contended. Modern styles and ways of life needed their missionaries. Advertising men were modernity's "town criers." They brought good news about progress. . . .

New industries were surging to the forefront in the 1920s. Nearly all of the glamor industries of the era—automobiles, radio, chemicals, movies, drugs, and electrical refrigeration—had established . . . a "face-to-face relationship" with the consuming public. Industrial giants like General Electric and Westinghouse, once primarily suppliers of equipment to other industries, increasingly sold products directly to individual consumers. The special modernity of advertising agents seemed exemplified by their strategic position on the interface of this dynamic new relationship between big business and its public. . . .

Advertisers thus celebrated the complexities and interdependencies of modern society, seeking to further rationalize the operations of the marketplace, to lubricate its mechanisms, and to achieve greater control over its functioning. With the maturing of industrialization, the consumer remained the most unpredictable and thus the most disruptive element in the economic system. If advertising agents could induce consumers to answer their needs by depending on more products offered them impersonally through the marketplace and could educate them to a predictable and enthusiastic demand for new products, then they would enhance the rationality and dynamism of the modern business system. . . .

The exhilaration created by the new pace of technological change and economic activity coexisted with deep anxieties about social disorder—anxieties symbolized by prohibition, immigration restrictions, and warnings of the dangers posed by the "new woman" and "flaming youth." Jazz, bobbed hair, cosmetics, the hip flask, and sexual frankness all flouted traditional moral standards and seemed to threaten family stability and paternal authority. The new media of movies and radio were nationalizing American culture, creating the specter of a country whose masses could be easily swayed by the latest fad.

Ad creators seized on the public's sense of an exciting yet disconcerting new tempo, reinforcing and amplifying this perception for their own purposes. They welcomed the economic forces that were propelling advertising toward an enhanced position of power and status in the society, and they explored strategies for transforming their clients' products into plausible solutions to the anxieties and dilemmas that arose from the pace of life and the scale of institutions in the new era. In the process, American advertising matured in style and content, gradually assuming what we now recognize as distinctly modern forms. . . .

Perhaps more than any other institution, American advertising adapted itself to the possibilities for exercising both a dynamic and a stabilizing influence during such an age. Advertising served preeminently as the spokesman for modernism. It exalted technological advances and disseminated the good news of progress to the millions. It promoted urban lifestyles and sought to educate consumers to master the new complexities of social interaction. But the very social and technological changes which advertising glorified also placed a burden of proof on those who wished to reassure an anxious public that society still operated on a comprehensible human scale—a scale within which people could expect their individual needs to be recognized and catered to. . . .

. . . Advertising, by linking itself with civilizing influences, could thus serve a redemptive function. It would not only improve the economic well-being of the consumer masses; it was destined to raise their cultural and intellectual standards as well. . . .

. . . Advertisements were *secular* sermons, exhortations to seek fulfillment through the consumption of material goods and mundane services. . . .

Any hope for uplilft, for the missionary effect of the advertising writer, would have to come, if at all, not from the impact of the advertisements on the consumer's mind but from the new behavior and tastes that the ownership of products would induce. Since the products themselves would be the agents of uplift, advertisers could best carry out their mission as modernizers and civilizers by employing the most effective means—including frivolous entertainment . . . to put the products in the consumer's hands. In serving the cause of modernity, American advertising modernized its techniques. Ironically, it did so by responding to some of the most archaic qualities of a seemingly unsophisticated, emotional, intimacy-hungry public. . . .

. . . [R]eaders found themselves schooled in one of the most pervasive of all advertising tableaux of the 1920s—the parable of the Democracy of Goods. According to this parable, the wonders of modern mass production and distribution enabled every person to enjoy the society's most significant pleasure, convenience, or benefit. The definition of the particular benefit fluctuated, of course, with each client who employed the parable. But the cumulative effect of the constant reminders that "any woman can" and "every home can afford" was to publicize an image of American society in which concentrated wealth at the top of a hierarchy of social classes restricted no family's opportunity to acquire the most significant products. By implicitly defining "democracy" in terms of equal access to consumer products, and then by depicting the everyday functioning of that "democracy" with regard to one product at a time, these tableaux offered Americans an inviting vision of their society as one of incontestable equality.

In its most common advertising formula, the concept of the Democracy of Goods asserted that although the rich enjoyed a great variety of luxuries, the acquisition of their *one* most significant luxury would provide anyone with the ultimate in satisfaction. For instance, a Chase and Sanborn's Coffee tableau, with an elegant butler serving a family in a dining room with a sixteen-foot ceiling, reminded Chicago families that although "compared with the riches of the more fortunate, your way of life may seem modest indeed," yet no one—"king, prince, statesman, or capitalist"—could enjoy better coffee. . . .

The social message of the parable of the Democracy of Goods was clear. Antagonistic envy of the rich was unseemly; programs to redistribute wealth were unnecessary. The best things in life were already available to all at reasonable prices. . . .

. . . The Great Depression of the early 1930s, however, presented the American dream of individual success through equal access to ample opportunities with its most formidable challenge. Not only had advertising writers served as public spokesmen for a business system now brought under suspicion; they were now engaged, in their own agencies and corporate departments, in an increasingly desperate personal struggle for survival and success. . . .

. . . [C]opywriters recognized the centrality of the success creed to the dilemmas of depression-era Americans. But advertisers made no effort to learn popular attitudes in order to mirror them. Rather, they invested themselves with a responsibility for moral leadership. By implicitly defining all other responses to the depression as cowardly, they sought to give a recommitment to hard work the force of a moral imperative. The appeal to courage did not invite a close examination of circumstances; rather it short-circuited any depression-inspired questions about the functioning and credibility of the American dream. . . .

. . . Depression advertising *looked* different. Of course, strategies for brand differentiation always insured that some advertisers would seek distinctive images by bucking style trends. But no one can glance through the advertisements of a 1932 issue of a popular magazine and mistake the prevalent style for that of a 1928 issue. Depression advertising was distinctively "loud," cluttered, undignified, and direct. . . .

Eventually these economic and occupational pressures were bound to affect the style and content of advertising copy. Advertisers did not like to become the bearers of bad news; still, they needed to make the messages about their products "newsworthy." To do so often meant to show how the product—in price, function, or symbolic value—was particularly necessary or attractive "in these times.". . .

. . . No single trend in advertising content characterized even the gravest years of the early 1930s. Even in 1933, most national advertisements offered no direct reflection of the existence of the depression. But gradually, more and more advertisers sought to empathize with, and perhaps to reflect, public concerns about econonomizing and job insecurity and popular yearnings for compensatory satisfactions. . . .

. . . [T]he parable of the Democracy of Goods gained even greater use as consolation. Psychologically, the depression could be overcome through compensatory satisfactions. Certain products, affordable by all, could provide pleasures no millionaire could surpass. "One joy you can afford," insisted Vigoro fertilizer, "is a Beautiful Garden." "Here—write like a millionaire!" beckoned the American Pencil Company. "A millionaire may ride in a sportier car, live in a richer home, and work at a bigger desk . . . but he can't write with a better pencil than *you* can. . . . And the price is ten cents, to everyone." Copywriters promoted easily affordable Edgeworth Pipe Tobacco not merely as a compensating pleasure but as a depression-inspired rediscovery of the truly satisfying. To the "thousands who had been swept away from the calmness and composure of pipe smoking by the speed of the Prosperity Era," Edgeworth offered an escape from "the tensions of work and business problems" and a return to "the solid things of life.". . .

The parable of the Democracy of Goods, including its dramatic depression versions, promised compensations for the lack of self-sufficiency and personal control inherent in the scale of a life lived among the multitudes. This parable offered consumers a sense of significant participation in the society, on an equality with the most privileged citizens, through specific and often trivial acts of consumption. In so doing, it brushed aside the question of whether average citizens could hope to retain the qualities of political participation and economic self-determination that they might have enjoyed in a society of smaller scale.

The Concerns of American Consumers

Many advertisers were convinced that American consumers were, quite literally, the "great unwashed." Their ads emphasized cultural values that society now considered to be of critical importance——appearance, cleanliness, pleasant odor, and fresh breath. As the prosperous years of the 1920s gave way to the Great Depression of the 1930s, ad writers increasingly emphasized these values, certain that they would make the difference in the continual struggle in this new era of unemployment and poverty. Excerpted from Juliann Sivulka, Soap, Sex, and Cigarettes: A Cultural History of American Advertising *(Belmont, CA, 1998), 158, 160, 162-63, 166-68, 199-201.*

What we know as mouthwash first sold as a "breath deodorant." Sales for the general antiseptic Listerine, invented by a St. Louis druggist named J. W. Lambert, moved slowly until Milton Feasley and Gordon Seagrove of the firm's Chicago ad agency, Williams & Cunnyngham, promoted the product as a remedy for bad breath. One simply did not talk about such personal matters

---

Excerpts reprinted from *Soap, Sex and Cigarettes: A Cultural History of American Advertising*, by Juliann Sivulka, 1998, Wadsworth Publishing Company.

in polite company, so the agency used the medical-sounding "halitosis" instead. Copywriter Milton Feasley created the halitosis idea in 1922. One expression of the concept became on[e] of the best-known advertising headlines: "Often a bridesmaid but never a bride." The headline continued with different copy and illustrations for three decades. For example, this classic 1925 ad created new anxieties:

> Edna's case was really a pathetic one. Like every woman, her primary ambition was to marry. Most of the girls of her set were married—or about to be. Yet not one possessed more grace or charm or loveliness than she. And as her birthdays crept gradually toward that tragic thirty-mark, marriage seemed farther from her life than ever. She was often a bridesmaid but never a bride.
>
> That's the insidious thing about halitosis (unpleasant breath). You, yourself, rarely know when you have it. And even your closest friends won't tell you.

But the friendly Listerine adviser could. Listerine worked as a "breath deodorant" and halted "food fermentation in the mouth and [left] the breath sweet, fresh, and clean."

Further installments of the dramatic Listerine campaign presented other social disasters, from missed invitations to ruined marriages, that supposedly could happen to anybody. One 1926 ad asked: "Was this a hint? This was the third time it had happened in a month: he the head of the concern, finding one of these advertisements on his desk, marked for his attention, no signature."

The campaign proved so successful that people's behavior changed. The morning mouthwash soon became as popular as the morning shower. To further boost sales, Listerine creatively introduced other uses for the product: a dandruff cure, an after-shave tonic, a cold and sore throat remedy, an astringent, and a deodorant; Listerine even developed its own brand of cigarettes. Annual ad expenditures for Listerine products rose from $100,000 in 1922 to $5 million in 1928, with Listerine generating a net $4 million profit over the same period.

With Listerine as a model, ad campaigns revolving around "advertising by fear" or "whisper copy" fostered new anxieties and contributed solutions every day. Yet all the ads carefully masked the "unmentionable" in sober, medical-sounding terms.

For example, Absorbine Jr. effectively treated the fungus "Tinea Trichophyton" (athlete's foot), Pompeiian massage cream eliminated "comedones" (blackheads), and Spencer corsets corrected "lordosis" (faulty posture).

Lever Brothers, the makers of Lifebuoy and Lux soap in Cambridge, Massachusetts, also were inspired by Listerine's ploy of creating a problem (halitosis) and then providing a solution. The company revised its advertising copy to reflect this stronger selling approach.

Since 1902 Lifebuoy had been advertised as "the soap that cleans and disinfects, purifies—at one operation." In 1928, however, a Lifebuoy soap ad assured consumers that the product would "protect" them from an even greater social disgrace: "B.O."—short for "Body Odor." Similarly, Lux originally had been promoted as a wonderful new product for "laundering fine fabrics"; and by the mid-1920s it could also preserve "soft, youthful, lovely feminine hands." In the early 1930s, however, Lever Brothers dramatically shifted gears and adopted a stronger sell. Lux could now prevent "undie odor": "She never omits her Daily Bath, yet wears underthings a SECOND DAY." As these stop-smelling pitches ran, business boomed for Lever Brothers.

Advertising the new product Kotex, made by Cellucotton Products Co. in Chicago, proved yet another delicate task. How did one mention the truly unmentionable? With the topic of menstruation a taboo, the early ads succeeded without using any descriptive words in the headline. A 1921 Kotex ad read: "Simplify the laundress problem," referring to the unwelcome chore of laundering soiled cloths or rags. "Kotex are good enough to form a habit, cheap enough to throw away, and easy to dispose of," explained the copy. In 1927 the Lord & Thomas agency claimed: "The Safe Solution of Women's Greatest Hygienic Problem, over 80 percent of the better class of women in America today employ Kotex" a product that "thoroughly deodorizes." Through friendly chatter the Kotex ads assured modern women of the value and convenience of the product while delicately avoiding an intimate discussion of feminine hygiene. Yet Kotex faced still another problem: women were too embarrassed to ask for the product by name. To address this issue, later Kotex ads included a new marketing device. Plain brown wrappers camouflaged the name Kotex on the packages; merchants displayed the product on the counter so a woman simply picked it up and left the money.

Once women did not have to ask for the product by name, sales rose. . . .

Selling the Cigarette Habit

The selling of cigarettes proved to be advertising's ultimate triumph of the decade. At that time many people considered cigarette smoking an undesirable habit. Moralists blasted cigarettes, referring to them as "coffin nails" and "gaspers." Henry Ford deemed cigarette smokers unemployable in a 1914 pamphlet. Others held that the cigarette smokers were most likely criminals, neurotics, or possibly drug addicts. The war and multimillion-dollar advertising campaigns changed all that. During and after World War I, cigarettes gained wider acceptance when both soldiers and civilians found smoking cigarettes to be more convenient, cheaper, and more sanitary than chewing tobacco.

To this audience R. J. Reynolds in Winston-Salem, North Carolina, directed its first nationally marketed cigarette, called Camel. The brand quickly achieved market dominance with an upscale-priced smoke that delivered a new tobacco taste. In no time George Washington Hill's American Tobacco Company in North Carolina created a richer, sweeter tobacco product, Lucky Strike cigarettes. The three major brands (Chesterfield was the third) then slugged it out for the market lead from 1917 until after World War II.

Hill hired hard-sell expert Albert J. Lasker of the Lord & Thomas agency and told him to do whatever was necessary to win the cigarette war. As a result, Lucky Strike advertising broke all previous records. Hill's enormous ad expenditures also brought the Lord & Thomas agency back into the ranks of the major agencies. In 1929 alone the American Tobacco Company accounted for over one-fourth of the agency's $40 million in billings. . . .

Hill, urged on by Lasker, jumped at the chance to reach an untapped audience—women—who would double the potential market. Until now advertising had supported the notion that the pleasures of smoking were for men only. But a number of women took up smoking during World War I as cigarette tobacco became milder and easier to use than the roll-your-own varieties (although the filter had not yet been invented). Still, society did not consider smoking an acceptable social practice for women.

Throughout the decade women smokers remained a controversial issue. For example, many colleges prohibited women from smoking on campus. Women also found themselves unable to smoke in railroad diners, in many smoking rooms in train stations, and on board ships. By the mid-1920s, however, some colleges had established smoking rooms, while streetcars, railroads, and shipping lines liberalized their regulations. Some railroads opened their smoking cars to women despite men's complaints that women occupied their seats; others installed separate smoking compartments for men and for women or allowed women to smoke in the dining car.

Advertising further fueled this cultural revolution. One 1912 ad for Velvet Tobacco showed a "respectable" woman sitting with a man who was smoking; "I wish I were a man," she mused, suggesting that she might like to smoke. Some ads hinted at this daring idea, while others took a more direct approach. In 1926 the Newell-Emmett agency daringly presented a poster showing a romantic moonlit seaside scene and a man lighting his Chesterfield with a woman perched beside him saying, "Blow some my way." These four words shocked many people. Yet Chesterfield resolutely carried on with its campaign, paving the way to the vast women's market. Hill and Lasker quickly sensed an opportunity for the Lucky Strike brand and pitched the female audience, appealing to women's growing sense of independence.

The Lucky Strike advertising campaign incorporated several major innovations. First, Hill was concerned that women were resisting the green packaging because it clashed with their clothes (the original pack had a red bull's-eye on a dark green background until 1942, when it changed to red on white). To solve the problem, he hired Edward L. Bernays, a public relations pioneer, who promoted the color green as fashionable in fashion shows so that the dark green Luckies packages would complement women's ensembles. Hill also used celebrities from the entertainment world, such [as] film stars, crooners, and jazz musicians, to promote his cigarettes. And for the first time women endorsed the product and popularized the image of the fashionable lady who, while she indeed smoked, still appeared stylish and respectable. Lucky Strike campaigns particularly favored testimonials from operatic sopranos, actresses, and society matrons, who attested to the positive effect Luckies had on their voices. One slogan ("Reach for a Lucky instead of a sweet") even drew protests from the candy industry. . . . Many marketers believe that this "sweet" campaign created more women smokers than any other single advertising effort. . . .

A "Hard Sell" for Hard Times

Advertising had helped spur the business boom in the 1920s, and some observers suggested that it could even prevent future economic downfalls. That is, advertising could best reverse the "depression state of mind" by hammering out messages of reassurance. But advertising had failed to stem the onset of the Depression, and agencies soon felt the tremors of the stock market crash. . . .

Economic and professional concerns eventually affected the look and content of advertising in the early 1930s. Cost-conscious advertisers used color and illustrations sparingly, substituting extensive text in a multitude of typefaces to grab attention. Louder headlines, strident hard-sell copy, and gross exaggerations appeared as pseudoscientific arguments and appeals to emotion. Ads especially capitalized on consumers' intensified economic and personal insecurities. . . .

Advertisers worked hard to show how their client's product was necessary or attractive in terms of price, function, or value. They also sought to empathize with the Depression-wracked public's concerns about economizing and employment. In the process admakers found two appeals of immense value. One obvious tactic was a blatant emphasis on price. Although hardly a new idea, these economy appeals intensified in the early 1930s, as evidenced by the emergence of supermarkets and ads featuring price as the attention-getting element. The other tactic tapped into consumers' economic insecurities. . . .

A heavy emphasis on dollar figures gave some national advertisements the look of retail ads. Some automobile ads even employed the traditional bargain-offer format that featured a crossed-out price. Other ads emphasized the potential savings associated with purchasing a given product. For instance, an ad for Hoover vacuum cleaners boasted: "The richest woman in the world can have no finer electric cleaner than any woman can have and for as little as $4.50 down." A Fabray window shade ad argued that people should not throw away filthy window coverings, but instead should wash them: "Now, Window Shades That

Are Really Washable . . . Yet Cost Only 45 Cents." Listerine toothpaste ads suggested another method to cope with tough times: "See what you can buy with the $3 you save" (that is, the money one saved after a year of buying a Listerine product at 25 cents a tube rather than other brands at 50 cents). Listerine ads listed potential uses of the money—purchases ranging from galoshes and underwear to milk and other staples. The economic appeal also addressed the mushrooming demand for "something for nothing," as contests, premiums, prizes, and two-for-one promotions appeared everywhere.

At the same time, advertisers' attempts to sell more products reflected their growing desperation. Traditional slice-of-life stories tapped emotions such as guilt, fear, shame, and blame to reinforce advertising appeals. These ads conveyed a common message: "If you don't buy this product, you'll be sorry."

Unease Over the Effects of Advertising

Michael Schudson tends to be critical of advertising's influence over American society. Still, he claims that advertisers have been unable to cause profound changes in social values. In this passage, he discusses the relationship between cigarette advertising and the increase in smoking among women during the 1920s. Excerpted from Advertising, the Uneasy Persuasion: Its Dubious Impact on American Society *(New York, 1984), 43, 179-80, 183, 192, 197, 207, 235-37.*

Here I speak only of advertising's specific power to sell specific goods, and that power is clearly limited. . . .

. . . I will develop this point through a case study of the growing popularity of the cigarette in the 1920s and, in doing so, will make a second point: that major consumer changes are rarely wrought by advertising. Advertising followed rather than led the

---

spread of cigarette usage and it was the convenience and democracy of the cigarette, coupled with specific, new opportunities for its use, that brought the cigarette into American life. . . .

The spread of cigarette smoking, particularly among women, was one of the most visible signs of change in consumption practices in the 1920s, and one that has been cited frequently as evidence of the new powers of advertising and marketing. Between 1918 and 1940, American consumption grew from 1.70 to 5.16 pounds of cigarette tobacco per adult. During the same period, advertising budgets of the tobacco companies bulged, movies pictured elegant men and women smoking, and public relations stunts promoted cigarettes.

Some contemporary observers concluded that advertising *caused* the increase in cigarette smoking among women. For instance, in 1930, Clarence True Wilson, board secretary of the Methodist Episcopal Church, declared: "If the advertising directed to women ceased, it is probable that within five years the smoking woman would be the rare exception." Scholars in recent years have accepted a similar view. Erik Barnouw, for instance, holds that advertising was responsible for bringing women into the cigarette market.

This conclusion is difficult to sustain for a number of reasons, the most obvious of which is that tens of thousands of women began smoking cigarettes in the 1920s *before* a single advertisement was directed toward them. It is more accurate to observe that cigarette smoking among women led tobacco companies to advertise toward the female market than to suggest that advertising created the market in the first place. The mass media played a role in spreading the cigarette habit among women, but it was primarily the information conveyed in news stories, not the persuasion attempted in advertisements, that helped in the first instance to legitimate smoking among women in the 1920s. . . .

Meanwhile, cigarette manufacturers were cautious in appealing directly to women. Curtis Wessel, editor of the *United States Tobacco Journal*, wrote in 1924 that "all responsible tobacco opinion" found the habit of women smoking so "novel" that "it would not be in good taste for tobacco men as parties in interest to stir a particle toward or against a condition with whose beginnings they had nothing to do and whose end, if any, no one can foresee."

When advertisers did begin to address women directly, they did so cautiously. The first notable cigarette ad directed toward women was a Chesterfield ad in 1926 showing a romantic couple at night, the man smoking, the woman sitting next to him, with the caption, "Blow Some My Way." Most ads for cigarettes, even ads with an audience of women in mind, showed only men smoking. The *New Yorker* in 1926 printed a full page ad for Miltiades Egyptian cigarettes that featured a drawing captioned, "After Theatre," with a man and a woman in evening dress. The man is smoking and says to the woman, "Somehow or other Shakespeare's heroines seem more feminine in modern garb and smoking cigarettes. . . . " He advises her to exercise care in choosing a cigarette—but she, as usual, is not shown smoking. A Camel cigarette ad in *Time* in 1926 shows two men lighting up, two women looking on. An ad in *Time* for Fatima Turkish Cigarettes claims, "It's What the Younger Crowd Thinks About It!" and shows a man and a woman waterskiing, but only the man smoking. A Camel cigarette ad in *The Outlook* in 1927 shows two men and a woman at a nightclub, both men smoking and the woman not smoking. . . .

. . . The cigarette was . . . a focus of anxiety and antagonism toward the "new woman" and the changing sex roles she embodied. Cigarette advertising provided a way to legitimate and naturalize women's smoking. It was a weapon in the fight among tobacco companies for market share, of course, but it was, like most advertising, conservative, venturing to challenge established ways in the population only when evidence of new market patterns was in plain view. Despite the importance of the commercial interests involved in spreading the use of cigarettes among women, the change that occurred was a cultural one. It was made possible by changes in the cigarette product itself, by World War I's transformation of social habits, and by a new class of women who sponsored the cigarette in its political and social battles. In the 1920s, a cigarette in the hands of a woman meant a change in the language of social interaction. Such changes may be vigorously contested. They were at that time, just as they have been more recently when "Ms" and "he or she" entered the spoken language and came to be used, at least in some circles, naturally. That advertising has played a role since the late 1920s in promoting smoking among women should not blind us to the fact that this change in consumption patterns, like many others, has roots deep in cultural change and political conflict that advertising often responds to but rarely creates. . . .

This cigarette case study has tried to reach a little deeper, to recognize the social roots of significant changes in consumption patterns and to characterize what a change in consumer activity might signify. It also has served as a reminder that advertising generally works to reinforce consumer trends rather than to initiate them. Critics of advertising in the 1920s and today have regarded the adoption of cigarette smoking by women as a clearcut proof of the power of persuasive advertising to dramatically change consumer habits. It is not so; the matter turns out to be not so obvious at all. . . .

. . . Perhaps, [the defenders of advertising and marketing] admit, there are things wrong with a consumer culture, but advertising is not responsible for them. Marketing, they say, merely identifies and responds to human needs and does not—cannot—create the motivations that propel the race of consumption. They are appalled that critics imagine they have such overwhelming powers. They easily brush off criticism that attributes to advertising untold magical influence, extraordinary psychological sophistication, or primary responsibility for creating a consumer culture. They show that they work to reach people already predisposed to the product they are selling, that their appeals stress solid product information as often as they engage in emotional manipulation, and that the consumer is so fickle and the world so complex that their best-laid plans go astray as often as not.

All of this is true. But it is a much less sturdy defense of marketing than it appears. . . .

First, marketers do not actually seek to discover what consumers "want" but what consumers want *from among commercially viable choices*. . . . Marketers keep the consumer in mind only to the degree that the consumer defines his or her own prospects in terms agreeable to marketers. Thus consumers are not asked if they would prefer public television to advertising-supported television or public transportation to private automobiles or government-supported health care to private physicians.

Developers survey consumers to find out what kind of housing project they prefer, but they do not ask if a public park would be more desirable. . . .

. . . In short, the consumers the marketers listen to are not persons, not citizens, but thin voices choosing from among a set of predetermined options. The "people" the marketers are concerned with are only those people or those parts of people that fit into the image of the consumer the marketer has created.

Second, marketers do not listen to all people equally. There is nothing democratic or populist about an approach that listens ten times as carefully to the person with $10,000 in discretionary income as to the person with $1,000. But that is what marketers do. The point is to make money, not to please people. The marketers keep their eyes on the main prize—pocketbooks, not persons. This yields an array of consumer choices top heavy in luxury, and it sometimes works directly to diminish the array of goods available to the person of modest means. For instance, in the competition for the affluent person's dollar, more and more extras become standard equipment on automobiles and other products, and the low-income consumer has no choice but to go deeper into debt to pay for the simplest model, now weighted with superfluous "standard" equipment. In Third World countries, national and multinational corporations provide a highly inappropriate array of products for local needs because they serve largely the very small affluent population in those nations. This is especially noticeable and dangerous in an area like that of health care: "Since middle-income and rich consumers represent the main market for modern drugs, pharmaceutical companies concentrate on furnishing remedies for middle-class ailments like general fatigue, headaches, and constipation rather than for low-income diseases like leprosy, filariasis, and tuberculosis."

Third, marketers wrongly assume that since "good advertising kills a bad product," they can do little harm; people will only buy what they find satisfying. This works, as I have argued, only if people have enough information available to know what the range of possibilities is and how to purchase wisely. This is not true for many populations: poor people, children, Third World peoples, people entering new social roles, people with limited time or uncertain emotional stability for making decisions. Even with educated, middle-class adults, where the product sold is complex and where the normal adult is not able to make informed comparisons among products, advertising or other marketing practices can lead people to buy things that they do not need, things that will not "satisfy" their desires, and things that are not good for them.

Questions

1. *How does the advertising and marketing process work? If you were an advertising executive, how would you introduce a new product to the buying public?*

2. *According to advertising executives, what kinds of problems bothered Americans during the 1920s? Did their concerns remain the same, or did new problems emerge during the 1930s? How did advertisers attempt to "solve" these problems?*

3. *Were advertisers simply trying to earn a paycheck by selling more products, or did they have more altruistic motives? Did advertisers feel that Americans would be better off if they consumed more products and, if so, why and how?*

4. *Compare and contrast how Sivluka and Schudson treat cigarette advertising to women. Why did cigarette consumption among women grow so dramatically during the 1920s? Were advertisers responsible for this change, or were other factors involved?*

WORDS AND IMAGES:
ADS AND ADVERTISERS
DURING THE 1920s AND 1930s

Although advertising executives spent much of their time publicizing products, many also publicized themselves and their profession. Since many Americans initially regarded advertising as little better than fraud, it is hardly surprising that ad writers attempted to convince the American people that advertising was a legitimate profession. Sometimes they went well beyond that, often claiming that advertising was central to social harmony and continued economic prosperity in the United States. Only advertisers, they said, could adequately direct the enormous flows of manufactured consumer goods from the factories to the consumer; only advertisers could predict and regulate the buying patterns of American consumers.

The best evidence of the advertisers' craft lies in ads themselves. These ads primarily appeared on the new medium of the radio and in national circulation magazines. Radio ads lose much of their appeal when transcribed into text, but print ads remain quite persuasive. For many advertisers, these ads were not just sales pitches; they were works of art, and a testimony to the skills of advertising copywriters and illustrators. Many of those involved in the advertising industry thought of themselves as artists and, like artists, they tapped into a deep well of human emotions—desire, love, happiness, fear, and insecurity. Many of those themes, so readily identifiable in ads from the 1920s and 1930s, still appear in today's far more technically sophisticated advertisements, although often more subtly. One thing has changed, though. Ads in the 1920s and 1930s did not target impressionable children and adolescents to nearly the same extent as they do today.

An Advertising Executive in Action

While many advertising executives wrote accounts of their professional and personal lives, these tend to be rather shallow and one-dimensional. One of the best first-person descriptions of the day-to-day activities of an ad executive comes from Fairfax M. Cone, With All Its Faults: A Candid Account of Forty Years in Advertising *(Boston, 1969), 90-92, 94-97.*

The half-dozen Roos Bros. stores, in San Francisco and the San Francisco Bay area . . . were characterized even then by a policy of innovation that approached audacity. The Roos stores were the first in the country to advertise "wardrobes" rather than "suits" for men. These were based on the combinations that were possible with matching coat and trousers and complementary and contrasting sports jackets and slacks. Just so, Roos Bros. discovered a gold mine that unlike most of the diggings in California has been an unfailing producer every year since.

Colonel Robert Roos was a brilliant, irascible potentate who moodily ran his satrapy from a black-walled, white-carpeted throne room whose doors were electrically opened and closed, and at whose bar the very simplest agreements were generally sealed only after long and often tempestuous arguments, but in rare old scotch or bourbon.

I very nearly was not invited to sample either one.

It was strictly a hunch on the part of the Colonel's advertising manager that brought me to the inner sanctum at all. The hunch belonged to an extraordinary woman. Her name is Eleanor Lyons. She never, to my knowledge, has had an advertising idea that wasn't practical and worthwhile, because that is the way her mind works. You could almost watch it under her nicely coiffed, prematurely gray hair. She knew precisely what she wanted and she outlined it in broad terms. Then she let you work out the details.

What she wanted from us was advertising that would give the Roos stores some of the aura of authority that Kenneth Collins had built into the advertising for Macy's in New York.

"There must be something better, something more important, than merely another retail clothier shouting low prices," Eleanor Lyons insisted. "There must be a way to establish an important character, a unique personality, to be an institution, like Macy's. Or, if you won't laugh, like Tiffany."

I said I thought there was. And I told Eleanor Lyons that I thought I knew how to do this.

But when I was let into the Colonel's black office, through the electric doors, I wasn't so sure that I wasn't out of my depth. Wanting not to seem cocky (which I certainly didn't feel) I ventured the opinion that Roos Bros. was doing a mighty good advertising job as things stood.

"You couldn't be more right," the Colonel boomed. "One hundred thousand dollars a month right. Twelve hundred thousand dollars a year right. It is a crazy idea of this dear girl that some advertising agency can do something for us that we ourselves can't do much better. Tell me what it is that we should expect from some advertising agency that has never sold a necktie or a suit.

"Nothing," the Colonel said, answering his own question. "Nothing. Absolutely nothing."

The answer in the man's mind appeared to be clear; as far as he was concerned the matter was settled. But the distaste with which the Colonel had spit out the words "advertising agency," and on "some" advertising agency that was obviously Lord & Thomas, made it necessary for me to make him eat those words if I could.

By trying to be polite, I had let Eleanor Lyons down badly. I hadn't been adroit enough to follow the lead she had given me, and the Colonel had pounced on my pleasantry and turned it against both of us. He was a hard man to sell, and I hadn't helped his lady at all.

It was midday on a Friday when Colonel Roos coldly pressed a button in a panel on his desk and opened the way out of his office. I wished that I might never have to see him again; but Eleanor Lyons had told me that the man knew Albert Lasker very well, and I knew that I would have to make another try, disagreeable as this might be.

On Monday I telephoned him to say that I wanted to see him. "I want to show you a newspaper advertisement," I said. "It will show you how to do everything Eleanor Lyons was trying to tell you and all she wants to do in advertising, and it will do everything you're already doing well better than you've ever done it."

I didn't sound like me even to myself. But the Colonel's unwillingness to listen to me after my soft opening three days before had made me furious. Also, there was the possible involvement of Albert Lasker in the affair. I was a new, insecure young manager, and I couldn't have his friend casting doubts about me.

"All right," the Colonel said, with what seemed a great effort. "I'll see what you've got, but I haven't much time." And off I started with my exhibits.

The idea that had come to me in Eleanor Lyons's office had grown on me on Friday night, in bed, which is where I have always done my best work, particularly under pressure, and most particularly when angry. I had written the full-page newspaper advertisement on Saturday, and had it laid out and illustrated on Sunday by a puzzled young art director named Harry Fletcher who couldn't understand why he should give up a picnic with his girl for a cranky non-client.

In the beginning, I was only working to square myself with Eleanor Lyons and to build up my case if I had to use it for Albert Lasker; but by the time I got the Colonel on the telephone on Monday morning I had no doubt that I would accomplish both my objectives at Colonel Roos's expense. What I planned to do was show the man the advertisement I had made, get his acknowledgment that the idea was good for a long series, then make him an elaborate gift of it and depart on my high horse.

When I showed him the advertisement he stared at it for several minutes, saying nothing. Then he got up from behind his enormous black desk and standing between the two silk flags that flanked it at the rear, the stars and stripes of the United States and the flag of his own California National Guard regiment, the Colonel cleared his throat and said, with full military dignity, "I knew you would come through."

I had hoped to win the day. But I only tied it. Colonel Roos had known very well that I would react to his taunts; for despite his dislike of agencies (and their fees, in this case) he wanted Eleanor Lyons to have her way.

The advertisement, which was framed at top and bottom with an institutional promise from Roos Bros., and which told the story of the featured merchandise in specific terms of design and manufacture instead of the generalities and tired expletives that were the rule in retail men's clothing advertising, became the pattern for a series that ran unchanged in format for almost ten years. . . .

Our second venture into the retail field, triggered by our success with Roos Bros., proved to be more educational than lucrative. This was with the Safeway stores which, traditionally, had run large newspaper advertisements that were really no more than price listings (the private label product accounts being handled independently and apart from the shopper pages).

The shopper advertisements were almost repulsively ugly, and a little research indicated to us that most housewives paid a minimum of attention to the listings except to scan the lines of heavy black type for real bargains. Where there were no deeply cut prices the advertisements, even in full facing pages, apparently had no tangible effect. They merely kept the stores' name before the public.

No one who was a passionate follower of Albert Lasker could believe that this was truly advertising. Or that the prodigious space that was involved couldn't be made more productive.

Again we set to work, as we had with the sterile Roos Bros. advertisements, to transform the Safeway newspaper pages into something that rewarded readers for their attention. By designing the pages in orderly columns and reducing the extra bold type, we made space for menu suggestions, recipes, party hints, even diets; and facts about Safeway's procurement of all the items of fresh produce, meat and dairy products that were available at Safeway stores on an exclusive basis.

It didn't matter, we reasoned, where one bought Wheaties or Bisquick or Carnation milk or Jell-O; wherever these well-known products were purchased they were the same. Moreover, Safeway's private labels and usually lower prices on similar packaged groceries had a long way to go to prove superiority. On the other hand, it was possible to show persuasive and memorable reasons why meat and produce at Safeway were fresher and more select because of Safeway's tremendous buying ability and its massive private transportation system that hurried food to market. We reasoned that if we attracted customers for these good reasons, they would buy the nonexclusive groceries at the same time.

We asked people to take note of the Safeway trucks they passed on the highways at night, bringing huge quantities of fresh fruit and vegetables and meat and milk to market. And we mentioned the courtesy of the road that the drivers of those trucks exhibited.

What we undertook was a kind of public relations advertising. We tried to make friends by being friendly, rather than by continuously assaulting the newspaper readers with fat black type in a cascade of prices that tumbled together dry groceries, laundry products, candy, disinfectants, small hardware, shoe polish, cheese, etc., in an inebriate jumble.

But if the Safeway management thought well of our efforts, the store managers had very different ideas. Years later, as a director of Montgomery Ward & Company, I encountered the same lack of interest in public relations advertising. The conclusion I drew was that most store managers are like most salesmen. They are usually so price-conscious, so demoralized by lower price competition whenever it raises its little pointed head, so demanding of a price advantage that they think of little else. . . .

Our noble experiment with Roos Bros. was a notable failure at Safeway. There was no Eleanor Lyons who was dissatisfied with the advertising situation the way she had been, there was no Colonel Roos to back her up, however testily. Not until a dozen years later, when Franklin J. Lunding and George Clements of the Jewel Tea Company initiated similar advertising in Chicago was the idea vindicated. Fresh, informative advertising gave the Jewel stores an inviting character that was followed up by alert, carefully trained managers and department heads, and Jewel became the dominant food distributor in the area. . . .

Advertising as a Religion

Bruce Barton was a partner in several New York City advertising agencies. While he was perhaps one of the best known advertisers in the United States, he was not highly regarded within the advertising profession. Instead, his fame comes from a most unusual book, in which he asserts that advertising agencies—and advertising executives—are entitled to positions of special influence in American society. The Man Nobody Knows: A Discovery of the Real Jesus *(Indianapolis, 1925),* 23, 27, 92, 104, 107, 143, 124-26, 129-30, 138-40, 146-47, 149, 153, 162-63, 177.

He [Jesus] picked up twelve men from the bottom ranks of business and forged them into an organization that conquered the world.

When the man had finished his reading he exclaimed, "This is a man nobody knows."

"Some day," said he, "some one will write a book about Jesus. Every business man will read it and send it to his partners and his salesmen. For it will tell the story of the founder of modern business." . . .

Nowhere is there such a startling example of executive success as the way in which that organization [of the twelve disciples] was brought together. . . .

Having gathered together his organization, there remained for Jesus the tremendous task of training it. . . .

. . . Assuredly there was no demand for a new religion; the world was already over-supplied. And Jesus proposed to send forth eleven men and expect them to substitute his thinking for all existing religious thought! . . .

Surely no one will consider us lacking in reverence if we say that every one of the "principles of modern salesmanship" on which business men so much pride themselves, are brilliantly exemplified in Jesus' talk and work. . . .

It would be easy to multiply examples, taking each of his parables and pointing out the keen knowledge of human motives on which it is based. In a later chapter we shall have something more to say of these parables—the most powerful advertisements of all time. . . .

. . . The parable of the Good Samaritan is the greatest advertisement of all time. . . .

I am not a doctor, or lawyer or critic but an advertising man. As a profession advertising is young; as a force it is as old as the

Excerpts reprinted from *The Man Nobody Knows: A Discovery of the Real Jesus*, by Bruce Barton, 1924, Grosset & Dunlap Publishers.

world. The first four words ever uttered, "Let there be light," constitute its charter. . . .

. . . In the first place he [Jesus] recognized the basic principle that all good advertising is news. . . .

Can you imagine the next day's issue of the *Capernaum News*, if there had been one?

PALSIED MAN HEALED
JESUS OF NAZARETH CLAIMS RIGHT TO
FORGIVE SINS

PROMINENT SCRIBES OBJECT
"BLASPHEMOUS," SAYS LEADING CITIZEN.
"BUT ANYWAY I CAN WALK," HEALED MAN
RETORTS

[another example]

PROMINENT TAX COLLECTOR JOINS
NAZARETH FORCES

MATTHEW ABANDONS BUSINESS TO PROMOTE
NEW CULT
* * *
GIVES LARGE LUNCHEON . . .

These are Jesus' works, done in Jesus' name. If he were to live again, in these modern days, he would find a way to make them known—to be advertised by his service, not merely by his sermons. One thing is certain: he would not neglect the market-place. Few of his sermons were delivered in synagogues. . . .

No; the present day market-place is the newspaper and the magazine. Printed columns are the modern thoroughfares; published advertisements are the cross-roads where the sellers and the buyers meet. Any issue of a national magazine is a world's fair, a bazaar filled with the products of the world's work. . . . That every other voice should be raised in such great market-places, and the voice of Jesus of Nazareth be still—this is a vital omission which he would find a way to correct. He would be a national advertiser today, I am sure, as he was the great advertiser of his own day. . . .

. . . Every advertising man ought to study the parables of Jesus in the same fashion, schooling himself in their language. . . .

. . . How often you must read and read before you discover just what it is that the advertiser wants you to do. Jesus had no introductions. . . .

. . . A sixty-eight word prayer, he said, contained all that men needed to say or God to hear. What would be his verdict on most of our prayers and our speeches and our advertisements? . . .

Much brass has been sounded and many cymbals tinkled in the name of advertising; but the advertisements which persuade people to act are written by men who have an abiding respect for the intelligence of their readers, and a deep sincerity regarding the merits of the goods they have to sell. . . .

But what interests us most in . . . [the] one recorded incident of his boyhood is the fact that for the first time he defined the purpose of his career. He did not say, "Wist ye not that I must practise preaching?" or "Wist ye not that I must get ready to meet the arguments of men like these?" The language was quite different, and well worth remembering. "Wist ye not that I must be about my father's *business*?" he said. He thought of his life as *business*. What did he mean by business? To what extent are the principles by which he conducted his business applicable to ours? And if he were among us again, in our highly competitive world, would his business philosophy work? . . .

So we have the main points of his business philosophy:

1. Whoever will be great must render great service.
2. Whoever will find himself at the top must be willing to lose himself at the bottom.
3. The big rewards come to those who travel the second, undemanded mile.

The GREATEST MOTHER in the WORLD

 Stretching forth her hands to all in need; to Jew or Gentile, black or white; knowing no favorite, yet favoring all.

Ready and eager to comfort at a time when comfort is most needed. Helping the little home that's crushed beneath an iron hand by showing mercy in a healthy, human way; rebuilding it, in fact, with stone on stone; replenishing empty bins and empty cupboards; bringing warmth to hearts and hearths too long neglected.

Seeing all things with a mother's sixth sense that's blind to jealousy and meanness; seeing men in their true light, as naughty children — snatching, biting, bitter—but with a hidden side that's quickest touched by mercy.

Reaching out her hands across the sea to No Man's land; to cheer with warmer comforts thousands who must stand and wait in stenched and crawling holes and water-soaked entrenchments where cold and wet bite deeper, so they write, than Boche steel or lead.

She's warming thousands, feeding thousands, healing thousands from her store; the Greatest Mother in the World—the RED CROSS

Every Dollar of a Red Cross War Fund goes to War Relief

World War I redeemed the image of advertising in America. Federal government agencies and charities like the Red Cross employed ad agencies to create national advertising campaigns that effectively persuaded Americans to give money, save food, join the military, or, more ominously, to hate everything German.

By the late 1800s, the most visually enticing ads extolled the virtues of patent medicines—"cure-alls" that really cured almost nothing, and were often harmful and occasionally lethal. These ads tainted the image of advertising in general, and consumers often equated advertising with fraud.

Nineteenth-century advertisements were primarily descriptive in nature. Instead of creating demand for a product, they merely informed buyers that certain items were available for purchase. There was little expectation that ads would actually help to create demand for a product.

One of the hallmarks of modern advertising is that it promises a vast array of intangible benefits—love, happiness, excitement—if the consumer will only buy the product. This ad, for the Borden Company, explicitly guarantees "happiness" and also offers romance, marriage, and sex—a considerable list of benefits from a can of sweetened condensed milk, to say the least. Also notice how ads from the 1920s used far more text, and correspondingly smaller visuals, than modern ads, and how they reinforced existing social values (a woman must be a good cook in order to land a husband).

During the 1920s "Chain stores" like Piggly Wiggly (we would call them "supermarkets" today) radically changed shopping patterns. Shoppers, accustomed to the limited choices of corner stores and street vendors, had to be taught how to read labels and then choose products from the shelf, rather than ask a grocer to assemble their order. Many shoppers found this new way of shopping almost incomprehensible— one chain store owner found that no one would use his new shopping carts until he paid "fake" shoppers to push carts around the store, thus showing the actual customers how to manage this unfamiliar technology. Ads also eased the public's anxiety about these new stores.

"Yeast builds resistance,"

says PROF. DOCTOR PAUL REYHER

famous lecturer at the University of Berlin

"THE MEDICINAL USES of yeast are many-sided. There is a high percentage of Vitamin B in yeast... Vitamin B bears a very close relation to the proper functioning of the nervous system. It also improves the appetite, regulates metabolism, promotes growth and raises the body's power of resistance to every kind of infection... One can see, therefore, that yeast contains a remarkable healing factor."

ANOTHER of the great medical leaders of Europe to add his voice to the movement of health preparedness is Prof. Dr. Paul Reyher, of the University of Berlin.

Dr. Reyher has made an exhaustive study of yeast. His findings extend new hope to all who suffer from indigestion, headaches, nervousness, depression, too frequent colds and sore throat—sure signs of constipation and lowered vitality.

In a recent survey throughout the United States, half the doctors reporting said they prescribed fresh yeast for constipation and its attendant ills.

Fleischmann's Yeast is fresh. Unlike dried or killed yeast it contains millions of living, active yeast plants. As these live yeast plants pass daily through your system, they rouse the muscles that control elimination, combat harmful poisons. Your digestion improves. Your skin clears.

Eat three cakes of Fleischmann's Yeast every day, one cake before each meal or between meals, plain or in water (hot or cold). To get full benefit from yeast you must eat it regularly and over a sufficient period of time. At all grocers and many leading cafeterias, lunch counters and soda fountains. Buy two or three days' supply at a time, as it will keep in a cool, dry place. Start now!

Write for latest booklet on Yeast in the diet—free. Health Research Dept. C-128, The Fleischmann Company, 701 Washington St., New York, N.Y.

FROM THROAT TO COLON is one continuous tube. 20% of the start here. Poisons from clogged intestines easily spread through the system, lowering resistance to disease. But here yeast acts as nature. Yeast builds resistance," says Dr. Reyher. It keeps the entire intestinal tract clean, active and fresh. Eat Fleischmann's Yeast regularly.

PROF. DR. PAUL REYHER

Lecturer, University of Berlin, on Vitamins, X-Ray and Pediatrics; Director, Children's Hospital, Berlin, which he built and equipped. The Germans refer to this hospital as "the jewel box" because of its perfect appointments and beauty of structure.

UNIVERSITY OF BERLIN, where Dr. Reyher is a noted lecturer.

FLEISCHMANN'S YEAST
for HEALTH

In a decade when many Americans increasingly believed that the values of science and "modernity" were becoming more important than those of religion, advertisers attempted to depict their products as both modern and scientific. Although the Fleischmann Company, manufacturers of brewers' yeast, suffered during the early years of Prohibition, an ad campaign stressing the scientific and health values of yeast saved the company and made Fleischmann's Yeast a household name.

Ad writers consulted a medical dictionary and discovered the word "halitosis." This ominous-sounding word meant nothing worse than bad breath, but Listerine ads suggested that this "flaw" would consign women to a lifetime of spinsterhood.

He had to fight himself so hard...
he didn't put it over

YES, he was his own worst enemy. His appearance was against him and he knew it. Oh why had he neglected the bath that morning, the shave, the change of linen? Under the other fellow's gaze it was hard to forget that cheap feeling. There's self-respect in soap and water. The clean-cut chap can look any man in the face and tell him the facts—for when you're clean, your appearance fights *for you*.

There's self-respect in SOAP & WATER

PUBLISHED BY THE ASSOCIATION OF AMERICAN SOAP AND GLYCERINE PRODUCERS, INC., TO AID THE WORK OF CLEANLINESS INSTITUTE

Many advertisers sincerely believed that they had a mission to teach ordinary Americans how they could improve their lives through consumption. At a time when many Americans bathed no more than once a week, the looming "conscience" figure in this ad reminds the consumer that daily bathing with soap and water will lead to success at the workplace. Advertisers sought to uplift less-fortunate Americans who, in this case, quite literally constituted the "great unwashed masses."

The emerging value system of the 1920s placed less emphasis on "old" values like honor, duty, morality, and character, and greater emphasis on "new" values of individualism, achievement, personality, and appearance. The Camay ad says nothing about the character of the woman at the left of the picture, but says everything about her appearance. This she owes to Camay—"the soap of beautiful women"— which promises not only radiant skin but also the intangible benefits of excitement, romance, and sex. The scowling women to the right will never enjoy these benefits, because they use some other soap—can we assume, by extension, that all other soaps must be "the soap of ugly women?"

The man on the sofa may be a millionaire, or a Nobel laureate, or even the president of the United States. But he will never prevail in affairs of the heart because he has committed the unforgivable sin of wearing ungartered socks (in an age before elastic, men used calf garters to hold up their socks). Once again, the ad's emphasis is on the readily identifiable external values of image and appearance, not the older internal values of character and honor.

"She looks old enough to be his mother"

"Read this little book *carefully*, dear. . . . It explains things so much better than I can"

These ads for Lysol blend the 1920s interest in appearance with the desire of ad writers to be advisers and confidants for the supposedly uneducated American buying public. Both ads offer a free booklet "The Scientific Side of Health and Youth" (note the emphasis on science and on the intangible value of youth) that both pushed Lysol and helped the company track the readership of its print ads in various publications. In "Read this little book carefully," a mother is admitting that a distant and faceless corporation is better equipped than she to give her daughter advice on "feminine hygiene." It should be pointed out that, during the 1920s, one of the typical, if unacknowledged, uses of Lysol was as a post-coital spermicidal douche.

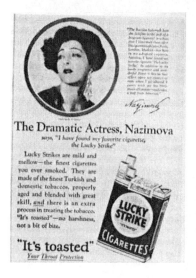

The 1926 Chesterfield "Blow some my way" ad marked a milestone in advertisers" efforts to gradually erode social taboos against women smoking in public. While the woman is not so radical as to light her own cigarette, she is receptive to the idea of inhaling her mate's second-hand smoke. Foreign women, like the Russian actress Nazimova, were often perceived as being more exotic than American women, and less subject to social taboos against smoking. Again, the advertisers' intent was to gradually render female smoking acceptable to mainstream Americans. By the end of the 1920s women openly reached for Lucky Strikes and other brands, though whether advertising caused this behavioral shift or was instead a product of it remains open to debate.

Few concepts better illustrate the social consciousness of ad writers than the idea of the democracy of goods. Many ad writers were genuinely troubled by the seemingly inescapable tendency of capitalism to create wide disparities in income and wealth (which worked against the cherished notion of "all men are created equal.") Some reasoned that they could help to create a democracy of goods—a society in which all Americans would be equal because they consumed the same products, or goods. The working-class man in the center (note his characteristic cap) does not feel resentment toward the unseen owner of the luxury car, and he certainly does not exhibit any desire to overthrow the capitalist system in favor of socialism or communism—each of which were very real alternatives in industrialized countries at that time—merely because both social classes have access to the same tires.

As the surface prosperity of the "Roaring Twenties" gave way to the hardships of the Great Depression, most Americans placed more emphasis on saving money rather than on acquiring the latest and greatest products. This Listerine toothpaste ad lists a price—almost unthinkable during the 1920s—and shows how thrift consumers can save enough money to buy important items for their families.

With fully a quarter of the American workforce unemployed during the depression, ad writers prayed on parents' fears that their children would fail in life, unless . . . Union Central life insurance could prevent an adolescent from being one of the forty-two out of forty-three children who failed in life, and caffeine-free Postum would save a child from the humiliation of being the class dunce.

Questions

1. *Does Fairfax Cone's account of his career match your expectations of the advertising industry? Did Cone work closely with the firms he was promoting, or were there tensions between this particular advertiser and his clients? What does this say about a possible "conspiracy" between advertisers and corporate managers to control the American consumer?*

2. *Why would Bruce Barton write a book like* **The Man Nobody Knows**? *Why would he compare ad writers to Jesus and his disciples?*

3. *How are the print ads similar to those seen in magazines today? How are they different? What key themes and issues emerge in the print ads? Have these themes changed since the 1920s and 1930s?*

4. *Pay particular attention to the ad for Goodyear tires. This ad reflects advertisers' notion of a "democracy of goods;" namely, that we are all equal through the products (goods) that we consume. Do you agree with the message of the ad that the working-class couple on the left should be happy and content because the tires on their inexpensive car are "just the same" as those on the Rolls Royce being polished by the chauffeur? Does this ad suggest that advertisers were trying to bury class conflict (i.e., rich vs. poor) beneath a flood of consumer products? Do you see evidence today (in sneaker ads, for example) that lower-class Americans are being told that products are more important that meaningful social change?*

FURTHER READING

David M. Potter's path-breaking work, **People of Plenty: Economic Abundance and the American Character** *(Chicago, 1954) traces the development of the American consumer culture. Daniel Pope,* **The Making of Modern Advertising** *(New York, 1983), often considered one of the "standard" works of advertising history, provides a solid overview of the development of that profession, and of its effects on American society. For advertising in wartime (often simply labeled "propaganda"), see Frank W. Fox,* **Madison Avenue Goes to War: The Strange Military Career of American Advertising, 1941–45** *(Provo, Utah, 1975). Stuart W. Ewen offers a harsh critique of the social impact of advertising, arguing that a conspiracy of corporate executives and ad writers distorted consumption patterns in* **Captains of Consciousness: Advertising and the Social Roots of the Consumer Culture** *(New York, 1976). Other useful works include Stephen Fox,* **The Mirror Makers: A History of American Advertising and Its Creators** *(New York, 1984), T. J. Jackson Lears,* **Fables of Abundance: A Cultural History of Advertising in America** *(New York, 1994), and Richard S. Tedlow,* **New and Improved: The Story of Mass Marketing in America** *(New York, 1990).*

The Expulsion
and Relocation of
Japanese Americans in
World War II

Michael Les Benedict

INTRODUCTION

On 7 December 1941, following years of growing tension between Japan and the United States, Japan launched a surprise bombing of Pearl Harbor, the home port of the United States Pacific fleet. Japan's allies, Germany and Italy, quickly joined it in declaring war on the United States, bringing the Americans fully into World War II.

Claiming that Japanese and Japanese Americans on the Pacific coast were sympathetic to Japan and preparing to aid Japanese air raids and even invasion, many people there called for their expulsion from the coast. Within two months the government of the United States ordered all persons of Japanese ancestry—both aliens and "non-aliens" (that is, citizens)—to leave a large swath of territory along the Pacific coast. This included both Japanese immigrants (called Issei or "first generation") and their children (Nisei or "second generation"). The small number previously identified as pro-Japan by U.S. intelligence agencies were interned at special locations. Over 100,000 others who had nowhere to go and no means of support outside of their homes in California, western Oregon, and western Washington were expelled from the region and taken to "relocation" camps in a process military authorities called "controlled evacuation." While German Americans had been subject to harassment during World War I, and both German and Italian aliens were interned during World War II, the scope of the forced Japanese evacuation was unprecedented. Moreover, unlike German and Italian immigrants, who could acquire American citizenship after five years' residence, Japanese immigrants had been barred from acquiring American citizenship by laws that limited naturalization to white immigrants and those of African descent.

After the war, more and more Americans came to doubt the practical and legal justification for wrenching Japanese and Japanese Americans from their homes and sending them to the relocation camps. Many of the relocated Japanese were outraged; after the war some returned to Japan rather than continue to live in the United States. The vast majority who remained did little to protest their treatment after the war, but by the 1970s many Japanese Americans demanded apologies and restitution. After a long struggle, Congress passed the Civil Liberties Act of 1988, acknowledging the injustice of the "controlled evacuation" and making reparations. The readings that follow describe the evacuation and relocation program, the reaction of the people subjected to it, life in the camps, and the demand for redress.

THE JAPANESE RELOCATION: EVENTS AND ATTITUDES

Most historians have condemned the expulsion and relocation of the Japanese and Japanese Americans during World War II, attributing the decision to domestic racism, fear of the "Yellow Peril" in foreign affairs, and the hysteria surrounding the sneak attack on Pearl Harbor. But some of those who supported the evacuation policy and a few modern analysts still defend the decision. The following readings provide a more detailed account of events and their effect on the forced evacuee. The readings demonstrate the continuing disagreement over whether the policy was justified.

A Daughter of an Evacuee Describes the History of the Expulsion and Relocation

In this essay, Donna K. Nagata, whose grandparents and parents were relocated, gives an overview of the history of the evacuation. Abridged from Donna K. Nagata, Legacy of Injustice: Exploring the Cross-Generational Impact of the Japanese American Internment *(New York, 1993), 1–15.*

The Decision to Evacuate

Japanese Americans recognize February 19 as the official Day of Remembrance for the Internment. On that date in 1942, President Franklin D. Roosevelt signed Executive Order 9066, ten weeks after the Japanese attacked Pearl Harbor. The order provided the secretary of war and his designated officers with the authority to exclude all persons, both citizens and aliens, from designated areas in order to provide security against sabotage or espionage. The army took charge of implementing Executive Order 9066 by removing all Japanese Americans from the West Coast of the United States, placing them first into temporary "assembly centers" and later into concentration camps located in desolate areas of the country. No formal charges were brought against the Japanese Americans, and there was no opportunity for an individual review of their loyalty.

The stated rationale for Executive Order 9066 concerned national security; removal of Japanese Americans from the West Coast was necessary to provide safeguards against espionage or sabotage. The order was signed at a time when the military activities of Japan generated increased concern in the United States. The Japanese struck the Malay Peninsula, Hong Kong, Wake and Midway islands, and the Philippines on the same day they attacked Pearl Harbor. By the time Executive Order 9066 was signed, they had successfully taken Guam, Wake Island, most of the Philippines, and Hong Kong. Rumors that the Pearl Harbor attack had been aided by ethnic Japanese in Hawaii ran rampant in newspapers and on radio, fueled by a December 12, 1941, press report from Secretary of the Navy Frank Knox. Although Knox falsely stated that Japanese spies operated in Hawaii prior to the Pearl Harbor attack, his press statements "carried considerable weight and gave credence to the view that ethnic Japanese on the mainland were a palpable threat and danger." In an atmosphere of paranoia and general panic, Japanese American fishing boats were accused of signaling Japanese submarines with their lights, and Japanese American farmers were suspected of planting their fields in rows pointing to nearby airports.

The fears for American security were not founded on fact. Intelligence reports, including those from the Federal Bureau of Investigation (FBI) and Naval Intelligence, concluded that mass incarceration was *not* a military necessity. Indeed, many of the fears were founded in racial prejudice evident both in the public and within the military itself. The views of Lieutenant General John L. DeWitt, who recommended the exclusion of Japanese from the West Coast, illustrate the extremity of this prejudice. DeWitt was in charge of West Coast security under Secretary of War Henry L. Stimson. Encouraged by both Major General Allen W. Gullion, the provost marshal for the army, and Colonel Karl R. Bendetsen, chief of Gullion's Aliens Division, he pressured the Department of Justice to adopt stricter enemy alien controls and informed Secretary of War Stimson that there were "indications that ethnic Japanese were organized and ready for concerted action within the United States." DeWitt saw the evacuation as a military necessity because he saw no distinction between the Japanese and Japanese Americans. Ethnic heritage alone determined one's loyalty. Transcripts of a conference between DeWitt and newspaper reporters on April 14, 1943, recorded him stating bluntly to reporters that "a Jap is a Jap" and on February 14, 1942, five days before the signing of Executive Order 9066, he stated to Secretary Stimson:

> In the war in which we are now engaged racial affinities are not severed by migration. The Japanese race is an enemy race and while many second and third generation Japanese born on United States soil, possessed of the United States citizenship, have become "Americanized," the racial strains are undiluted. That Japan is allied with Germany and Italy in this struggle is no ground for assuming that any Japanese, barred from assimilation by convention as he is, though born and raised in the United States, will not turn against this nation when the final test of loyalty comes. It follows that along the Pacific Coast over 112,000 potential enemies, of Japanese extraction, are at large today.

In an incredible "catch-22," DeWitt also noted that "the very fact that no sabotage has taken place to date is a disturbing and confirming indication that such action will be taken."

Research suggests that U.S. intelligence had monitored Japanese immigrants and their activities *before* the war, and as early as August 1941, Army Intelligence inquired about the possibility of arresting and detaining those civilians who were American citizens. Prior to Pearl Harbor there were also government officials who considered the use of Japanese in America as "barter" and "reprisal" reserves in case the United States needed to trade "prisoners of war" or wanted to ensure the humane treatment of American soldiers who were held as prisoners.

Individuals did oppose DeWitt's recommendations, but such opposition was neither unified nor focused. Both the Justice Department and J. Edgar Hoover of the FBI proposed that restrained actions would be preferable to a mass evacuation. Secretary of War Stimson, Assistant Secretary of War John J. McCloy, and Attorney General Francis Biddle also disagreed with DeWitt's plans but did not protest them vigorously. However, stronger political forces pressed for mass internment along with DeWitt.

That the motivations behind the internment could not be justified simply on the basis of military necessity was evident when contrasting the sequence of events in Hawaii with those on the mainland. The military interned only 1% of the Japanese population in Hawaii, which was significantly closer to Japan, compared with more than 90% of the Japanese Americans on the mainland. Several factors contributed to the differential treatment of the Hawaiian Japanese. Japanese Americans composed a significant portion, more than one-third, of Hawaii's population, and the territory's population was more pluralistic and ethnically tolerant than the mainland. Anti-Asian sentiment, although present, did not occur at the levels evident along the West Coast. Because they were so numerous, an internment of all Japanese Americans would severely hamper day-to-day functioning on the islands. In addition, General Delos Emmons of the War Department, the commanding general of Hawaii, urged a restrained response to the presence of ethnic Japanese, recommended that the size of the areas prohibited to Japanese Americans be reduced, and objected to the exclusion of persons not actually or potentially dangerous. The difference in treatment between the Hawaiian and mainland Japanese Americans is striking. . . .

The racism underlying the internment did not emerge suddenly, for although Executive Order 9066 may serve as an official "beginning" to the internment, decades of anti-Asian prejudice prior to World War II set the context for its inception. As [historian Roger] Daniels notes, the Japanese were initially welcomed in the mid-1800s in Hawaii as a source of cheap labor on sugar plantations. The Chinese, who had been brought earlier to Hawaii as a source of inexpensive labor, came to be seen as problematic when their numbers increased. By the 1800s, Japanese labor groups were recruited in large numbers from Hawaii to come to the mainland and work in agriculture.

As the numbers of Japanese increased on the mainland, so did the levels of prejudice and hostility around them. The media portrayed the Japanese as a "yellow peril," and by 1908, the Gentleman's Agreement (an executive agreement between the United States and Japan) restricted immigration from Japan. The Gentleman's Agreement prevented the immigration of Japanese men but did allow for a significant number of Japanese women to immigrate as picture brides and begin families in this country. However, in 1924 the Immigration Act effectively stopped all Japanese immigration until 1965. These immigration restrictions had important long-term consequences in defining the demographics of the Japanese American community, isolating Japanese couples in the United States and creating a population with "unique age distributions" and distinct age peaks for each generation. For example, by 1940 the Issei (first-generation Japanese immigrant) men were generally between the ages of 50 and 64, whereas the Issei women tended to be approximately 10 years younger. Most of their U.S.-born children (the Nisei) were born between 1918 and 1922.

Pre-World War II discrimination against the Japanese was also evident in other forms of anti-Japanese legislation. Antimiscegenation laws prohibited Japanese Americans from intermarrying with whites. In addition, Japanese were considered "aliens ineligible for citizenship," and the 1913 Alien Land Law in California (where the vast majority of mainland Japanese lived) barred such aliens from purchasing land and owning property. In fact, Japanese immigrants could not become citizens until 1952.

Economic competition fueled anti-Japanese sentiment along the West Coast prior to the war. More than 50% of all Japanese men along the West Coast made their living through agriculture, forestry, and fishing. In 1940, Japanese American farms in California, Washington, and Oregon numbered over 6,000 and comprised a total of 250,000 acres. Most were small family businesses that specialized in "a labor-intensive, high-yield agricultural technique as opposed to the resource-intensive, low-yield agriculture characteristic of American farming." Altogether, these farms were valued at $72.6 million, and the productivity of the Japanese

Soldiers guarding Japanese and Japanese-Americans at Santa Anita Park, where evictees were gathered for relocation to desert camps. (Courtesy of The National Archives.)

American farmers benefitted the West Coast. Nonetheless, their success threatened many white American groups. Fears that the Japanese farmers were driving whites out of business heightened negative feelings, as did the erroneous perception that the Japanese population was exploding and creating a "yellow peril." Records show that, in reality, the Japanese farmers in California were not displacing existing farmers.

Years of the anti-Japanese sentiment prior to World War II set the emotional and economic stage for the removal of Japanese Americans. Then came the shock of Pearl Harbor, which crystallized these views into a panic. Not surprisingly, the majority of citizens favored harsh treatment of Japanese Americans. In March 1942, the National Opinion Research Center found that a vast majority of the public supported internment. Ninety-three percent of those questioned approved of the relocation of Japanese aliens, and 60% favored the evacuation of U.S. citizens as well. Two-thirds thought that once the Japanese Americans were incarcerated, they should not be allowed to move freely within the camps, but rather they ought to be kept "under strict guard like prisoners of war." Additional polls revealed that more than half of those sampled wanted to send all Japanese Americans to Japan after the war.

Those who had typically advocated for civil rights also remained silent or endorsed the internment orders. A majority of members of the Northern California Civil Liberties Union actually *favored* the evacuation orders in the spring of 1942. Japanese Americans clearly were excluded from the moral community of most other Americans at that time. Moral exclusion occurs when "individuals or groups are perceived as *outside the boundary in which moral values, rules, and considerations of fairness apply.* Those who are morally excluded are perceived as nonentities, expendable, or undeserving; consequently, harming them appears acceptable, appropriate, or just." Japanese Americans, viewed as treacherous, racially inferior, and unassimilable, were easily excluded. On the other hand, German and Italian Americans, who were racially similar to the dominant group, much more numerous, and politically powerful, did not suffer the extreme pressures toward mass incarceration; they remained within the boundaries of inclusion.

The Evacuation Process

Pearl Harbor affected Japanese Americans immediately. On the night of December 7, 1941, the FBI arrested approximately 1,500 Issei aliens who were considered to be potentially disloyal. Virtually all the leaders of Japanese American communities were removed, often with no explanation or indication of their fate. The void in leadership within the communities left Japanese Americans with few options. . . . [T]here was no political group in the larger community to support a resistance of the internment orders. As a result, the vast majority of Japanese Americans "played a passive role—waiting to see what their government would do with them."

Initially, General DeWitt attempted to implement a plan of "voluntary" resettlement. According to the plan, Japanese Americans would be restricted from military zones of the West Coast . . . [see map] but free to move outside of those zones. Data from the U.S. army indicated that approximately 5,000 individuals chose this option and "voluntarily" migrated east between March and October of 1942, in addition to an uncounted number who fled the

West Coast between December 7, 1941, and March 1942. The plan, however, was destined to fail. It was impossible for Issei and Nisei to sell their businesses and homes quickly. Many had no funds with which to move because their monies had been frozen by the government. They feared the hostility of an unknown destination. Japanese Americans could easily be recognized wherever they went, and interior states such as Idaho and Wyoming were no more welcoming than West Coast states. Recognizing the inad-

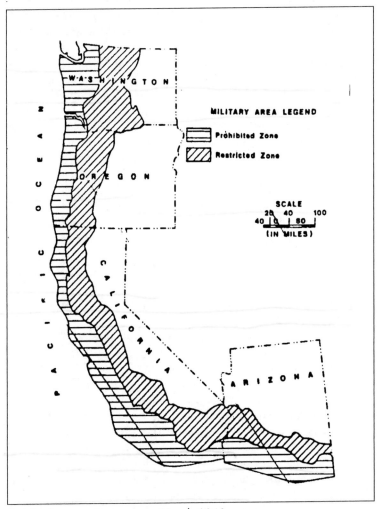

Original evacuation zones, March 1942.

equacy of the voluntary relocation program, the government took control over the evacuation process and implemented a plan for compulsory removal of Japanese Americans.

Because it was impossible to evacuate and relocate such a large group of people at the same time, the Japanese Americans first had to be transported to temporary "assembly centers." Later, when the more permanent camps were built, the internees would be moved again. The evacuation to assembly centers was carried out under military supervision of the army between March and August of 1942. Although there were Japanese Americans who were aware of the potential for some kind of evacuation, the army typically withheld details about the impending move, leaving little time or information for preparations. Many were given but a few days' notice that they would be leaving their homes. They took what they could carry. The economic losses stemming from the enforced evacuation were tremendous. Real estate, cars, appliances, farm equipment, crops ready for harvest, and personal possessions were sold for a fraction of their worth or simply left behind in haste. The fact that the military would not inform the Japanese Americans of their destination made the decision of what to bring more difficult. Families did not know whether to pack for cold or warm climates.

Throughout the evacuation families wore impersonal numbered tags. Travel by train or bus to the assembly centers was stressful and dehumanizing. Some trains had inadequate food supplies. Window shades blocked out the scenery, and passengers could not tell their whereabouts. As armed guards patrolled the trains, gossip arose that the military planned to take the Japanese Americans to an isolated area and shoot them.

After traveling hours without clear information about their destination or what fate lay in store for them, the internees arrived at the assembly centers. Sixteen of the hastily converted assembly centers were located in California, and an additional three were in Washington, Oregon, and Arizona. Many were located at race tracks and fairgrounds, where the Japanese Americans lived in horse stalls and animal quarters. Although whitewashed, they still smelled of manure. A family of eight was squeezed into a 20- by 24-foot space, four persons into an 8- by 20-foot space. Married couples often shared one large space, living in sections partitioned by a hanging sheet. Inadequate food, sanitation, and medical facilities proved equally problematic. Military police with ma-

Evicted Japanese and Japanese-Americans forced to leave the small town of Byron, California, May 2, 1942. (Courtesy of The National Archives.)

chine guns guarded the perimeter of the centers, while internal police instituted curfews, roll calls, and searches within the camps.

Although most internees lived with their families at the assembly center, others arrived without their complete family. Often, the father or husband had been taken by the FBI prior to the evacuation, but in other circumstances families were separated from loved ones who were institutionalized or incapacitated. Non-Japanese spouses of interracial couples also faced internment if they wanted to remain with their husband or wife.

Although assembly centers were labeled "temporary," the Japanese Americans remained in the centers for an average of 3 months. Then, at the end of May 1942, the process of uprooting began again. This time the long, tiresome train rides ended at the more permanent concentration camps. These 10 camps . . . were located in barren areas outside the exclusion area.

Many Japanese Americans hoped that the concentration

camps (euphemistically called "relocation centers") would provide better living conditions than the assembly centers. Unfortunately, the conditions were not significantly better. Barbed wire and armed guards persisted, as did the harsh living conditions. No camp housed less than 7,000 internees, and the largest held over 18,000. Barrack-style housing was constructed specifically for the purpose of containing the Japanese Americans. Each "block" consisted of 12 to 14 barracks, a communal mess hall, toilet and bath facilities, a laundry, and a recreation hall. A barrack measured approximately 20 by 100 feet and was divided into four to six rooms. At Topaz, a camp that was typical of the others, rooms ranged in size from 20 feet by 8 feet, to 20 feet by 24 feet. Each room contained one family. Sparse furnishings included a cot, a coal-burning stove with no coal, and a light bulb hanging from the ceiling. There was no running water. Internees braved extreme temperatures throughout the year. In the deserts, where many of the camps were located, winter temperatures could reach as low as 35 below zero and summers could be as high as 115 degrees. Dust storms arose frequently.

The War Relocation Authority (WRA), a newly formed civilian agency, was responsible for the camps. It planned to act as a facilitator of the resettlement rather than a warden for prisoners and proposed a policy that would entitle the Japanese Americans to the same treatment as other American citizens. As noted in the CWRIC [Commission on Wartime Relocation and Internment of Civilians] final report, however, the actual experience of the Japanese Americans fell far short of this initial goal. The institutional mess-hall meals were minimally adequate. Dairy items were in continual shortage, and some centers had no meat for several days each week. Facilities for the sick, elderly, and mothers with infants were particularly poor. The WRA did prepare special meals for those with health problems, but the elderly and sick who needed the special meals might have to walk a mile three times a day to get them because the meals were prepared in a building separate from the mess halls. The shortage of medical care, evident in the assembly centers, also continued. At one point, the camp in Jerome, Arkansas, had only seven doctors to provide care to 10,000 people. Epidemics of dysentery, typhoid, and tuberculosis were reported in several camps.

The Japanese Americans had meager opportunities for work while interned and performed a variety of jobs: Many worked in agriculture or food preparation, while others constructed camouflage nets or operated sawmills. According to the 1982 [CWRIC] . . . , the WRA encouraged their participation because they hoped that outsiders would view such work as a sign of Japanese American loyalty. However, a strict limit on earnings was set. Camp internees could earn no more than $19.00 a month, regardless of whether they worked as nurses or field workers. In contrast, a white WRA librarian might earn $167.00 a month in camp.

Some 30,000 Japanese American children attended public school at the time of the internment. Although inadequate numbers of textbooks, equipment, and trained teachers severely limited what could be accomplished, both the Issei and older Nisei remained committed to providing an education for the young internees. Within weeks, the Japanese American residents themselves set up kindergarten and English classes, even in the temporary assembly centers. However, once the internees were transferred to the more permanent concentration camps, the WRA made little effort to retain the educational initiatives from the assembly centers and instead instituted inadequate and paternalistic educational policies. . . . Approximately 600 Caucasian American teachers, 50 certified Japanese American teachers, and 400 Japanese American assistant teachers eventually taught in the camps.

The WRA's system of governance gave it veto power over all legislative activities. It also barred the Issei from holding elected office and created conflicts between the Issei and Nisei generations by placing greater official authority in the hands of the children and disenfranchising their parents. Such a structure directly opposed Japanese cultural values of filial piety and deference to one's elders.

Other government policies produced friction among internees. In early 1943, all Japanese Americans over age 16 in the camps were required to answer loyalty questions. These questions were to serve two purposes. First, they would be used to help camp authorities process internees requesting work furloughs and resettlement outside the camps. Second, because the government had decided to open enlistment into the armed forces to Japanese Americans in 1944, a system was needed by which "loyal" and "disloyal" Japanese could be distinguished. To accomplish this latter task, army officers and WRA staff distributed questionnaires to all draft-age males that contained two critical questions about loyalty. Question 27 asked, "Are you willing to serve in the armed forces of the United States on combat duty, wherever ordered?" Question 28 asked, "Will you swear unqualified allegiance to the United States of America and faithfully defend the United States from any or all attack by foreign or domestic forces, and forswear any form of allegiance or obedience to the Japanese emperor, or any other government, power or organization?" The answers to the required questions were then used in registering Nisei men for the draft. The Issei and women internees were required to answer loyalty questions as well, although Question 27 was rephrased to ask whether they were willing to serve in the WACS or Army Nurse Corps.

The loyalty questionnaire raised significant and painful conflicts for Issei and Nisei alike and again demonstrated the government's blatant insensitivity to the circumstances of the Japanese Americans. The Issei struggled over Question 28. To answer "yes" would require them to renounce their Japanese nationality. Yet, because they were legally prevented from becoming American citizens, this would leave them without a country of citizenship at all! On the other hand, an answer of "no" would be seen as disloyal and could lead to being transferred to another camp and separated from one's children who were citizens of the United States. The loyalty oath essentially asked the Issei to "voluntarily assume stateless status," a request that was "a clear violation of the Geneva convention."

Loyalty questions concerned the Nisei as well. Some wondered if Question 28 were a trick question, since forswearing allegiance to the emperor might also be construed as admitting that allegiance had once existed. Question 27 asked them to fight for the country that had so unjustly imprisoned them. Tensions and debates over how to respond to the loyalty questions arose between family members and friends. In the end, the majority of internees (87%) answered the question with an unqualified "yes." Qualified answers and unanswered questions were interpreted as "no's." The approximately 8,000 who answered "no" to both Question 27 and 28 were considered "disloyals" and eventually shipped to a special high-security camp at Tule Lake. There the so-called "no-no's" joined individuals who wished to expatriate or repatriate to Japan.

By January 1944, following the loyalty questionnaire, the government reinstituted the draft for Japanese Americans. According to the selective service, approximately 23,000 Nisei served during World War II. About half came from the continental United States, and among these were 2,800 Nisei inductees from the camps. Some of the young Nisei males willingly joined the armed forces. The all-Japanese American 100th Battalion and the 442nd Regimental Combat Team, composed of volunteers from Hawaii and the camps, became famous for their bravery and loyalty. Other Nisei contributed to the war effort through their service in the intelligence or by acting as interrogators of Japanese war prisoners in combat. Ironically, the Japanese heritage that made them targets for suspected disloyalty had become an asset.

Dissension and Resistance

The outstanding service record of Japanese Americans who served in the military might lead one to believe that all internees supported the recruitment effort. Other statistics, however, indicate that there were Nisei who did not accept military service as a positive alternative. Twenty-two percent of the total Nisei males eligible for the draft refused to answer "yes" to both of the loyalty questions. In addition, the army eventually recruited only 1,208 volunteers from the camps. The proportion of volunteers from the noninterned Hawaiian Japanese was significantly higher. Daniels also points out that many Japanese American soldiers who fought in Europe were farmers. White farmers of draft age would have received deferments as "essential agricultural workers," but no such occupational deferments were available to Japanese Americans. And while the 442nd Regiment and 100th Battalion were exemplary combat units, Company K, another all-Nisei unit, was plagued by low morale and insubordination. Not all Nisei welcomed the draft as a sign of reinstated rights. For them, the loyalty questionnaire and the draft represented additional insults to their citizenship and rights. At the Heart Mountain camp, some 85 men were indicted and convicted for draft resistance.

Draft resistance represented only one example of the Japanese American disillusionment. Renunciation of citizenship represented yet another. By January 1945, over 5,000 Nisei had renounced their American citizenship. Some regretted their decision several months later when an end to the war appeared near and the Justice Department announced that Nisei renunciants would be deported to Japan while their Issei parents would be relocated in the United States. Eventually, after negotiating considerable legal and bureaucratic complexities, all who wished to invalidate their renunciations were able to do so. Other Japanese Americans filed for repatriation (in the case of aliens) or expatriation (in the case of citizens) to Japan.

> In the assembly and relocation centers, applications to go to Japan had been one of the few nonviolent ways to protest degrading treatment. During three years of rising humiliation, 20,000 people chose this means to express their pain, outrage and alienation, in one of the saddest testaments to the injustice of exclusion and detection. . . . The cold statistics fail . . . to convey the scars of mind and soul that many carried with them from the camps.

As was the case with the renunciants, most repatriation and expatriation applicants eventually remained in the United States. It is nonetheless sobering that 4,724 Japanese Americans actually left the camps for Japan.

Resettlement

Beginning in 1943, Nisei who answered "yes" to the loyalty oath but did not enlist in the service began receiving clearance to leave the camps for areas outside the restricted zones of the West Coast. Resettlement was a slow process. Those who left the camps were given one-way transportation costs and $25 to begin a new life. Young Nisei between the ages of 15 and 35 relocated in cities such as Chicago, Denver, and New York and took whatever form of work they could find. Many became domestics or performed other forms of manual labor. Between 2,300 and 2,700 ended up working at Seabrook Farms in New Jersey. These individuals were influenced by farm recruiters who went to the camps to solicit resettlers by feedback from trial groups sent from the camps and letters from those already resettled in Seabrook.

Although resettlement had been a goal of the WRA from early on in the internment, there were many reasons why the Japanese Americans were reluctant to leave the camps. In addition to experiencing the physical and emotional stress of imprisonment, many were fearful to leave the camps and distrustful of resettlement offers. This was especially true of the older Issei. Government records showed that by January 1945, only one of six Issei had left the camps, and it was not until June 1946 that all camps (with the exception of Tule Lake, where hearings on detainees were held) closed. . . .

. . . Greater than two-thirds of those who left the camps eventually returned to their previous region of residence. Both those who resettled in cities away from the West Coast and those who returned to their home towns faced many adjustments. [Historian Tetsuden] Kashima, in fact, refers to the resettlement years between 1945 and 1955 as a crisis period for Japanese Americans, a time when they were forced to readjust to a normal life after the camps, find jobs and a place to live, and confront an often hostile environment. Most found their original neighborhoods greatly changed. Areas that had once been the "Japantowns" and centers of Japanese American community life had, over the war years, become occupied by other ethnic minority groups. In addition, anti-Japanese sentiments remained high, and 31 major attacks on California relocatees were reported between January and June of 1945.

We have seen that by spring of 1943, following the loyalty review of internees, there was evidence that the incarceration of the Japanese Americans was not a military necessity. Yet, many Japanese Americans remained in the camps through 1945. Why was this so? The following quote taken from the CWRIC report provides the sobering answer to this question:

> . . . the President was unwilling to act to end the exclusion until the first Cabinet meeting following the Presidential election of November, 1944. The inescapable conclusion from this . . . pattern is that the delay was motivated by political considerations. By the participants' own accounts, there is no rational explanation for maintaining the exclusion of loyal ethnic Japanese from the West Coast for eighteen months after May, 1943—except political pressure and fear.

From the beginnings of the decision to evacuate, to the closing of the camps, the Japanese Americans were the victims of racial, economic, and political injustices. By the end of the internment, with their community dispersed across the country, their lives would never be the same.

A Defense of the Relocation Policy

In the following selection, Dwight D. Murphey, a lawyer who has written on social and political philosophy, defends the relocation policy, arguing that it was justified and that conditions in the camps were good. From Dwight D. Murphey, The Dispossession of the American Indian—And Other Key Issues in American History *(Washington, D.C., 1995), 31-35, 39-41.*

On February 19, 1942, President Franklin D. Roosevelt signed Executive Order 9066. This authorized the establishment of military areas from which people of all kinds could be excluded. Lt. General John L. DeWitt was appointed the military commander to carry out the Executive Order. In March, Gen. DeWitt declared large parts of the Pacific Coast states military areas in which no one of Japanese descent would be allowed to remain. The exclusion order affected Japanese-Americans living on the West Coast by forcing them to move inland. Its only effect upon those who already lived inland was to bar them from going to the quarantined areas on the West Coast. . . .

A short-lived plan originally was to assist the Japanese-Americans in a process by which they would move inland "on their own recognizance" as individuals and families. [Karl R.] Bendetsen [who directed the evacuation for the government] says that "funds were provided for them [and] we informed them . . . where there were safe motels in which they could stay overnight." This was ended almost immediately, by late March, however . . . the need for a more organized system became apparent when most of the Japanese-Americans were not able to make arrangements to relocate quickly even with some help. A second reason was that the governors of western states (reflecting public opinion in their states) objected strongly to thousands of people of Japanese origin moving into their states without oversight. . . .

Relocated Japanese-Americans play baseball at the Lone Pine Relocation Camp, with other residents looking on. (Courtesy of The Library of Congress.)

This led to the "assembly center phase," during which the evacuees were moved to improvised centers such as race tracks and fairgrounds along the West Coast pending the construction of ten "relocation centers" in eastern California, Arizona, Utah, Idaho, Wyoming, Colorado, and as far east as Arkansas. . . .

Hastily improvised and purely temporary quarters for thousands of people who have been uprooted from their homes on short notice could not have been pleasant. There is no incongruity, however, between this and the fact, also true, that the government worked with the evacuees to take extraordinary measures to make the centers as comfortable as possible. In the short time they existed, some centers opened libraries; movies were shown regularly; there were Scout troops, arts and crafts classes, musical groups, and leagues for basketball and baseball. Three hundred and fifty people signed up for a calisthenics class at Stockton. All had playgrounds for children, and one even had a pitch-and-putt golf course. The centers were run almost entirely by the Japanese-Americans themselves.

As the ten relocation centers became ready, the evacuees were moved to them from the assembly centers. These were under the jurisdiction of the War Relocation Authority. . . . It is worth noting that no families were ever separated during the process.

As with the assembly centers, the critics find fault with much about the relocation centers. For example, the health care has been the subject of continuing dispute. Dillon Myer [director of the War Relocation Authority (WRA), which supervised the camps], however, says that "the professional care was excellent [and] was free."

There were messhalls for meals, and a large number of community enterprises, which included stores, theaters, hairdressers, community theaters, and newspapers. There was ping-pong, judo, boxing, badminton, and sumo wrestling. Again, there were basketball and baseball leagues (along with some touch football). The Santa Fe center had "gardens, two softball diamonds, two tennis courts, a miniature nine-hole golf course, a fenced forty-acre hiking area, . . . classes in calligraphy, Chinese and Japanese poetry. . . ." The Massachusetts Quakers sponsored art competitions. Libraries featured Japanese-language sections. There were chapters of the American Red Cross, YMCA, YWCA, Boy Scouts, and Girl Scouts. State Shinto, with its emperor-worship, was barred, but otherwise the evacuees worshiped as they pleased. The government paid a salary equal to an American soldier's pay ($21 per month) to those who worked in the centers.

Each of the camps (except Tule Lake . . .) had fully accredited schools through the high school level. There were nursery schools, kindergarten, the teaching of instrumental music, school choruses, achievement testing, high school newspapers and annuals, dances, active Parent-Teacher Associations, student councils and class officers. . . .

Much of the credit for the livability of the centers goes to the Japanese-Americans themselves, whose energy and intelligence immediately made the best of the situation. This was accomplished in an active relationship with the WRA.

Subject to a veto that the WRA could exercise, each relocation center was governed internally (as had been the assembly centers) by the Japanese-Americans themselves, who elected representatives from each block.

Even before the relocation centers became filled, college-age students began to leave to attend American universities. By the beginning of the fall semester in 1942, approximately 250 students had left for school, attending 143 colleges and universities. By the time the war was over, 4,300 college-age students were attending more than 300 universities around the country (though not on the West Coast). Scholarships were granted based on financial ability. Foundations and churches funded a "National Japanese American Student Relocation Council" to help with college attendance.

The centers were intended, as their name suggests, to be places in which the evacuees could stay while they were being relocated around the country. Myer says "never was there any policy of confinement for the duration." . . . That is why the camps were called "relocation centers" rather than "internment camps."

Many of the evacuees, however, remained in the centers for the duration of the war. Critics attribute this to a lack of alternatives, as though the evacuees were trapped, but Bendetsen credits the fact that life was acceptable within the centers. "Many elected to stay in the relocation centers while being gainfully employed in nearby pursuits in the general economy . . . The climate of hostility which presented intractable problems in the very early phases had long since subsided." . . .

The critics of the evacuation often argue that there was no demonstrated military necessity for it. The Report of the Commission on Wartime Relocation speaks of "the clamor" by California officials for protective action, and says that "these opinions were not informed by any knowledge of actual military risks." The extensive critical literature mocks the perception of danger, suggesting that it was a figment of hysterical imaginations.

But this is nonsense. The danger was apparent to anyone who considered the situation. Earl Warren, as attorney general of California, testified before a select committee of Congress (the "Tolan Committee") on February 21, 1942, and submitted letters from a number of local officials. Some pointed to the vulnerability of the water supply and of the large-scale irrigation systems: "It would be absolutely humanly impossible," one of them wrote, "for the small force now available in the sheriff's office to make even a pretense of guarding this tremendous farm territory and the irrigation system." Another pointed out that "a systematic campaign of incendiarism would cause terrific disaster" during the California dry season from May until October. . . .

In addition to the civilian population, there was much that was important militarily and economically along the West Coast; it was clearly exposed; and there were few means to defend it. This was enough in itself to create a critical emergency, to be met as humanely but as effectively as possible. It should not be necessary for the American government to have known specifically of plans for espionage and sabotage.

Just the same, there *was* definitive evidence of Japan's intent to exploit (and actual exploitation of) the situation. On December 4, 1941, the Office of Naval Intelligence reported a Japanese "intelligence machine geared for war, in operation, and utilizing west coast Japanese." On January 21, 1942, a bulletin from Army Intelligence "stated flat out that the Japanese government's espionage net containing Japanese aliens, first and second generation Japanese and other nationals is now thoroughly organized and working underground," according to the testimony of David D. Lowman, a retired career intelligence officer who has written extensively on declassified intelligence from World War II. . . .

Amazingly, the Commission ignored the most important source of information about espionage, which is the dispatches sent by the Japanese government to its own officials before and during the war. U. S. Navy codebreakers had broken the Japanese diplomatic code in 1938, and the decoded messages were distributed, on a basis "higher than Top Secret," to a small handful of the very highest American officials under the codename "MAGIC." Lowman testified in 1984 that "included among the diplomatic communications were hundreds of reports dealing with espionage activities in the United States and its possessions." . . .

Several officials within the Roosevelt administration opposed the evacuation of the Japanese-Americans from the West Coast, but Lowman makes a telling point: that the President, the Secretary of War, the Army Chief of Staff, the Director of Military Intelligence, the Secretary of the Navy, the Chief of Naval Operations, the Director of Naval Intelligence, and the Chiefs of Army and Navy Plans—all of whom received MAGIC—*favored* evacuation. It was those who did not have knowledge of the Japanese dispatches who found it possible, somewhat incongruously in light of the self-evident factors I have mentioned, to doubt the military necessity.

Questions

1. *What role did racism play in encouraging the government to order the forced relocation of Japanese and Japanese Americans from the Pacific coast? Do you think that military necessity alone can explain the decision? Do you think that government officials' perception of military necessity alone can explain the decision?*

2. *Does Dwight Murphey's justification of the expulsion and relocation policy help you to understand the feelings of those who supported it in 1941?*

3. *How persuasive do you find Murphey's defense of the government's policy? Did the fears and evidence of Japanese disloyalty that Murphey describes justify mass relocation? Explain.*

4. *Defenders of the evacuation of Japanese Americans from the Pacific coast describe their transfer to the relocation camps as "voluntary." Nagata, like many who have described the events, refers to the relocation as "internment," suggesting the transfer was involuntary. How voluntary does it appear to have been? If you are unsure, keep this question in mind as you read the original documents that follow.*

5. *Defenders of the evacuation and relocation policy point out that Japanese and Japanese Americans were treated much better than enemy aliens in Germany and Japan. How does this affect your evaluation of the expulsion and relocation policy?*

THE JAPANESE RELOCATION:
DOCUMENTS AND
FIRST-HAND ACCOUNTS

After their release from the relocation camps, few of the residents were willing to describe their experiences. For some the memory was too painful. Many adult Japanese considered their time in the camps to be a mark of shame, to be hidden. Moreover, many Japanese and Japanese Americans had been taught not to express anger openly. But over time, Japanese Americans—especially the younger generation—began to describe their experiences and express their outrage. The following documents and first-hand accounts describe their experiences and the actions of the United States government.

Executive Order 9066

After several months of debate within his administration, on 19 February 1942, President Franklin D. Roosevelt signed an executive order authorizing the military to relocate the Japanese and Japanese Americans living on the West coast. Did the president allege any actual evidence of sabotage or disloyalty? Excerpted from U.S. House of Representatives, Report of the Select Committee Investigating National Defense Migration (hereafter cited as Tolan Committee), House Report No. 2124, 77th Cong., 2d sess. (1942), 314.

WHEREAS the successful prosecution of the war requires every possible protection against espionage and against sabotage to national defense material, national defense premises, and national defense utilities. . . .

Now, therefore, by virtue of the authority vested in me as President of the United States, and Commander in Chief of the Army and Navy, I hereby authorize and direct the Secretary of War, and the Military Commanders who he may from time to time designate, whenever he or any designated Commander deems such action necessary or desirable, to prescribe military areas in such places and of such extent as he or the appropriate Military Commander may determine, from which any or all persons may be excluded, and with respect to which, the right of any person to enter, remain in, or leave shall be subject to whatever restrictions the Secretary of War or the appropriate Military Commander may impose in his discretion. The Secretary of War is hereby authorized to provide for residents of any such area who are excluded therefrom, such transportation, food, shelter, and other accommodations as may be necessary, in the judgment of the Secretary of War or the said Military Commander, and until other arrangements are made, to accomplish the purpose of this order.

An Evacuation Order

The following was the first of the evacuation orders that forced over 100,000 Japanese Americans from their homes on the West coast and led to their relocation to camps in the interior. Abridged from Tolan Committee, House Report No. 2124, *332–33.*

Civilian Exclusion Order No. 1
Headquarters, Western Defense Command and Fourth Army, *Presidio of San Francisco, California, March 24, 1942.*

1. Pursuant to the provisions of Public Proclamations Nos. 1 and 2, this headquarters, dated March 2, 1942, and March 16, 1942, respectively, it is hereby ordered that all persons of Japanese ancestry, including aliens and nonaliens, be excluded from that portion of Military Area No. 1 described as "Bainbridge Island," in the State of Washington,

on or before 12 o'clock noon, P. W. T., of the 30th day of March 1942.

2. Such exclusion will be accomplished in the following manner:

   (a) Such persons may, with permission, on or prior to March 29, 1942, proceed to any approved place of their choosing beyond the limits of Military Area No. 1 and the prohibited zones established by said proclamations or hereafter similarly established, subject only to such regulations as to travel and change of residence as are now or may hereafter be prescribed by this headquarters and by the United States Attorney General. Persons affected hereby will not be permitted to take up residence or remain within the region designated as Military Area No. 1 or the prohibited zones heretofore or hereafter established. Persons affected hereby are required on leaving or entering Bainbridge Island to register and obtain a permit at the Civil Control Office to be established on said Island at or near the ferryboat landing.

   (b) On March 30, 1942, all such persons who have not removed themselves from Bainbridge Island in accordance with Paragraph 1 hereof shall, in accordance with instructions of the Commanding General, Northwestern Sector, report to the Civil Control Office referred to above on Bainbridge Island for evacuation in such manner and to such place or places as shall then be prescribed.

   (c) A responsible member of each family affected by this order and each individual living alone so affected will report to the Civil Control Office described above between 8 a. m. and 5 p. m. Wednesday, March 25, 1942.

3. Any person affected by this order who fails to comply with any of its provisions or who is found on Bainbridge Island after 12 o'clock noon, P. W. T., of March 30, 1942, will be subject to the criminal penalties provided by Public Law No. 503, 77th Congress, approved March 21, 1942, entitled "An Act to Provide a Penalty for Violation of Restrictions or Orders with Respect to Persons Entering, Remaining in, Leaving, or Committing Any Act in Military Areas or

Zone", and alien Japanese will be subject to immediate apprehension and internment.

J. L. DE WITT,
Lieutenant General,
U.S. Army, Commanding

The Uchida Family is Evacuated

Like many other community leaders, Yoshiko Uchida's father, Dwight Takashi Uchida, the manager of a leading department store serving the Japanese community in Berkeley, California, was arrested and interned immediately after the bombing of Pearl Harbor. His family, including his daughter Yoshiko, a student at the University of California, remained in Berkeley until ordered to evacuate on 21 April 1942. From Yoshiko Uchida, Desert Exile: The Uprooting *of a Japanese American Family (Seattle, 1982), 58–60, 62.*

Each day we watched the papers for the evacuation orders covering the Berkeley area. On April 21, the headlines read: "Japs Given Evacuation Orders Here." I felt numb as I read the front page story. "Moving swiftly, without any advance notice, the Western Defense Command today ordered Berkeley's estimated 1,319 Japanese, aliens and citizens alike, evacuated to the Tanforan Assembly Center by noon, May 1." (This gave us exactly ten days' notice.) "Evacuees will report at the Civil Control Station being set up in Pilgrim Hall of the First Congregational Church . . . between the hours of 8:00 A.M. and 5:00 P.M. next Saturday and Sunday."

This was Exclusion Order Number Nineteen, which was to uproot us from our homes and send us into the Tanforan Assembly Center in San Bruno, a hastily converted racetrack.

All Japanese were required to register before the departure date, and my sister, as head of the family, went to register for us.

She came home with baggage and name tags that were to bear our family number and be attached to all our belongings. From that day on we became Family Number 13453.

Although we had been preparing for the evacuation orders, still when they were actually issued, it was a sickening shock.

"Ten days! We have only ten days to get ready!" my sister said frantically. Each day she rushed about, not only taking care of our business affairs, but, as our only driver, searching for old crates and cartons for packing, and taking my mother on various errands as well.

Mama still couldn't seem to believe that we would have to leave. "How can we clear out in ten days a house we've lived in for fifteen years?" she asked sadly.

But my sister and I had no answers for her.

Mama had always been a saver, and she had a tremendous accumulation of possessions. Her frugal upbringing had caused her to save string, wrapping paper, bags, jars, boxes, even bits of silk thread left over from sewing, which were tied end to end and rolled up into a silk ball. Tucked away in the corners of her desk and bureau drawers were such things as small stuffed animals, wooden toys, *kokeshi* dolls, marbles, and even a half-finished pair of socks she was knitting for a teddy bear's paw. Many of these were "found objects" that the child in her couldn't bear to discard, but they often proved useful in providing diversion for some fidgety visiting child. These were the simple things to dispose of.

More difficult were the boxes that contained old letters from her family and friends, our old report cards from the first grade on, dozens of albums of family photographs, notebooks and sketch pads full of our childish drawings, valentines and Christmas cards we had made for our parents, innumerable guest books filled with the signatures and friendly words of those who had once been entertained. These were the things my mother couldn't bear to throw away. Because we didn't own our house, we could leave nothing behind. We had to clear the house completely, and everything in it had either to be packed for storage or thrown out.

We surveyed with desperation the vast array of dishes, lacquerware, silverware, pots and pans, books, paintings, porcelain and pottery, furniture, linens, rugs, records, curtains, garden tools, cleaning equipment, and clothing that filled our house. We put up a sign in our window reading, "Living room sofa and chair for sale." We sold things we should have kept and packed away foolish trifles we should have discarded. We sold our refrigerator, our dining room set, two sofas, an easy chair, and a brand new vacuum cleaner with attachments. Without a sensible scheme in our heads, and lacking the practical judgment of my father, the three of us packed frantically and sold recklessly. Although the young people of our church did what they could to help us, we felt desperate as the deadline approached. Our only thought was to get the house emptied in time, for we knew the Army would not wait.

Organizations such as the First Congregational Church of Berkeley were extremely helpful in anticipating the needs of the panic-stricken Japanese and provided immediate, practical assistance. Families of the church offered storage space to those who needed it, and we took several pieces of furniture to be stored in the basement of one such home. Another non-Japanese friend offered to take our books and stored more than eight large cartons for us. In typical Japanese fashion, my mother took gifts to express her gratitude to each person who helped us. . . .

By now I had to leave the university, as did all the other Nisei students. We had stayed as long as we could to get credit for the spring semester, which was crucial for those of us who were seniors. My professors gave me a final grade on the basis of my midterm grades and the university granted all Nisei indefinite leaves of absence.

During the last few weeks on campus, my friends and I became sentimental and took pictures of each other at favorite campus sites. The war had jolted us into a crisis whose impact was too enormous for us to fully comprehend, and we needed these small remembrances of happier times to take with us as we went our separate ways to various government camps throughout California.

A Description of a Camp

Minoru Yasui, a California-born lawyer and U.S. Army reserve officer, refused to report for relocation. He was taken from his home in Oregon, interned with 3,000 other Japanese Americans in Portland for five months, and then transported to the Minidoka camp in Idaho. Abridged

The belongings of relocated Japanese and Japanese-Americans, piled behind the barbed-wire fence at the Salinas Relocation Center. (Courtesy of The Library of Congress.)

from John Tateishi, And Justice for All: An Oral History of the Japanese American Detention Camps *(New York, 1984), 76–77.*

We arrived late afternoon, at some isolated siding in the desert area, north of Twin Falls, although we did not know where we were. No houses were in sight, no trees or anything green— only scrubby sagebrush and an occasional low catcus, and mostly dry, baked earth. There was a slight rise to the north, and one could not see to the horizon.

Baggage was unloaded and piled up next to the road, and Army trucks were rolling in, kicking up huge clouds of dust. People came off the train, were lined up and loaded into the trucks, and went off into the distance. The seats were hard planks, and after riding all day on the train, most were sore and tired.

We had left the dark, dank confines of a livestock barn hoping to breathe the fresh, open air. But because the virgin desert had been bulldozed and disturbed by men and machinery, instead of fresh air, we got to breathe dust. I remember groups of women getting off the train, looking bewildered. After the lush greenness of the Willamette Valley, to see the sterile, dusty desert which was to be our home "for the duration," many sat on the baggage in the middle of nowhere and wept. . . .

We saw again the barbed-wire fences, the watchtowers, guard houses, the MP detachments, the administration housing, warehouse areas, and block after block of black, tar-paper barracks, about 120 feet long and about 20 feet wide. I remember that at least the mess halls and kitchens were completed, and that evening we had hot meals, perhaps spam and canned vegetables. The barracks were supplied with army cots with metal springs, and we got padding-filled ticks and a couple of army blankets. There was a potbellied stove, and each block had a coal depot. One bare bulb hung from the center of the room. There were real composition-board ceilings but the walls were unfinished with open two-by-four studs. The floor was wood, and single layered, so one could see the earth below, through the cracks. The smaller units for childless couples were on the end of the building, with two windows on each side, or a total of four windows. There was only one entrance to each unit. No chairs or tables were furnished; however, later the evacuees scrounged scrap lumber and built chairs, tables, bunk beds, dressers, and other things. But only those who were handy with tools could do this. The internee wives with small children were not always able to furnish their rooms comfortably. There was, however, a great deal of sharing and exchange going on.

The Loyalty Questionnaire

In February 1943 the government began to register the people it had relocated to camps. To facilitate the release of those considered loyal and to encourage loyal Japanese Americans to enlist in the armed forces, the government prepared a questionnaire to accompany registration. Question 27 asked Nisei men if they were willing to serve in the armed forces in combat wherever ordered. Question 28 amounted to a loyalty oath— asking respondents to reaffirm allegiance to the United States and renounce allegiance to Japan. In the camps, Japanese Americans divided bitterly about how to respond. In the end about 5,000 refused to take the oath of allegiance and refused to express a willingness to fight for the United States against "any or all" of its enemies, including Japan. Extremists among the refusers worked to foment resistance to American authorities among camp residents, resorting at times to violence and intimidation. The following describes how Frank Chuman, a California-born law student in the Manzanar camp in the California desert, anguished over what to do. Taken from John Tateishi, And Justice for All: An Oral History of the Japanese American Detention Camps, *230–32.*

I didn't get the full brunt of the anti-Japanese hostility which was a hell of a good thing, because when I went to Manzanar there was a delayed reaction for me. What the hell am I doing in camp? I thought. While I was very busy working in the hospital, I said to myself, Why should the United States Government doubt our loyalty to the United States? We haven't done anything to justify this kind of treatment. Certainly not myself and certainly none of the others that I know of. And yet here I am in a camp of ten thousand people—men, women, and children. So I began to think to myself, because I had studied law—constitutional law and constitutional rights and due process and equal protection and all the rest of it—Jesus Christ, we've been deprived of our constitutional rights. There's been no accusations against me, and yet I'm suspect and I'm arbitrarily told to go into a camp. It's completely in violation of my rights. . . . And I really got angry and very, very upset at the United States Government for doing this kind of thing to not only me, but all Japanese Americans. I really got upset.

The Army recruiting team came into Manzanar around the early part of 1943. We had a big meeting in this mess hall of all persons eligible for military duty with two white soldiers and a person of Japanese ancestry, and this guy was trying to persuade us all to volunteer for the Army, and I'm not too sure whether I got up and spoke back to him or whether I said it in my own mind, but I said, "Why should we fight for the United States Government as soldiers, when the United States Government distrusts us? Why do they now want us to serve when they consider us to be disloyal? Why do they want us to serve when they have taken us out of our homes and schools and businesses, and now they want us to become loyal to the United States? It doesn't make sense, and so far as I'm concerned I'm not going to do anything to go into the

United States Army until the United States Government does something to remedy this unjust situation." I cannot remember whether I stood up and said it or whether I felt it.

In any event, that's the way it was. In the latter part of 1943, this questionnaire came out sponsored by the WRA, and in that questionnaire it had something like "request for relocation" as well as the questionnaire. It was in two parts. And there were these questions 27 and 28, "Are you willing to foreswear any allegiance to any foreign potentate and say that you are loyal to the United States?" and, "Are you willing to bear arms for the United States?" The first answer that I gave to both questions was no. I was so goddamned mad at that questionnaire. It was insulting, impugning without any evidence, just from the top down that there was something that made us Japanese Americans suspect in loyalty, allegiance, that we wouldn't fight for the government and saying now you're going to fight. They don't have to push it down my throat—are you willing to bear arms to defend the United States? That's so goddamned obvious that I would do that that it just really made me angry. . . .

I did not remain a no-no, because all of a sudden I thought to myself, after I had said that, I regretted it, because it wasn't my true feelings. There was no way that I could hate the United States Government, but I was goddamned angry at them for doing things like that about us.

The Supreme Court Upholds Japanese Relocation: *Korematsu* v. *U.S.* (1944)

Several Japanese Americans resisted the government exclusion orders in order to challenge their constitutionality in the courts. In 1943 the Supreme Court sustained a curfew applying to all people of Japanese ancestry along the Pacific Coast. A year later, to the dismay of civil libertarians, it upheld Executive Order 9066 and the relocation program instituted under its authority. Abridged from Korematsu v. U.S., *323 US 214, (1944), 216, 218–20, 233–34, 240, 242.*

Opinion of the Court

It should be noted, to begin with, that all legal restrictions which curtail the civil rights of a single racial group are immediately suspect. That is not to say that all such restrictions are unconstitutional. It is to say that courts must subject them to the most rigid scrutiny. Pressing public necessity may sometimes justify the existence of such restrictions; racial antagonism never can. . . .

. . . [E]xclusion of those of Japanese origin was deemed necessary because of the presence of an unascertained number of disloyal members of the group, most of whom we have no doubt were loyal to this country. It was because we could not reject the finding of the military authorities that it was impossible to bring about an immediate segregation of the disloyal from the loyal that we sustained the validity of the curfew order as applying to the whole group. In the instant case, temporary exclusion of the entire group was rested by the military on the same ground. The judgment that exclusion of the whole group was for the same reason a military imperative answers the contention that the exclusion was in the nature of group punishment based on antagonism to those of Japanese origin. . . .

We uphold the exclusion order as of the time it was made and when the petitioner violated it. . . . In doing so, we are not unmindful of the hardships imposed by it upon a large group of American citizens. . . . Citizenship has its responsibilities as well as its privileges, and in time of war the burden is always heavier. Compulsory exclusion of large groups of citizens from their homes, except under circumstances of direst emergency and peril, is inconsistent with our basic governmental institutions. But when under conditions of modern warfare our shores are threatened by hostile forces, the power to protect must be commensurate with the threatened danger. . . .

MR. JUSTICE MURPHY, dissenting.
This exclusion of "all persons of Japanese ancestry, both alien and non-alien," from the Pacific Coast area on a plea of military necessity in the absence of martial law ought not to be approved. Such exclusion goes over "the very brink of constitutional power" and falls into the ugly abyss of racism. . . .

. . . [I]t is essential that there be definite limits to military discretion, especially where martial law has not been declared.

Individuals must not be left impoverished of their constitutional rights on a plea of military necessity that has neither substance nor support....

. . . No one denies, of course, that there were some disloyal persons of Japanese descent on the Pacific Coast who did all in their power to aid their ancestral land. Similar disloyal activities have been engaged in by many persons of German, Italian and even more pioneer stock in our country. But to infer that examples of individual disloyalty prove group disloyalty and justify discriminatory action against the entire group is to deny that under our system of law individual guilt is the sole basis for deprivation of rights. . . . To give constitutional sanction to that inference in this case, however well intentioned may have been the military command on the Pacific Coast is to adopt one of the cruelest of the rationales used by our enemies to destroy the dignity of the individual and to encourage and open the door to discriminatory actions against other minority groups in the passions of tomorrow....

. . . All residents of this nation are kin in some way by blood or culture to a foreign land. Yet they are primarily and necessarily a part of the new and distinct civilization of the United States. They must accordingly be treated at all times as the heirs of the American experiment and as entitled to all the rights and freedoms guaranteed by the Constitution.

The Government Reinvestigates

In response to agitation by Japanese Americans in the 1970s and renewed public interest in the events surrounding Japanese exclusion and relocation, Congress established a commission to investigate the subject. After taking testimony from those who organized and administered the program, those subjected to it, and historians of it, the Commission concluded that the exclusion and relocation had been unjustified and unjustifiable. It recommended a formal apology and restitution. Excerpted from Personal Justice Denied: Report of the Commission on Wartime Relocation and Internment of Civilians *(Washington, D.C., 1982), 2–3, 18.*

This policy of exclusion, removal and detention was executed against 120,000 people without individual review, and exclusion was continued virtually without regard for their demonstrated loyalty to the United States. Congress was fully aware of and supported the policy of removal and detention; it sanctioned the exclusion by enacting a statue which made criminal the violation of orders issued pursuant to Executive Order 9066. The United States Supreme Court held the exclusion constitutionally permissible in the context of war, but struck down the incarceration of admittedly loyal American citizens on the ground that it was not based on statutory authority.

All this was done despite the fact that not a single documented act of espionage, sabotage or fifth column activity was committed by an American citizen of Japanese ancestry or by a resident Japanese alien on the West Coast.

No mass exclusion or detention, in any part of the country, was ordered against American citizens of German or Italian descent. Official actions against enemy aliens of other nationalities were much more individualized and selective than those imposed on the ethnic Japanese.

The exclusion, removal and detention inflicted tremendous human cost. There was the obvious cost of homes and businesses sold or abandoned under circumstances of great distress, as well as injury to careers and professional advancement. But, most important, there was the loss of liberty and the personal stigma of suspected disloyalty for thousands of people who knew themselves to be devoted to their country's cause and to its ideals but whose repeated protestations of loyalty were discounted—only to be demonstrated beyond any doubt by the record of Nisei solders, who returned from the battlefields of Europe as the most decorated and distinguished combat unit of World War II, and by the thousands of other Nisei who served against the enemy in the Pacific, mostly in military intelligence. The wounds of the exclusion and detention have healed in some respects, but the scars of that experience remain, painfully real in the minds of those who lived through the suffering and deprivation of the camps.

The personal injustice of excluding, removing and detaining loyal American citizens is manifest. Such events are extraordinary and unique in American history. For every citizen and for American public life, they pose haunting questions about our country and its past. . . .

The promulgation of Executive Order 9066 was not justified by military necessity, and the decisions which followed from it—detention, ending detention and ending exclusion—were not driven by analysis of military conditions. The broad historical causes which shaped these decisions were race prejudice, war hysteria and a failure of political leadership. Widespread ignorance of Japanese Americans contributed to a policy conceived in haste and executed in an atmosphere of fear and anger at Japan. A grave injustice was done to American citizens and resident aliens of Japanese ancestry who, without individual review or any probative evidence against them, were excluded, removed and detained by the United States during World War II.

The Civil Liberties Act of 1988

In response to the report of the Commission on Wartime Relocation and Internment of Civilians, on 10 August 1988, Congress passed the Civil Liberties Act of 1988. The act requested the president to issue pardons to those convicted of violating the curfew, exclusion, and relocation orders; authorized restitution in the amount of $20,000 to every person expelled, interned, or relocated; and set up a fund to finance educational programs to inform the public about the expulsion and relocation "so as to prevent the recurrence of any similar event." Taken from U.S. Statutes at Large, *vol. 102, 1988 (1990), 903–4.*

SEC. 2. STATEMENT OF THE CONGRESS.

(a) WITH REGARD TO INDIVIDUALS OF JAPANESE ANCESTRY.—The Congress recognizes that, as described by the Commission on Wartime Relocation and Internment of Civilians, a grave injustice was done to both citizens and permanent resident aliens of Japanese ancestry by the evacuation, relocation, and internment of civilians during World War II. As the Commission documents, these actions were carried out without adequate security reasons and without any acts of espionage or sabotage documented by the Commission, and were motivated largely by racial prejudice, wartime hysteria, and a failure of political leadership. The excluded individuals of Japanese ancestry suffered enormous damages, both material and intangible, and there were incalculable losses in education and job training, all of which resulted in significant human suffering for which appropriate compensation has not been made. For these fundamental violations of the basic civil liberties and constitutional rights of these individuals of Japanese ancestry, the Congress apologizes on behalf of the Nation.

Questions

1. *Many non-Japanese tried to help their Japanese and Japanese American neighbors as they were forced to leave the Pacific Coast. Should they have done more? What more could they have done?*

2. *Should the Nisei have resisted the relocation program more forcefully? What might have inhibited such resistance?*

3. *Why did some of the Japanese and Japanese Americans in the relocation camps refuse to reaffirm their allegiance to the United States and refuse to agree to fight in the armed forces when presented with Questions 27 and 28 of the registration questionnaire in 1943? How would you have answered the questions?*

4. *On what basis did the Supreme Court sustain the constitutionality of Japanese expulsion and relocation in* **Korematsu** *v.* **U.S.?** *On what basis did Justice Murphy disagree? Do you think an occurrence similar to Japanese relocation could take place in a future time of war? Do you think the Supreme Court might intervene?*

5. *Do you think it was appropriate for Congress to apologize formally for the actions taken during World War II? Do you think the formal apology and the Civil Liberties Act might deter similar actions by government in the future? Explain.*

FURTHER READING

Page Smith, Democracy on Trial: The Japanese American Evacuation and Relocation in World War Two *(New York, 1995) is a balanced chronicle of the events leading up to the relocation of the Japanese and their experiences afterwards. Smith argues that perceived military necessity, rather than racism, motivated the government's decision. Roger Daniels takes the opposite view in* Concentration Camps USA: Japanese Americans and World War II *(New York, 1971). In* Justice at War *(New York, 1983), Peter H. Irons also argues that political considerations and the racism of the Pacific coast military leaders overcame the resistance to relocation on the part of some officials of the Roosevelt administration. John Tateishi compiled the remembrances of camp inmates in* And Justice for All: An Oral History of the Japanese American Detention Camps *(New York, 1984).* Righting a Wrong: Japanese Americans and the Passage of the Civil Liberties Act of 1988 *(Stanford, California, 1993), by Leslie T. Hatamiya, tells how crusaders secured compensation and the official apology of the United States government for its treatment of Japanese American citizens during World War II. Lillian Baker trenchantly defends the expulsion and relocation policy in* American and Japanese Relocation in World War II: Fact, Fiction & Fallacy *(Medford, Oregon, 1990).*

Nonviolence and the
Civil Rights Movement

Penny A. Russell

INTRODUCTION

Some histories of the civil rights movement begin in 1954 with the __Brown v. Board of Education__ *decision that struck down separate but equal in public education. Other writers insist that the movement began in August 1955 with the decision of an all-white Mississippi jury to set free the two white men who brutally tortured and murdered fourteen-year-old Chicago native Emmett Till for allegedly whistling at a white woman. Many scholars begin their analysis with Rosa Parks, Martin Luther King, Jr., and the Montgomery Bus Boycott that started in December 1955. Recently, a few scholars have searched for the origins of the movement in the decades before the 1950s.*

Historians also disagree on how to characterize the ideology, politics, strategies, and tactics of the movement. A few have insisted that the commonly used term "the civil rights movement" is inadequate because this social movement was concerned with more than securing citizenship rights for Blacks. Some people saw the movement as a search for community, others spoke of it as a religious crusade, and still others believed it was a battle for the soul of America. To understand how and why African-American activism and politics came to be one of the dominant forces in American life from the mid-1950s to the mid-1960s, you must understand the origins and the foundation of the civil rights movement.

African Americans attempted to mobilize mass movements before the 1950s. The first call for a march on Washington came in May 1941, twenty-two years before Martin Luther King, Jr., told the nation about his dream of equality for all people. In May 1941,

A. Philip Randolph urged African Americans to demonstrate in Washington for an end to discrimination in defense industries and in the military. The march was canceled only after President Franklin D. Roosevelt issued Executive Order 8802, which outlawed discrimination in employment in defense industries that held government contracts and created a Fair Employment Practices Committee (FEPC) to investigate companies that violated the order.

The mass movement that Randolph had wanted to create became a reality fourteen years later. On 1 December 1955, Rosa Parks left her seamstress job in a tailor shop, boarded a city bus for home, and was arrested for refusing to give up her seat to a white passenger, a violation of Alabama's segregation laws. In response, the Women's Political Council, a black women's organization that had been petitioning Montgomery's mayor about discrimination and segregation on the city buses, called for a boycott of the buses on 5 December when Parks's case went to trial. E. D. Nixon and other black men in Montgomery met to discuss the situation and they endorsed the idea of a boycott and called for a mass meeting on the night of 5 December as well.

The city buses were virtually empty of black riders on the morning of the boycott. That same afternoon, Nixon and other male leaders created the Montgomery Improvement Association and elected a young minister, Martin Luther King, Jr., as head of the organization. African Americans in Montgomery walked for a year, enduring intimidation, loss of employment, violence, and bombings until the U.S. Supreme Court declared Montgomery's bus segregation laws unconstitutional.

African-American college students became the leaders and innovators during the next phase of the movement. On 1 February 1960, Franklin McCain, David Richmond, Joseph McNeil, and Izell Blair, Jr., four black college students attending North Carolina Agricultural and Technical College in Greensboro, asked to be served at a Woolworth's lunch counter and refused to leave their seats when they were denied service. Their actions sparked sit-ins by black college students, who were sometimes joined by a few white students, all across the South. In mid-April 1960 local *student sit-in leaders met at Shaw University in Raleigh, North Carolina, and, with the assistance of Ella Baker of the Southern Christian Leadership Conference (SCLC), created the Student Nonviolent Coordinating Committee (SNCC) to organize their struggles against segregation.*

SNCC's first efforts to register African-American voters were in McComb, Mississippi, under the direction of Robert Moses, a Harlem school teacher who had attended graduate school at Harvard and who had worked with Ella Baker in the past. Despite intimidation, humiliation, violence, and arrests, SNCC members worked with local activists to establish voting rights projects in other communities in Mississippi where they supported the efforts of African Americans to register to vote. SNCC workers were often arrested for their actions and chose to serve their sentences instead of accepting bail. This was a dangerous choice, for African Americans were routinely beaten and mistreated in southern jails.

In April 1963, Martin Luther King, Jr., was arrested in Birmingham, Alabama. While he was incarcerated, in response to a letter from white clergymen, he composed the most famous statement on the philosophy of nonviolent direct action. They had accused King and the SCLC of promoting violence and argued that civil rights activists were outsiders who should not have come to the city. In his letter from jail, King explained the use of nonviolence and assured the clergymen that they would join African Americans in their protests if they knew how the police had tortured Blacks both in the streets and the jails of Birmingham.

Most African-American organizations involved in the struggle for social and political change from the mid-1950s to the mid-1960s adopted the philosophy of nonviolence and the tactics of nonviolent direct action. The definition of nonviolence and how it should be used differed from individual to individual and from group to group, but most civil rights activists agreed on the goals of their movement. They wanted to destroy segregation and transform the nation. They embraced the spirit of urgency that Martin Luther King, Jr., spoke about at the August 1963 March on Washington: "Now is the time to make real the promises of democracy; now is the time to rise from the dark and desolate valley of segregation to the sunlit path of racial justice; now is the time to lift our nation from the quicksands of racial justice to the solid rock of brotherhood; now is the time to make justice a reality for all God's children."

WAS IT MORE THAN
A CIVIL RIGHTS MOVEMENT?

In his search for the beginning of the civil rights movement, Adam Fairclough discovers a history of struggle against segregation dating back to the 1930s and reveals a long-forgotten period highlighted by the radicalism of the National Association for the Advancement of Colored People (NAACP). Arguing that civil rights activists constructed a radical, new kind of politics, Clayborne Carson shows the relationship between their politics and traditional sources of struggles against discrimination and segregation. He also argues for a new interpretation of the civil rights movement that questions established ideas about Martin Luther King, Jr., SNCC, and the ideological foundation of their strategies for social change. Both Fairclough and Carson are interested in the roots of this social movement and are dissatisfied with traditional analysis of this period.

When Did the Civil Rights Movement Begin?

Emphasizing "the courage and determination with which ordinary blacks challenged the status quo," Adam Fairclough finds activists in Louisiana using tactics in their struggle against segregation years before they would become common strategies used throughout the South in the early 1960s.

Excerpted from *Adam Fairclough,* "The Civil Rights Movement in Louisiana, 1939-54," *in* **The Making of Martin Luther King and the Civil Rights Movement,** *ed. Brian Ward and Tony Badger (Washington Square, New York, 1996), 15-19, 21-22, 26.*

In 1950, in the sweltering heat of a June evening, blacks gathered in a small church in the tiny hamlet of Lebeau, Louisiana, to hear a distinguished guest speaker talk to them about democracy. Alvin Jones held degrees from Columbia University and the University of Pennsylvania; a former schoolteacher, and until recently executive secretary of the New Orleans Urban League, he worked for the Louisiana Progressive Voters League, an off-shoot of the NAACP. A broad-shouldered, distinguished-looking black man in his late forties, Jones reminded the audience that St. Landry Parish, where the tiny hamlet of Lebeau stood, did not have a single black voter. He insisted that now was the time to remedy this situation. The following morning he accompanied five people to the parish court house in Opelousas, which housed the office of the registrar of voters. When they entered the room several policemen assaulted and chased them away. 'I was slugged with the butt of a gun and pounded with a pair of brass knuckles', Jones recounted. 'They left a hole in my head.' Dazed and bloody, he received first aid from a black doctor and then returned to New Orleans. Within eighteen months he was dead.

Although St. Landry Parish lay in the heart of the Acadian triangle, a Catholic area of south Louisiana often regarded as less racially oppressive than the northern, Protestant, half of the state, many blacks regarded it as one of Louisiana's worst. A few months earlier an alleged rapist, Edward Honeycutt, had escaped a lynching party only by diving into the Atchafalaya river. An NAACP lawyer who saw him after his recapture found the surliness of Honeycutt's jailers unnerving: 'I have never in my life experienced a more hostile situation.' Honeycutt's confession had been so obviously beaten out of him that the state supreme court ordered a retrial. (Convicted a second time, Honeycutt went to the electric chair.) A local Catholic priest told black civil rights lawyer A. P. Tureaud that whites in St. Landry Parish were 'immovably opposed' to black voting.

The beating of Alvin Jones, however, gave the NAACP an opportunity that it eagerly seized: here was a dramatic illustration

---

Abridged from "The Civil Rights Movement in Louisiana, 1939–1954" by Adam Fairclough as it appeared in *The Making of Martin Luther King and the Civil Rights Movement*, edited by Dr. Brian Ward and Dr. Tony Badger. Published by New York University Press, 1996. Reprinted by permission of the publisher.

Scenes like this one, where police armed with dogs, clubs, or fire hoses attacked unarmed and nonviolent black protesters, were common during the struggle for civil rights and raised awareness of the racism that permeated American society in the 1950s. (Courtesy of AP/Wide World Photos.)

of southern brutality that could advance the cause of black suffrage by goading the federal government into action. Under pressure from the Association, the Attorney General ordered the FBI to conduct a full investigation. But in a pattern that was becoming wearily familiar to civil rights activists, the 'G-men' drew a blank. The registrar of voters admitted that he *did* remember some kind of commotion in his office, but 'he was busy registering voters at the time and did not notice any of the details of the commotion.' Nothing fazed, blacks in St. Landry Parish pressed on with their quest for the ballot. Forming a local branch of the NAACP, they found three men willing to file suit in federal court against the registrar of voters. A few days after the litigation began, a deputy sheriff shot and killed one of the plaintiffs. The other two plaintiffs fled to the comparative safety of Baton Rouge.

White politicians in St. Landry, however, recognized that if the NAACP backed suit went to trial, the registrar of voters would probably lose. In 1950, in the first ruling of its kind in Louisiana, federal district judge J. Skelly Wright had ordered the registrar of Washington Parish to enrol black applicants; two years later judge Gaston Porterie slapped a similar injunction on the registrar of Bossier Parish, in the northern part of the state. Black determination and NAACP pressure paid off: in 1953, for the first time since the wholesale disfranchisement of the black population in 1898-1904, blacks started to vote in St. Landry Parish. Indeed, black registration soared. It soon exceeded 80 per cent and composed two-fifths of the total electorate. Blacks helped to elect a new sheriff, a new mayor, and a new city council.

To any student of the civil rights movement this is a familiar tale; it could have happened in any one of hundreds of counties throughout the length and breadth of the South. Yet, because this particular story unfolded between 1950 and 1954—before *Brown v. Board of Education*, before the Montgomery bus boycott, before the civil rights movement 'began'—the name of Alvin Jones is absent from the list of martyrs that is inscribed on the Civil Rights Memorial in Montgomery. Nor will Jones's name be encountered in any of the standard histories of the civil rights movement.

When *did* the civil rights movement begin? Precisely when the term 'civil rights movement' became common currency is unclear. Historians commonly use it to describe the wave of black protest that swept the South between 1955 and 1965. Those were the years when black southerners, even in the most oppressive areas of the Deep South, challenged white supremacy head-on. They developed an insurgency so insistent, so broadly based and so morally appealing that they overcame every obstacle that white racists threw at them—legal repression, economic coercion, physical brutality, and murder. The civil rights movement achieved a decisive breakthrough in the long struggle for racial equality. It tore up the fabric of segregation and transformed the South's political landscape. The words 'civil rights movement' carry such specific connotations of time, place and character that they immediately conjure up powerful images: images of sit-ins and freedom rides, of mass meetings and demonstrations; above all, images of Martin Luther King Jr on his heroic journey from Montgomery to Memphis.

Yet, in many parts of the South an organized struggle against white supremacy developed much earlier, and had already made giant strides by the time of the Montgomery bus boycott. In a few short years, for example, St. Landry Parish had undergone a dramatic transformation. So had hundreds of other southern counties.

The breakthroughs came earlier and faster in Louisiana than elsewhere in the South. . . .

These gains did not simply flow from federal court decisions: they also reflected the courage and determination with which ordinary blacks challenged the status quo. Moreover, many acts of opposition utilized direct action tactics. . . .

Baton Rouge, the state capital, witnessed the most striking example of direct action. There, in June 1953, blacks boycotted city buses to protest against segregation laws that compelled them to stand over empty seats that had been reserved for whites. An ad hoc organization, the United Defense League, coordinated the boycott, and a young Baptist minister, Theodore J. Jemison, led it. . . . During the week-long protest, hardly any blacks rode the city buses. 'Operation Free Lift', a car pool made up of about a hundred private vehicles, ferried people to and from work.

The Baton Rouge bus boycott did not gain much national attention; it was too short-lived. Nor did it achieve any great victory: blacks soon accepted a compromise that embodied a more equitable form of segregation. They then made the tactical error of challenging segregation in the state rather than the federal courts, losing the case. Even so, the fact that the boycott happened at all, and that it took place in the heart of the Deep South, was immensely significant. An entire black community had been speedily and effectively mobilized in a protest against segregation.

Such examples of pre-1955 direct action are not, perhaps, all that surprising. Historical epochs do not come in neatly-wrapped chronological parcels; there is always overlapping and fuzziness around the edges. . . .

. . . Nevertheless, the central assertion of this paper is that the 'Montgomery-to-Selma' account of the civil rights movement, which focuses almost exclusively on the period 1955 to 1965, needs to be extended and revised. As Gerald Horne has argued, this narrative has become a historical myth. It is a myth not in the sense of being untrue, but in the sense of providing a simplified version of history that is readily comprehensible, morally edifying and politically acceptable. 'The traditional myth', writes Horne, 'is centred on Martin Luther King, Jr, with Rosa Parks and the Student Non-Violent Coordinating Committee playing pivotal and supporting roles. All of a sudden, in the mid-1950s—during a period, we are told, for some reason otherwise somnolent—Negroes, led by Dr. King and assisted by brilliant attorneys . . . started marching and getting their rights.' This is a caricature, of course, but we can recognize various elaborations of that myth in many, if not most, histories of the civil rights movement. . . .

Here is another advantage of a longer perspective: by examining specific black communities over time the remarkable depth and duration of black protest becomes evident. As historians redirect their gaze from the top leadership of the civil rights movement to the grass roots activists, and away from the few famous confrontations toward the many unheralded struggles, we can see how the work of SNCC, CORE [Congress of Racial Equality] and SCLC in the 1960s depended upon the efforts of 'local people' . . . who had been organizing and struggling for many years. And we can recognize that the civil rights movement began to take shape in the 1930s and 1940s. . . .

The example of Louisiana suggests that one can find, if one only looks, a long and continuous history of black organization and protest in many cities, towns and counties. For many local activists the struggle for civil rights was not merely a year-by-year affair but often a decade-by-decade one. And for many who joined the NAACP it was a lifetime commitment. . . .

The NAACP supplied, in most cases, the core element of continuity in local black activism. Yet, historians have until quite recently both neglected and underestimated that organization. In most histories of the civil rights movement it receives short shrift, virtually disappearing from sight after *Brown* v. *Board of Education* save for an occasional comment disparaging its effectiveness. . . .

Assessments of the NAACP's effectiveness circa 1960, however, must take into account the segregationist counter-attack known as Massive Resistance. In 1956 ultra-segregationists across the South unleashed a campaign to smash the NAACP. This onslaught almost succeeded. . . .

Hence the generation of 1960 encountered the NAACP in an enfeebled state. Moreover, they usually knew little of the history of the civil rights struggle in particular local communities and made little effort to find out. What happened in 1956, let alone 1946, was ancient history. Historians, however, should not be so present-minded. . . . Southern whites tried to destroy the NAACP not because the organization was ineffective, but because its combination of courtroom action, political pressure and popular mobilization was proving all *too* effective. It would be a great irony if Massive Resistance achieved a posthumous triumph by erasing the NAACP's golden age from the history books. . . .

The relationship between the pre-Montgomery and post-Montgomery phases of the civil rights struggle is a complex one. But an awareness of discontinuities, and an appreciation for the distinctive qualities of the Montgomery-to-Selma years, does not lessen the argument for treating the two periods as inextricably linked. Instead of viewing 1940 to 1955 as a mere prelude to something much bigger, we should see it as the first act of a two-act drama.

. . . . In 1940, lynching was still an ever-present threat; by 1955 it had become such a rarity that each incident evoked national condemnation and international opprobrium. In 1940 southern whites were still implacably opposed to black voting; by 1955 the areas of hard-core white resistance were increasingly isolated. I am not arguing, of course, that the voter registration and direct action campaigns of the 1960s were a mere mopping-up operation. I am simply asserting that the registration of one and a quarter million black voters between 1944 and 1956 represent an achievement of equal magnitude and significance.

As King was the first to acknowledge, his leadership was created by, and responded to, the aspirations and activism of ordinary people. By the same token, ordinary people became stronger and more courageous when they found a leader such as King. The Montgomery bus boycott and the emergence of King were critically important in intensifying black protest. But they also represented a further stage in a struggle that went back ten, fifteen, twenty years. And these earlier years were just as critical; they should not be lightly passed over. At stake is more than the remembrance of civil rights martyrs like . . . Alvin Jones; more than the apportioning of credit to this or that organization. At stake is our understanding of what shaped and propelled the most important social movement of twentieth-century America.

Rethinking African-American Politics and Activism

Clayborne Carson argues that King's awareness "of the potential power of non-violent tactics when used by militant, disciplined practitioners in close association with mass movements" marked an important change in black political thought and activism.

Taken from Clayborne Carson, "Rethinking African-American Political Thought in the Post-Revolutionary Era," in The Making of Martin Luther King and the Civil Rights Movement, *ed. Brian Ward and Tony Badger (Washington Square, New York, 1996), 117-22.*

Although the ideas that emerged from the African-American activism of the 1950s and early 1960s are often seen as precursors to the black power and New Left radicalism of the late 1960s, they can best be understood as the outgrowth of efforts by King, by youthful organizers of the SNCC, and other civil rights activists to create radical alternatives to both traditional black nationalism and Marxism. Once Rosa Parks's defiance of southern segregation thrust King into a leadership role, he and other activists began change that departed from mainstream liberalism and from the two main ideological traditions of militant African-American struggle—that is, black nationalism and Marxism.

King's alternative radicalism was constructed, first of all, on the foundation of social gospel Christianity, especially the African-American variant of this tradition to which his father and grandfather had contributed. Reviving this tradition of prophetic dissent, King publicly criticized Cold War liberalism and capitalist materialism while also rejecting communism. Acknowledging in *Stride Toward Freedom: The Montgomery Story* that the works of Karl Marx had reinforced his long-held concern 'about the gulf between superfluous wealth and abject poverty', King charged that capitalist materialism was 'always in danger of inspiring men

Abridged from "Rethinking African-American Political Thought in the Post Revolutionary Era" by Clayborne Carson as it appeared in *The Making of Martin Luther King and the Civil Rights Movement,* edited by Dr. Brian Ward and Dr. Tony Badger. Published by New York University Press, 1996. Reprinted by permission of the publisher.

Shown here being arrested for leading a civil rights demonstration, the Reverend Martin Luther King, Jr. pioneered the use of nonviolent protest for racial justice in America. (Courtesy of Black Star Stock Photo.)

to be more concerned about making a living than making a life.' His version of social gospel Christianity also incorporated socialist ideas as well as anti-colonial sentiments spurred by the African independence movements.

In short, King made an important contribution to what later became known as liberation theology, which has enabled activists around the world to redefine widely held spiritual beliefs that are often used as supports for the status quo. . . . King understood that Christianity could serve either as a basis for African-American accommodation or for resistance. As a privileged insider within the largest African-American denomination, he fought an uphill struggle to transform the black church into an institutional foundation for racial struggles.

King also continued the efforts of Howard Thurman, James Farmer, Benjamin Mays, James Lawson and others to combine social gospel Christianity with Gandhian ideas of non-violent struggle. . . . Under the guidance of more experienced Gandhians, such as Bayard Rustin, Glenn Smiley and Lawson, King came to recognize that Gandhian non-violence represented more than simply a tactical option for oppressed people. He became increasingly aware of the potential power of non-violent tactics when used by militant, disciplined practitioners in close association with mass movements. Moreover, he discerned the importance of the ethos of non-violence as a cohesive force within the black struggle and as a spiritual foundation for what Gandhians called the Beloved Community.

At the beginning of the 1960s, the activists associated with SNCC were more willing than King to explore the radical implications of social gospel Christianity and Gandhism. At the time of SNCC's founding, however, many young black activists were drawn more to Lawson than to King. Having tutored Nashville student activists in Gandhian principles, Lawson encouraged SNCC activists to transform the lunch-counter sit-ins into a 'nonviolent revolution' to destroy 'segregation slavery, serfdom, paternalism', and 'industrialization which preserves cheap labour and racial discrimination.' Although some SNCC activists later abandoned Lawson's idealism in favour of instrumental rather than philosophical rationales for non-violence, those in the group continued to see themselves as involved in a freedom struggle rather than simply in an effort to achieve civil rights reforms. Several of the graduates of Lawson's Nashville workshop—especially Diane Nash, James Bevel and John Lewis—were more tactically audacious than was King, who often backed away from confrontations that lacked federal legal sanction or were likely to result in violence.

Moreover, SNCC workers quickly moved from conventional liberalism toward their own distinctive radicalism, which was more secular and innovative than King's Christian Gandhianism. SNCC field secretaries, especially those working with Bob Moses in Mississippi, resisted ideological conformity and derived their evolving worldview from their experiences as community organizers in the Deep South. SNCC developed a distinctive style of community organizing that self-consciously avoided the creation of new dependent relationships to replace the traditional racial dependencies of southern blacks. SNCC organizers were inspired by the example of Ella Baker, a woman who abhorred the elitism she had encountered as a field secretary of the NAACP and as the executive director of King's hierarchically organized SCLC. Rejecting King's charismatic leadership style, Baker encouraged the development of 'group-centered leaders' rather than leader-centered groups. SNCC's notion of organizing emphasized the development of grassroots leaders. SNCC organizers often stated, and some of them actually believed, that their job was to work themselves out of a job and that organizers should never seek leadership positions for themselves.

SNCC's radicalism was greatly influenced by the example of activists of earlier generations. Although SNCC workers generally avoided Marxian sectarianism, they borrowed tactics and rhetoric from the dedicated Communist Party organizers who had played significant roles in southern black movements of the pre-1960 era. SNCC also borrowed from Miles Horton and Septima Clark at the Highlander Folk School in Tennessee and from the Students for a Democratic Society, although SDS was more influenced by SNCC than vice versa. Finally, during the period after 1963, SNCC borrowed ideas from Malcolm X and the black nationalist tradition, most notably concepts of consciousness-raising and institution-building.

During the first half of the 1960s, King and the college-student organizers in SNCC were, in their different ways, responsible for mobilizations of large masses of black people willing to confront white authority on a scale unequalled during the last half of the decade. These militant mobilizations compelled a reluctant federal government to enact civil rights legislation, and they established a foundation for a fundamental restructuring of African-American participation in the electoral politics of the United States.

Nevertheless, by the mid 1960s, many SNCC activists, recognizing the need to move beyond civil rights reform to address issues of poverty and political powerlessness, adopted the black power slogan. Initially, the slogan represented an extension of SNCC's organizing efforts in the deep South, but after it became popularized by Stokely Carmichael the slogan came to symbolize a sharp break with SNCC's past. Rather than continuing to develop the radicalism of the early 1960s, many black power advocates abandoned the radical perspectives that grew out of the civil rights movement in favour of racial separatist ideologies. Veterans of SNCC's earlier organizing efforts, such as Carmichael, were embittered by their experiences and abandoned interracialism and non-violence as guiding principles. As the black power proponents pursued the mirage of a successful black nationalist revolution, they also abandoned many of the valuable insights that SNCC had acquired during its years of growth.

The key individual in this transformation of African-American political thought was Malcolm X. Malcolm's ideological contribution to the black power era would consist largely of his bitter critique of the non-violent civil rights movement; yet ironically, at the time of his assassination in February 1965, he was seeking to forge ties with King and SNCC organizers. While a member of Elijah Muhammad's Nation of Islam, Malcolm had supported his group's policy of non-engagement, which prevented members from joining in any protest activity. Even as he fiercely attacked King's strategy of non-violent resistance, however, Malcolm increasingly recognized that the Nation [of Islam] offered no real alternative to black people facing vicious white racists in the South. Unlike many of his posthumous followers, Malcolm realized that the militant racial rhetoric of his years in the Nation of Islam obscured the group's accommodationism. Indeed, he knew that the Nation of Islam was not above making deals with white people when it served the leaders' interests. Malcolm later admitted that in 1961, even while he criticized civil rights activists for working with white liberals, his own organization sent him to Atlanta to negotiate a mutual non-interference agreement with the Ku Klux Klan. . . .

After his break with the Nation of Islam, Malcolm publicly acknowledged the radical potential of what he called the grassroots forces of the civil rights movement. Rather than attempting to supplant the radical ideas that were emerging from the grassroots, Malcolm saw the need for a convergence of those ideas and his own version of revolutionary nationalism. . . . In March 1964, after leaving the Nation of Islam and establishing his own Organization of Afro-American Unity (OAAU), he immediately began reaching out to civil rights leaders he had once harshly criticized. . . .

Soon afterwards, in his 'Ballot or the Bullet' speech delivered in April 1964, Malcolm sought to erase the ideological boundaries that had previously separated him from the civil rights organizations: 'The political philosophy of black nationalism is being taught in the Christian church . . . in the NAACP . . . in CORE meetings . . . in SNCC . . . It's being taught everywhere'. Malcolm broadened his own political perspective as a result of his tour of several African nations, including Nigeria and Ghana, following the *Hajj* to Mecca. . . .

Returning to the United States, Malcolm established increasingly close links with the southern black struggle. In December

1964 he invited Fannie Lou Hamer and the SNCC Freedom Singers to be guests of honour at an OAAU meeting in Harlem. He also hosted a delegation of 37 teenage activists from the McComb Mississippi movement. On 1 February 1965, he sent a telegram to the head of the American Nazi Party, warning, 'I am no longer held in check from fighting white supremacists by Elijah Muhammad's separatist Black Muslim movement, and if your present racist agitation of our people there in Alabama causes physical harm to Reverend King or any other Black Americans . . . you and your KKK friends will be met with maximum physical retaliation. . . .' Malcolm also sought to make amends for his previous harsh personal criticisms of Martin Luther King Jr. A few weeks before his assassination, while in Selma, Alabama, to lend support to the ongoing voting rights struggle, he met Coretta Scott King and made clear that he did not want to make her husband's job more difficult, explaining that, if whites knew that Malcolm was the alternative, 'it might be easier for them to accept Martin's proposals.'

Despite Malcolm's effort to achieve an alliance of black nationalism and the civil rights movement, black power militancy after Malcolm's death was often characterized by hostility toward any black leader who advocated non-violent tactics and racial integration. Malcolm's call for liberation 'by any means necessary' became a rationale for the abandonment of militant Gandhian tactics, despite the fact that Malcolm himself came to realize the necessity of non-violent tactics as part of any sustained mass struggle. Serious ideological conflicts within the African-American political community undermined the unity Malcolm was attempting to achieve. This disunity culminated in violent clashes between militant blacks, such as the one that took place in January 1969, at UCLA, when members of Maulana Karenga's US group shot and killed two Black Panthers in the campus dining-hall. By the end of the 1960s, the rhetorical violence of many self proclaimed black revolutionaries had been transformed into self-destructive violence that ravaged the fabric of black communities. Initially the Panthers advised blacks to 'pick up the gun', but the drug dealers of the 1970s were far better armed and more ruthless than were the black revolutionaries of the 1960s. . . .

Ultimately, the black power movement of the last half of the 1960s promised more than the civil rights movement but delivered less. Black Power militants talked of power yet exercised only transitory power within black communities and none outside those communities. They proclaimed that they acted on behalf of African Americans whose needs had been ignored by the civil rights leaders, but black power militancy did not prevent a rapid deterioration in the economic status of the black masses during more than two decades since the late 1960s. Black power militants talked of revolution but the veterans of the black power movement have generally found ways of accommodating to the existing white-dominated social order. After Malcolm's assassination in 1965, the black power movement adopted many of his ideas, but the lasting contributions of the black power period were more significant in the intellectual and cultural rather than the political arena. Black power militancy survives not as insurgencies but as unthreatening expressions of Afrocentrism.

While failing to produce greater power for black people, black power militancy actually led to a decline in the ability of African-Americans to affect the course of American politics. The emergence of Stokley [Stokely] Carmichael and H. Rap Brown as nationally known black advocates of black power prompted more effective repression once J. Edgar Hoover's FBI recognized that the black struggle could be crippled through the elimination of a few leaders. Moreover, the rhetorical violence and racism of some black militants spurred the increasing popularity among whites of 'law and order' politics. Brown, in fact, helped to create the conditions that made it possible for Spiro Agnew to transform himself from a minor Maryland politician to Vice-President within little more than a year. In the larger context of American politics, the black power controversy encouraged a conservative political trend which has led to a Republican ascendancy in national electoral politics.

Questions

1. *What are the reasons that Adam Fairclough gave for reconsidering the beginning of the civil rights movement? Would Clayborne Carson agree with him?*
2. *Is it possible to combine Fairclough's and Carson's analyses to create a new narrative of the civil rights movement or are their ideas too dissimilar?*
3. *How does Carson's view of Martin Luther King, Jr., differ from popular views of King that are presented during the King holiday?*
4. *What are the major differences between the philosophical approaches of Martin Luther King, Jr., and Malcolm X?*

The Strategies of Nonviolence and the Dangers of Activism

These documents offer different views of nonviolence, activism, and resistance by African Americans. Some of these people, such as Rosa Parks, Malcolm X, and King, are familiar while others, such as Ella Baker, James Forman, or A. Philip Randolph, are not. These selections are a small example of the creativity and innovation that activists employed in their efforts to transform the United States into a nation where all citizens could enjoy justice, equality, and freedom.

A. Philip Randolph Calls for a March on Washington, 1941

A. Philip Randolph was the head of the Brotherhood of Sleeping Car Porters, a predominantly African-American labor union, an early civil rights activist, and publisher of **The Black Worker,** *a labor magazine. In this excerpt from his May 1941 call for a march on Washington, Randolph wanted "mass action that is orderly and lawful, but aggressive and militant, for justice, equality and freedom."*

Taken from "To March On Washington for Jobs and Equal Participation in National Defense," **The Black Worker,** *May 1941, p. 4.*

Greetings:

We call upon you to fight for jobs in National Defense.

We call upon you to struggle for the integration of Negroes in the armed forces, such as the Air Corps, Navy, Army and Marine Corps of the Nation.

We call upon you to demonstrate for the abolition of Jim-Crowism in all Government departments and defense employment.

This is an hour of crisis. It is a crisis of democracy. It is a crisis of minority groups. It is a crisis of Negro Americans.

What is this crisis?

To American Negroes, it is the denial of jobs in Government defense projects. It is racial discrimination in Government departments. It is widespread Jim-Crowism in the armed forces of the nation. . . .

What shall we do? . . .

With faith and confidence of the Negro people in their own power for self-liberation, Negroes can break down the barriers of discrimination against employment in National Defense. . . .

Most important and vital to all, Negroes, by the mobilization and coordination of their mass power, can cause PRESIDENT ROOSEVELT TO ISSUE AN EXECUTIVE ORDER ABOLISHING DISCRIMINATIONS IN ALL GOVERNMENT DEPARTMENTS, ARMY, NAVY, AIR CORPS AND NATIONAL DEFENSE JOBS. . . .

In this period of power politics, nothing counts but pressure, more pressure, and still more pressure, through the tactic and strategy of broad, organized, aggressive mass action behind the vital and important issues of the Negro. To this end, we propose that ten thousand Negroes MARCH ON WASHINGTON FOR JOBS IN NATIONAL DEFENSE AND EQUAL INTEGRATION IN THE FIGHTING FORCES OF THE UNITED STATES.

An "all-out" thundering march on Washington, ending in a monster and huge demonstration at Lincoln's Monument will shake up white America.

It will shake up official Washington.

It will give encouragement to our white friends to fight all the harder by our side, with us, for our righteous cause.

It will gain respect for the Negro people.

It will create a new sense of self-respect among Negroes. . . .

We summon you to mass action that is orderly and lawful, but aggressive and militant, for justice, equality and freedom.

From "To March on Washington for Jobs and Equal Participation in National Defense" by A. Philip Randolph as it appeared in *The Black Worker*, p. 4, May 1941.

Rosa L. Parks is Arrested in Montgomery, Alabama on 1 December 1955

In a 1977 interview Rosa Parks remembers that she told the city bus driver to "go on and have me arrested" for not giving up her seat to a white man who boarded the bus after her. In this selection, she discusses the events that ignited a community-wide protest.

Taken from Howell Raines, My Soul Is Rested: Movement Days in the Deep South Remembered *(New York, 1977), 40-42.*

As I got up on the bus and walked to the seat I saw there was only one vacancy that was just back of where it was considered the white section. So this was the seat I that I took, next to the aisle, and a man was sitting next to me. . . . The third stop is when all the front seats were taken, and this one man was standing and when the driver looked around and saw he was standing, he asked the four of us, the man in the seat with me and the two women across the aisle, to let him have those front seats.

At his first request, didn't any of us move. Then he spoke again and said, "You'd better make it light on yourselves and let me have those seats." At this point, of course, the passenger who would have taken the seat hadn't said anything. In fact, he never did speak to my knowledge. When the three people, the man who was in the seat with me and the two women, stood up and moved into the aisle, I remained where I was. When the driver saw that I was still sitting there, he asked if I was going to stand up. I told him no, I wasn't. He said, "Well, if you don't stand up, I'm going to have you arrested." I told him to go on and have me arrested.

He got off the bus and came back shortly. A few minutes later, two policemen got on the bus, and they approached me and asked if the driver had asked me to stand up, and I said yes, and they wanted to know why I didn't. I told them I didn't think I should have to stand up. After I had paid my fare and occupied a seat, I didn't think I should have to give it up. They placed me under arrest then and had me to get in the police car, and I was taken to jail and booked on suspicion, I believe. The questions were asked,

Rosa Parks' courageous challenge to segregated busing in Montgomery ignited a community-wide protest and proved to be one of the first major successes of the civil rights movement. (Courtesy of Bettmann/Corbis.)

the usual questions they ask a prisoner or somebody that's under arrest. They had to determine whether or not the driver wanted to press charges or swear out a warrant, which he did. Then they took me to jail and I was placed in a cell. In a little while I was taken from the cell, and my picture was made and fingerprints taken. I went back to the cell then, and a few minutes later I was called back again, and when this happened I found out that Mr. E.D. Nixon and Attorney and Mrs. Clifford Durr had come to make bond for me.

In the meantime before this, of course . . . I was given permission to make a telephone call after my picture was taken and fingerprints taken. I called my home and spoke to my mother on the telephone and told her what had happened, that I was in jail. She was quite upset and asked me had the police beaten me. I told her, no, I hadn't been physically injured, but I was being held in jail, and I wanted my husband to come and get me out. . . . He didn't have a car at that time, so he had to get someone to bring him down. At the time when he got down, Mr. Nixon and the Durrs had just made bond for me, so we all met at the jail and we went home.

Student Nonviolent Coordinating Committee Statement of Purpose

The Reverend James Lawson was a divinity student who was expelled from Vanderbilt University after sit-ins in the spring of 1960. Later that year he would be influential in the founding of the Student Nonviolent Coordinating Committee. In May 1960, he drafted the statement of purpose for the new organization that appeared in the first issue of the newspaper the students created, **The Student Voice 1** *(June 1960): 1.*

Statement of Purpose

"Carrying out the mandate of the Raleigh Conference to write a statement of purpose for the movement, the Temporary Student Nonviolent Coordinating Committee submits for careful consideration the following draft. We urge all local state or regional groups to examine it closely. Each member of our movement must work diligently to understand the depths of nonviolence.

We affirm the philosophical or religious ideal of nonviolence as the foundation of our purpose, the pre-supposition of our faith, and the manner of our action. Nonviolence as it grows from Judaic-Christian tradition seeks a social order of justice permeated by love. Integration of human endeavor represents the crucial first step towards such a society.

Through nonviolence, courage displaces fear; love transforms hate. Acceptance dissipates prejudice; hope ends despair. Peace dominates war; faith reconciles doubt. Mutual regards cancel enmity. Justice for all overthrows injustice. The redemptive community supercedes [supersedes] systems of gross social immorality.

Love is the central motif of nonviolence. Love is the force by which God binds man to himself and man to man. Such love goes to the extreme; it remains loving and forgiving even in the midst of hostility. It matches the capacity of evil to inflict suffering with an even more enduring capacity to absorb evil, all the while persisting in love.

From "Statement of Purpose" by Rev. James Lawson as it appeared in *The Student Voice*, June 1960.

By appealing to conscience and standing on the moral nature of human existence, nonviolence nurtures the atmosphere in which reconciliation and justice become actual possibilities."

Prepared by-Rev. J.M. Lawson, Jr. Saturday, May 14, 1960

Bigger Than A Hamburger

Ella Baker, executive director of the Southern Christian Leadership Conference, organized the student conference in Raleigh, North Carolina, from which SNCC emerged. She encouraged the student leaders attending the Raleigh conference to create their own organization where they would be free to work "to rid America of the scourge of racial segregation and discrimination—not only at lunch counters, but in every aspect of life."

Baker's ideas about leadership and community organizing were adopted by SNCC and they are presented in Ella J. Baker, "Bigger Than A Hamburger," Southern Patriot (June 1960): 1.

Raleigh, N.C.—The Student Leadership Conference made it crystal clear that current sit-ins and other demonstrations are concerned with something bigger than a hamburger or even a giant-sized Coke.

Whatever may be the difference in approach to their goal, the Negro and white students, North and South, are seeking to rid America of the scourge of racial segregation and discrimination—not only at lunch counters, but in every aspect of life.

In reports, casual conversations, discussion groups, and speeches, the sense and spirit of the following statement that appeared in the initial newsletter of the students at Barer-Scotia College, concord, N.C., were re-echoed time and again:

We want the world to know that we no longer accept the inferior position of second-class citizenship. We are willing to go to jail, be ridiculed, spat upon and even suffer physical violence to obtain First Class Citizenship.

By and large, this feeling that they have a destined date with

---

From "Bigger Than A Hamburger" by Ella J. Baker as it appeared in *The Southern Patriot*, June 1960.

freedom, was not limited to a drive for personal freedom for the Negro in the South. Repeatedly it was emphasized that the movement was concerned with the moral implications of racial discrimination for the "whole world" and the "Human Race."

"This universality of approach was linked with a perceptive recognition that "it is important to keep the movement democratic and to avoid struggles for personal leadership."

It was further evident that desire for supportive cooperation from adult leaders and the adult community was also tempered by apprehension that adults might try to "capture" the student movement. The students showed willingness to be met on the basis of equality, but were intolerant of anything that smacked of manipulation or domination.

This inclination toward group-centered leadership, rather than toward a leader-centered group pattern of organization, was refreshing indeed to those of the older group who bear the scars of the battle, the frustrations and the disillusionment that come when the prophetic leader turns out to have heavy feet of clay.

However hopeful might be the signs in the direction of group-centeredness, the fact that many schools and communities, especially in the South, have not provided adequate experience for young Negroes to assume the initiative and think and act independently accentuated the need for guarding the student movement against well-meaning, but nevertheless unhealthy, overprotectiveness.

Here is an opportunity for adult and youth to work together and provide genuine leadership—the development of the individual to his highest potential for the benefit of the group. . . .

In Jail in Greenwood, Mississippi

James Forman provides the following glimpse of life for SNCC activists in the Greenwood, Mississippi jail in his book The Making of Black Revolutionaries: A Personal Account *(New York, 1972), 299-301.*

April 2, 1963: We have been in jail one week today. Our morale is good, although there are serious undertones of a desire to be free among some members of the group. . . .

The cell in which we are being held is not so bad so far as American prisons go. (The entire penal system needs reforming.) We are eight in a cell with six bunks. We have two mattresses on the floor. There is an open shower, a sink, a stool. It took us two days to get a broom and five days to get some salt for our food. The inner cell in which we are "contained" is approximately 15' x 12'. Not much room is there? . . .

We are also improving our minds. We have been allowed to keep our books and we have sufficient cigarettes. I even have my pipe and some tobacco. Personally, I have tried to organize our lives. Do you expect anything else of me? We have occasional classes. Moses gave us an excellent math lecture the other day. I gave one lesson in writing and English. Guyot has delivered several in biology. We are always having discussions. Sometimes one of us will read a passage from a book and then we will discuss the meaning of it. We have had several stimulating conversations on Thoreau's essay on Civil Disobedience and Nkrumah's thoughts on Positive Action. . . .

My personal opinion as to the significance of our staying in jail follows: I am convinced that all the people connected with SNCC are busily engaged in protesting our unjust imprisonment. This is as it should be. I am also convinced that others sympathetic to the cause of Freedom are also alarmed at this travesty of justice. Only our bodies are confined to this cell. Our minds are free to think what we wish and we know our stay here will also pass away. Our imprisonment serves to dramatize to the nation and to the world that the black man does not even have the right to *try* to be an American citizen in some parts of our so-called democracy. Our jail-without-bail may also serve to remind others in the movement of the need for some of us to stay in jail to dramatize the situation.

On a local and state level it is important that we stay in jail, for people are remembered more by what they do than by what they say. We have been telling Mississippians that we must prepare to die. We have encouraged them to accept our beliefs. Thus it follows that we must lead by example rather than by words.

Letter from the Birmingham City Jail

King presents his ideas on the use of nonviolence and reminds the white clergymen that he is in Birmingham because "injustice anywhere is a threat to justice everywhere." This version of his famous letter is in Martin Luther King, Jr., *"Letter from Birmingham Jail," in* Why We Can't Wait *(New York, 1963), 77-83, 98-100.*

April 16, 1963

My Dear Fellow Clergymen:

While confined here in the Birmingham city jail, I came across your recent statement calling my present activities "unwise and untimely." Seldom do I pause to answer criticism of my work and ideas. If I sought to answer all the criticisms that cross my desk, my secretaries would have little time for anything other than such correspondence in the course of the day, and I would have no time for constructive work. But since I feel that you are men of genuine good will and that your criticisms are sincerely set forth, I want to try to answer your statement in what I hope will be patient and reasonable terms.

I think I should indicate why I am here in Birmingham, since you have been influenced by the view which argues against "outsiders coming in." . . . Several months ago the [local SCLC] affiliate here in Birmingham asked us to be on call to engage in a nonviolent direct-action program if such were deemed necessary. We readily consented, and when the hour came we lived up to our promise. So I, along with several members of my staff, am here because I was invited here. I am here because I have organizational ties here.

But more basically, I am in Birmingham because injustice is here. . . .

Moreover, I am cognizant of the interrelatedness of all communities and states. I cannot sit idly by in Atlanta and not be concerned about what happens in Birmingham. Injustice any-where is a threat to justice everywhere. We are caught in an inescapable network of mutuality, tied in a single garment of destiny. Whatever affects one directly, affects all indirectly. Never again can we afford to live with the narrow, provincial "outside agitator" idea. Anyone who lives inside the United States can never be considered an outsider anywhere within its bounds.

You deplore the demonstrations taking place in Birmingham. But your statement, I am sorry to say, fails to express a similar concern for the conditions that brought about the demonstrations. . . .

In any nonviolent campaign there are four basic steps: collec-tion of the facts to determine whether injustices exist; negotiation; self-purification; and direct action. We have gone through all these steps in Birmingham. There can be no gainsaying the fact that racial injustice engulfs this community. Birmingham is prob-ably the most thoroughly segregated city in the United States. Its ugly record of brutality is widely known. Negroes have experi-enced grossly unjust treatment in the courts. There have been more unsolved bombings of Negro homes and churches in Bir-mingham than in any other city in the nation. These are the hard, brutal facts of the case. On the basis of these conditions, Negro leaders sought to negotiate with the city fathers. But the latter consistently refused to engage in good-faith negotiation. . . .

You may well ask: "Why direct action? Why sit-ins, marches and so forth? Isn't negotiation a better path?" You are quite right in calling for negotiation. Indeed, this is the very purpose of direct action. Nonviolent direct action seeks to create such a crisis and foster such a tension that a community which has constantly refused to negotiate is forced to confront the issue. It seeks so to dramatize the issue that it can no longer be ignored. . . .

. . . My friends, I must say to you that we have not made a single gain in civil rights without determined legal and nonvio-lent pressure. Lamentably, it is an historical fact that privileged groups seldom give up their privileges voluntarily. . . .

We know through painful experience that freedom is never voluntarily given by the oppressor; it must be demanded by the oppressed. Frankly, I have yet to engage in a direct-action cam-paign that was "well timed" in the view of those who have not suffered unduly from the disease of segregation. For years now I have heard the word "Wait!" It rings in the ear of every Negro with piercing familiarity. This "Wait" has almost always meant "Never." We must come to see, with one of our distinguished jurists, that "justice too long delayed is justice denied." . . .

Before closing, I feel impelled to mention one other point in your statement that has troubled me profoundly. You warmly commended the Birmingham police force for keeping "order" and "preventing violence." I doubt that you would have so warmly commended the police force if you had seen its dogs sinking their teeth into unarmed, nonviolent Negroes. I doubt that you would so quickly commend the policemen if you were to observe their ugly and inhumane treatment of Negroes here in the city jail; if you were to watch them push and curse old Negro women and young Negro girls; if you were to see them slap and kick old Negro men and young boys; if you were to observe them, as they did on two occasions, refuse to give us food because we wanted to sing our grace together. I cannot join you in your praise of the Birmingham police department. . . .

I wish you had commended the Negro sit-inners and demonstrators of Birmingham for their sublime courage, their willingness to suffer and their amazing discipline in the midst of great provocation. One day the South will recognize its real heroes. They will be the James Merediths, with the noble sense of purpose that enables them to face jeering and hostile mobs, and with the agonizing loneliness that characterizes the life of the pioneer. They will be old, oppressed, battered Negro women, symbolized in a seventy-two-year-old woman in Montgomery, Alabama, who rose up with a sense of dignity and with her people decided not to ride segregated buses, and who responded with ungrammatical profundity to one who inquired about her weariness: "My feets is tired, but my soul is at rest." They will be the young high school and college students, the young ministers of the gospel and a host of their elders, courageously and nonviolently sitting in at lunch counters and willingly going to jail for conscience' sake. One day the South will know that when these disinherited children of God sat down at lunch counters, they were in reality standing up for what is best in the American dream and for the most sacred values in our Judaeo-Christian heritage, thereby bringing our nation back to those great wells of democracy which were dug deep by the founding fathers in their formulation of the Constitution and the Declaration of Independence. . . .

. . . Let us all hope that the dark clouds of racial prejudice will soon pass away and the deep fog of misunderstanding will be lifted from our fear-drenched communities, and in some not too distant tomorrow the radiant stars of love and brotherhood will shine over our great nation with all their scintillating beauty.

Yours for the cause of Peace and Brotherhood,
MARTIN LUTHER KING, JR.

To Mississippi Youth from Malcolm X

Malcolm X, originally Malcolm Little, took the surname X to represent the lost identity of African slaves. Malcolm became the main spokesman for the Nation of Islam during the 1950s. While in the Nation of Islam, he emphasized racial separatism and black self-reliance and was described by some as militant and extremist. He became disillusioned with and left the Nation of Islam in March 1964 and subsequently founded the Organization of Afro-American Unity (OAAU). From his break with the Nation of Islam in 1964 until his assassination in February 1965, he distanced himself from racial separatism and sought solidarity with the civil rights movement. In this excerpt from a speech on 31 December 1964, Malcolm presents his views on nonviolence and the movement in Mississippi.

Excerpted from Malcolm X, "To Mississippi Youth," in George Breitman, ed., Malcolm X Speaks: Selected Speeches and Statements *(New York, 1965), 138, 142-44.*

My experience has been that in many instances where you find Negroes talking about nonviolence, they are not nonviolent with each other, and they're not loving with each other, or forgiving with each other. Usually when they say they're nonviolent, they mean they're nonviolent with somebody else. I think you understand what I mean. They are nonviolent with the enemy. A person can come to your home, and if he's white and wants to heap some kind of brutality on you, you're nonviolent. . . . But if another Negro just stomps his foot, you'll rumble with him in a minute. Which shows you that there's an inconsistency there.

Condemned by many as a racist and extremist, Malcolm X, provided an important alternative to Martin Luther King's nonviolent tactics. (Courtesy of Bettmann/Corbis.)

I myself would go for nonviolence if it was consistent, if everybody was going to be nonviolent all the time. I'd say, okay, let's get with it, we'll all be nonviolent. But I don't go along with any kind of nonviolence unless everybody's going to be nonviolent. If they make the Ku Klux Klan nonviolent, I'll be nonviolent. If they make the White Citizens Council nonviolent, I'll be nonviolent. But as long as you've got somebody else not being nonviolent, I don't want anybody coming to me talking any nonviolent talk. . . .

In studying the process of this so-called [racial] progress during the past twenty years, we of the Organization of Afro-American Unity realized that the only time the black man in this country is given any kind of recognition, or even listened to, is when America is afraid of outside pressure, or when she's afraid of her image abroad. . . .

And today you'll find in the United Nations, and it's not an accident, that every time the Congo question or anything on the African continent is being debated, they couple it with what is going on, or what is happening to you and me, in Mississippi and Alabama and these other places. In my opinion, the greatest accomplishment that was made in the struggle of the black man in America in 1964 toward some kind of real progress was the successful linking together of our problem with the African problem, or making our problem a world problem. . . .

So we here in the Organization of Afro-American Unity are with the struggle in Mississippi one thousand per cent. We're with the efforts to register our people in Mississippi to vote one thousand per cent. But we do not go along with anybody telling us to help nonviolently. We think that if the government says that Negroes have a right to vote, and then some Negroes come out to vote, and some kind of Ku Klux Klan is going to put them in the river, and the government doesn't do anything about it, it's time for us to organize and band together and equip ourselves and qualify ourselves to protect ourselves. And once you can protect yourself, you don't have to worry about being hurt. . . .

If you don't have enough people down there to do it, we'll come down there and help you do it. Because we're tired of this old runaround that our people have been given in this country. For a long time they accused me of not getting involved in politics. They should've been glad I didn't get involved in politics, because anything I get in, I'm in it all the way. If they say we don't take part in the Mississippi struggle, we will organize brothers here in New York who know how to handle these kind of affairs, and they'll slip into Mississippi like Jesus slipped into Jerusalem.

Questions

1. *How did these people and organizations use nonviolent direct action? Do they have similar ideas about nonviolence?*
2. *What are some of the dangers that activists in the movement faced?*
3. *Did King and his allies, members of SNCC, and Malcolm X understand each others' views on nonviolence and activism? Was there any common ground between them?*
4. *Do these documents suggest that some people were more idealistic in the 1950s and 1960s? Why or why not?*
5. *Do you think that you could have been an activist like any of these people? What factors would encourage or inhibit you?*

Further Reading

Race & Democracy: The Civil Rights Struggle in Louisiana, 1915-1972 by Adam Fairclough (Athens, 1995) demonstrates that civil rights struggles began with the twentieth century. Two studies that analyze the indigenous roots of the movement and emphasize the roles of local leaders are Charles M. Payne, *I've Got the Light of Freedom: The Organizing Tradition and the Mississippi Freedom Struggle* (Berkeley, 1995); and John Dittmer, *Local People: The Struggle for Civil Rights in Mississippi* (Urbana, 1994). The best history of SNCC is still Clayborne Carson, *In Struggle: SNCC and the Black Awakening of the 1960s* (Cambridge, 1995); and there is a collection of fascinating interviews with organizers in *A Circle of Trust: Remembering SNCC*, ed. Cheryl Lynn Greenberg (New Brunswick, 1998). *But for Birmingham: The Local and National Movements in the Civil Rights Struggle* by Glenn T. Eskew (Chapel Hill, 1997) examines one of the most important civil rights campaigns of the 1960s. Belinda Robnett's *How Long? How Long? African-American Women in the Struggle for Civil Rights* (New York, 1997) is a long-awaited study of women's activism that provides a theoretical framework for exploring their unique roles in the movement. Biographies have provided some of the best scholarship on the movement, and the second volume of Taylor Branch's biography of King, *Pillar of Fire: America in the King Years, 1963-65* (New York, 1998), is now available. The life of a significant, but overlooked, woman who was responsible for running SNCC is eloquently presented in Cynthia Griggs Fleming, *Soon We Will Not Cry: The Liberation of Ruby Doris Smith Robinson* (Lanham, Maryland, 1998). A thoughtful comparison of the ideas of King and Malcolm X can be found in James H. Cone, *Martin & Malcolm & America: A Dream or a Nightmare* (Maryknoll, New York, 1992).

Dissent in the 1960s: Definitions and Context

Steven Conn

INTRODUCTION

Sex, drugs, and rock 'n roll.

For many people this has become the easiest way to summarize the tumultuous decade of the 1960s. Perhaps the most enduring images of those times remain hippies, flower children, rock music festivals, and be-ins. Needless to say this assessment of the decade as one dominated by dope-smoking hippies vastly oversimplifies. It obscures much about the nature of the dissent that took place during the 1960s. The easiest way to understand the nature of that dissent, and its role in shaping the 1960s, is to recognize and delineate three broad streams of youth and student activity that converged during the decade.

The first of these streams found its source in the American South and in the struggle for civil rights. Initially this movement based itself in black churches and other community institutions. Throughout the 1950s, the Southern Christian Leadership Conference (SCLC) had been the organizational heart of the civil rights movement. By the early 1960s, however, younger activists were challenging their elders for leadership of the movement. In February 1960, black college students led dramatic sit-ins at the segregated Woolworth's lunch counter in Greensboro, North Carolina. Later that year, the formation of the Student Non-Violent Coordinating Committee (SNCC) boldly announced the arrival of a new generation of civil rights activists.

By the second half of the decade, that younger generation had grown impatient with the slow progress of the civil rights movement and angry with the violent white backlash. A militant wing *of the black youth movement split from the older generation, following the banner of "Black Power." Under that banner, younger black activists experimented with increasingly militant and separatist politics, embodied most famously in the Black Panther Party, and with a variety of cultural expressions exploring ideas of black pride.*

The second stream originated in Port Huron, Michigan. There, roughly fifty college students from Ivy League and Big Ten universities gathered to form Students for a Democratic Society (SDS) in 1962. Their founding document, the **Port Huron Statement**, *offered an impassioned critique of an American society grown comfortably complacent. For these students, the nation they now inherited gorged itself on consumerism, and while it starved spiritually, it remained politically indifferent despite the ever-present threat of nuclear annihilation, and it trumpeted pompous patriotism even while black Americans fought their second-class status. SDS called on students to lead a reinvigoration of American politics through the mechanism of "participatory democracy." Hundreds of SDS chapters organized on campuses from coast to coast and these formed the backbone of what became known as the "New Left."*

The third stream formed in this context. The counter culture made its unofficial national debut in the summer of 1967 in San Francisco. In that summer, thousands of young people flocked to the Bay area to participate in the "Summer of Love." The summer began with the Monterey Pop Festival in June, which proved to be the first large-scale counter-cultural musical event. Throughout the late 1960s, large music festivals became unofficial conventions for counter-cultural rebels. The musical event that seemed to demonstrate most dramatically the promise of the counter culture took place near Woodstock, New York, in August 1969. For the most enthusiastic participants in the counter culture, Woodstock stood as a gentle alternative to the rest of American society. Some participants called themselves "Woodstock Nation."

The legacy of the counter culture is complicated and is still unfolding. For many involved, the counter culture really meant nothing more than sex, drugs, and rock. At the same time, such glib dismissals do not do justice to the sincerity and creativity with which some experimented with different ways of living and the depth to which they explored the connection between the personal and the political. The varieties of personal expression that college students today take for granted have their origins in the explorations of the counter culture. The counter culture did, for better or worse, alter the American social landscape.

To separate dissent in the 1960s into these three categories reflects, at some level, a convenience for historians. Surely these three broad groups involved different people, dealt with different issues, and employed different methods to achieve their goals. But it is also important to recognize that they overlapped in significant ways as well. There were certainly black hippies and those who believed in communal living and political engagement. The job for the historian is to analyze both the differences and the similarities.

THE LASTING IMPACT OF THE 1960S

Historians are only now beginning to evaluate the meaning of the dissent of the 1960s. Some of this history, in the form of personal memoirs, comes from those who participated; some comes from those who either opposed this activity at the time or who have repudiated it subsequently.

While there is an easy consensus that the radicals of the 1960s did not achieve their goals, and that they did not live up to the promises of their often super-heated rhetoric, it is also clear that the varieties of political and cultural dissent did transform American society. Exactly how remains the subject of this debate.

On one side are those who believe that the political experiments of the 1960s opened up American society fundamentally and irreversibly. These historians note that students and youth in the 1960s filled a political void left by the chilling somnolence of the McCarthyite 1950s and created space for democratic participation that had not been there before. They point to the flourishing of all kinds of grassroots move-ments—from feminism to environmentalism—in the 1970s as evidence that the terms of participation in politics and society had been profoundly changed.

On the other side, some historians believe that the demonstrations, marches, sit-ins, and later, violence, had little impact. Indeed, these historians argue, our exaggerated attention to those in the streets has hidden from view the development of a larger, deeper, and more signifi-cant conservative backlash. Hippies may have flocked to Woodstock in 1969, but Richard Nixon was in the White House. It is, finally, the legacy of conservatism that has proved more important in the last quarter of the twentieth century.

Another issue with which historians wrestle is how to consider the relationship between culture and politics. In many ways this question lies at the bottom of all the movements of dissent in the 1960s. Many of those who participated in these movements wanted both political and cultural change. In linking the two, they changed the way in which we see both. In this essay, historians Maurice Isserman and Michael Kazin attempt to evaluate both the failure and success of what they call "the new radicalism" to achieve both cultural and political goals. Excerpted from Maurice Isserman and Michael Kazin, "The Failure and Success of the New Radicalism," in The Rise and Fall of the New Deal Order, 1930-1980, *ed. Steve Fraser and Gary Gerstle (Princeton, New Jersey, 1989), 212-18, 220-27, 229, 235-37.*

Though the origins of the New Left can be traced back at least to the mid-1950s, radicalism only began to reemerge as a significant undercurrent on American campuses in 1960 when a heretofore obscure group called the Student League for Industrial Democracy (SLID) renamed itself Students for a Democratic Society (SDS). Under the leadership of two recent University of Michigan graduates, Al Haber and Tom Hayden, SDS became a small but increasingly influential network of campus activists. At its official founding convention, held in Port Huron, Michigan, in 1962, SDS adopted a manifesto declaring that the ideas and organizational forms familiar to earlier generations of Marxian radicals were outmoded. The "Port Huron Statement" dedicated SDS to the achievement of "participatory democracy" inside its own movement and within the larger society. Initially engaged on a wide variety of fronts, from civil rights to nuclear disarmament to university reform, by the mid-1960s, many SDS founders had left the campuses to concentrate on community organizing in the slums of northern cities. Ironically, just as SDS leaders began to forsake the campus, the Berkeley Free Speech Movement in the fall of 1964 and the Vietnam teach-in movement in the spring of 1965 signaled the growing responsiveness of college students to radical ideas.

The steady escalation of the war in Vietnam from the spring of 1965 up to the spring of 1968 spurred the growth of both a broadly based antiwar movement and of the campus New Left, and led the latter to adopt increasingly militant rhetoric and tactics. By the fall of 1967 the New Left had moved "from dissent to resistance." Teach-ins and silent vigils gave way to the seizure of campus buildings and disruptive street demonstrations. Under new and younger leadership SDS continued to grow, and eventually some of its original leaders, like Tom Hayden and Rennie Davis, were attracted back to antiwar organizing from the slums of Newark and Chicago.

In the aftermath of the bloody confrontations at the Chicago Democratic convention in the summer of 1968, and the indictment of Hayden, Davis, and six others for "conspiracy," most New Leftists abandoned whatever hopes they still cherished of reforming the existing political system. Declaring themselves allies and disciples of third-world Communist revolutionaries like Mao Zedong and Che Guevara, SDS leaders now conceived their principal role as one of "bringing the war home" to the "imperialist mother country." In 1969, SDS collapsed as small, self-proclaimed revolutionary vanguards squabbled over control of the organization, but the ranks of student radicals continued to increase through the 1969-70 school year. Polls showed that as many as

A variety of opposition groups gathered in Chicago to protest the Democratic National Convention. The demonstration turned into a bloody melee, which a subsequent investigation blamed largely on the actions of the police. (Courtesy of Corbis-Bettman.)

three quarters of a million students identified themselves as adherents of the New Left. The national student strike that SDSers had long dreamed of but had never been able to pull off became a reality in the spring of 1970. Spontaneously organized in response to the invasion of Cambodia and the killing of four students at Kent State University, it effectively paralyzed the nation's university system. . . .

. . . [I]n surveying the ruins of these successive political failures, it is striking that while "nothing" was accomplished by the New Left in its short life, everything was different afterward. If the years that followed the 1960s did not live up to the hopeful vision of the future sketched out in the Port Huron Statement, still they did not mark a return to the previous status quo. America certainly became a more politically and culturally contentious society because of what happened in the 1960s—and in some respects it also became a more just, open, and egalitarian one. On the coldest, darkest, and most reactionary days of the Reagan ascendancy, there was more radical belief and activity to be seen in the United States than was present anytime in the 1950s. As an organizational presence the New Left had vanished, but as a force in American political culture its impact continued to be felt.

The New Left was shaped by and came to embody a profound dislocation in American culture, and, in the end, it had more impact on the ideas that Americans had about themselves and their society than on structures of power that governed their lives. Young radicals articulated a critique of "everyday life" in the United States, which was, in time, taken up by millions of people who had little notion of where those ideas originated. In the course of the sixties and seventies, many Americans came to recognize and reject the prevalence of racial and sexual discrimination, to ask new questions about the legitimacy of established institutions and authority, and to oppose military adventures abroad. . . .

As a college education became the norm rather than a privilege, millions of young people found themselves in a new socially determined developmental stage that extended adolescence into the middle twenties or even later. By the early 1960s, "youth communities" had sprung up on the outskirts of college campuses, often in the cheap housing available on the edge of black ghettos. . . .

At precisely the moment when the first wave of the baby boom reached the college campuses, the southern civil rights movement exploded into newspaper headlines and the nation's consciousness through the use of an innovative strategy of mass, nonviolent civil disobedience. The 1960 southern sit-in movement, which attracted fifty thousand participants in the space of a few months, was sparked by four black college freshmen in Greensboro, North Carolina, who decided on their own to challenge the segregation of a Woolworth's lunch counter. Rennie Davis, a founder of SDS who was a sophomore at Oberlin College in 1960, recalled: "Here were four students from Greensboro who were suddenly all over *Life* magazine. There was a feeling that they were us and we were them, and a recognition that they were expressing something we were feeling as well and they'd won the attention of the country." . . .

In 1961, John F. Kennedy had sounded the call for a selfless dedication to the (vaguely defined) national cause, significantly posed in terms of individual choice: "Ask not what your country can do for you, ask what you can do for your country." The same spirit of self-sacrificing idealism that led many students to volunteer for the Peace Corps led others to the civil rights movement. . . .

. . . As the war and the protests it inspired escalated in the mid-1960s, SDS grew rapidly. . . . There were national headlines in the spring of 1965 when SDS's antiwar march attracted some twenty thousand participants. By the end of that school year, the SDS National Office (NO) was receiving a flood of letters from individuals and groups eager to affiliate, from places like Dodge City Community College in Kansas not previously known as loci of radical activity. It was no longer necessary for SDS to organize chapters: they organized themselves. Many recruits were members of preexisting local groups who sought access to the resources and prestige that only a national organization could provide. . . .

The NO set up a system of campus "travelers" and regional offices, but these did little more than service existing chapters, distribute literature, and make an occasional statement to the media. New members were seldom "converted" to SDS ideology. . . .

The SDS annual national conventions were important mainly as places where SDSers from around the country could make contacts and share experiences. Labored efforts to chart a coordinated national strategy (like an abortive "Ten Days to Shake the Empire" plan in 1968) were almost universally ignored by local chapters. To the extent that people in SDS chapters learned to speak a common language and pursue a common political agenda, they did so through a process of osmosis rather than central direction.

Just at the moment when it began to develop a significant national presence, SDS lost the ability to set its own agenda. Starting in 1965, SDS's concerns and the pace of its development were largely reactions to decisions being made in the White House and the Pentagon. The escalation of the Vietnam War thus simultaneously strengthened and weakened SDS. In the matter of a few months, it transformed the group from a small network of activists, most of whom knew one another, into a national movement with hundreds of chapters—and an organizational infrastructure that never managed to make the transition. And while the war galvanized protesters, it also bred frustrations and extremism in their ranks. Vietnam was a particularly volatile issue around which to build a mass movement. No partial victories or breathing spaces could be won: the movement would either force the government to end the war, or it would fail. As a result the peace movement, with the New Left at its core, constantly swung back and forth between near-millennial expectations and dark and angry despair.

As the political climate changed after 1965, so did the New Left's cultural style. The new members who flooded into SDS (dubbed the "prairie power" contingent because so many of them came from places other than the usual urban centers of radical strength) were less likely to share the theoretical sophistication or intellectual ambitions of the group's founding generation. The new breed tended to be unschooled in and impatient with radical doctrine, intensely moralistic, suspicious of "elitism" and "bureaucracy," and immersed in the new cultural currents running through college towns.

In January 1966, three members of the newly organized SDS chapter at the University of Oklahoma were among those arrested in a marijuana raid on a private party in Norman. Newspapers throughout the country picked up the story, linking SDS with pot-smoking. The Norman police chief unabashedly revealed to local reporters that his suspicions of the students had been aroused by their politics as much as their alleged drug use: "Several of these people have been active in the Society [SDS]. . . . One of them had a receipt showing he had just joined the SDS." High bail was set for all the defendants, and two of them were locked up incommunicado in a state mental hospital for observation because of their long hair. . . .

Steve Max and a few other "old guard" leaders of SDS . . . wanted the Norman chapter suspended until it had, through some unspecified procedure, reformed itself. In a subsequent letter, he reiterated, "If we don't start to draw the line someplace we are going to wind up with a federation of dope rings instead of a national political organization."

But sentiment in the hinterland seemed to run in a completely opposite direction. . . .

The Norman SDS chapter was not suspended. Moreover, within a few years, SDS would not simply regard the use of drugs as a question of individual choice but would endorse it as yet another emblem of the revolutionary disaffection of the young. "Our whole life is a defiance of Amerika," the newspaper of the Weatherman [a particularly militant] SDS faction exulted in 1969. "It's moving in the streets, digging sounds, smoking dope . . . fighting pigs." By the late sixties, marijuana and LSD were circulating freely at national SDS conventions. . . .

Earlier generations of radicals had derided capitalism as an anarchic, irrational system; the new radicals scorned the system because it was *too* rational, based on a soul-destroying set of technological and bureaucratic imperatives that stifled individual expression. From university reform, where the slogan was "I am a human being, do not fold, spindle or mutilate," to draft resistance, where the buttons read "Not with my life, you don't," the New Left championed a form of radical individualism that was authentically American in derivation and flavor—ironically, all too "American" for the organizational well-being of the movement. For this deeply rooted individualism prepared the way for the development of a movement cult of "confrontation." . . .

By the late 1960s, SDS had grown to as many as a hundred thousand loosely affiliated members, while tens of thousands more could be counted as supporters of the movement. But off-campus, the New Left's activities, and the increasingly outrageous and opaque language in which they were justified, found few supporters. Ronald Reagan spoke for many Americans when he declared in the midst of the People's Park disorders in Berkeley in 1969 (which left one spectator dead from police buckshot), "If it's a blood bath they want, let it be now." The ferocity with which authorities sought to crack down on campus protest only exacerbated the appeal of extreme rhetoric and doctrines within SDS. . . .

The demise of SDS did not retard the flowering of cultural radicalism. From campus towns to the "youth ghettos" of big cities and even to American military bases in Vietnam, a diffuse set of "countercultural" ideas, symbols, and behaviors circulated. "Liberation" was easy to achieve, since it was defined as the practice of a communal, playful, and sensual life-style. While they often ignored or explicitly rejected the politics advocated by "power-tripping" radicals, those immersed in the counterculture embraced beliefs the earlier New Left had first popularized. Alternative, participatory communities based on decentralized, small-scale technology and an ethic of loving mutuality had all been prefigured by the Port Huron Statement, the civil rights movement, and the SDS's community organizing projects. Garbed in apolitical dress, this vision continued to attract believers (many of them from working-class backgrounds) who never would have considered attending an SDS meeting. . . .

As the sixties ended, some radical leaders withdrew from the increasingly fractious realm of left-wing politics to join rural communes or mystical cults, or to embrace various "new age" therapies. . . . Paul Potter, a former SDS president, . . . recorded his own painful withdrawal from the movement in his 1971 book *A Name for Ourselves*. Potter reaffirmed his belief in the values and concerns that had initially led him to the New Left, but rejected organized politics as a means of achieving a better world:

> I am less involved in changing America. . . . This does not mean that I am less angry or upset or horrified by this country than before. If anything, I am more profoundly and intuitively aware, day to day, of what an ugly society this is and how desperately it needs change. But my information comes less and less from the papers—more and more from my own experience with it.

. . . New Leftists thus succeeded in transforming American politics—though not according to the sanguine script laid out at Port Huron. The continued influence of the movements of the 1960s has been most pronounced in five aspects of contemporary

American society: intellectual life, perceptions of race and of gender, foreign policy, and the language of politics itself. . . .

The politics of the two major parties also reflect the impact of sixties radicalism. The most direct influence appears within the Democratic party. In many areas, local Democratic activists began to move left during the 1968 presidential campaign and, in time, found their forces strengthened by an infusion of former New Leftists. By the 1980s, left Democrats represented a variety of "single-issue" movements—black, Chicano, feminist, environmentalist, peace, gay and lesbian, and elderly—as much as they did the party apparatus itself. . . . Liberal and radical Democratic activists helped transform Jesse Jackson into a serious candidate for president, promoted Geraldine Ferraro's vice-presidential nomination in 1984, and set the anti-interventionist tenor of the party's foreign policy debates. To the dismay of many party officials in the South, and those elsewhere nostalgic for the days of . . . Richard Daley [mayor of Chicago], "New Politics"-style Democrats increasingly supply the financial backing, political energy, and moral élan that keeps the party organization afloat.

Yet what gives life to one side also provides opportunity for the other. Since the 1960s, conservative Republicans have lured away traditional Democratic voters by portraying the GOP as the only safe haven for the white ethnic working class against the onslaught of the civil rights movement and the political and social insurgencies it spawned. After taking a Watergate-induced pause in the mid-1970s, this backlash intensified, as millions of white northern voters joined southerners in rejecting the presidential candidates of their own party whom they perceived as apostles of weakness abroad and captives of single-issue "special interests" at home. Meanwhile, the New Right was using the specter of a hedonistic, God-denying counterculture to raise funds and recruit activists. Thus both parties, each in its own way, still lived off energy generated in the 1960s. . . .

In ways both trivial and serious, the example, language, and actions of sixties radicals offered millions of Americans a way to express the discontent generated by the triple debacle of Vietnam, Watergate, and seventies stagflation. Often it was the New Left's style rather than its politics that wound up being recycled in the 1970s and 1980s. Some otherwise law abiding "right-to-life" demonstrators risked arrest blockading abortion clinics while singing, in paraphrase of John Lennon, "All we are saying / is give life a chance." Campus conservatives distributed leaflets accusing Gulf Oil of "corporate murder" because the firm does business with the pro-Soviet government of Angola. New Leftists succeeded in exposing the bankrupt policies of the liberal state in the 1960s. But that very success activated right-wing critics of liberalism who championed a "counterculture" of their own, based on biblical injunctions, the patriarchal family, and the economic homilies of nineteenth-century capitalism.

The contradictory legacy of the sixties thus provides evidence of both the failures and successes of the new radicalism— "failures" that were sometimes unavoidable, and sometimes self-inflicted, and "successes" that usually were unrecognized and were often the opposite of what was intended. [Historian] Richard Hofstadter wrote in *The Age of Reform* that while it may be "feasible and desirable to formulate ideal programs of reform, it is asking too much to expect that history will move . . . in a straight line to realize them." Despite the best efforts of the Reagan administration and the New Right, the 1980s did not represent a return to the "normalcy" of the 1950s. Young radicals never became serious contenders for state power, but the issues they raised and the language in which those issues were dramatized became the normal fare of American politics.

Questions

---

1. *What do Isserman and Kazin see as the most significant aspects of 1960s dissent?*
2. *What ironic legacies of the 1960s do they describe?*
3. *How would you evaluate the success or failure of dissent in the 1960s?*
4. *Why do you think the 1960s continue to loom so large in our national imagination?*

VOICES FROM THE 1960s

The young people who joined the various dissent movements of the 1960s made self-conscious efforts to define who they were and what they saw wrong with American society. Through poems, manifestos, books, and interviews they worked to explain their beliefs and to critique the social and political status quo. In the following selections, the leaders of the three main streams of dissent describe their goals and methods.

The Black Panther movement defined itself against the nonviolent tradition of the earlier civil rights movement. Stokely Carmichael and others rejected the methods of peaceful collaboration with white allies in favor of radical action. They linked racism, poverty, and America's foreign policy in Vietnam with the domestic repression of African Americans and called for armed struggle to replace the exploitative system.

Tom Hayden and other "New Left" activists believed in the possibility of constructive engagement in the political system as a means to create a more just society. Disillusioned with the perceived gap between American ideals and reality, these activists advocated wider political participation by the young in order to achieve social justice. Concentrating on the university as the focal point of activism, they hoped to bring these young people to the forefront of political mobilization.

Others rejected the possibility of constructive change in the status quo that the first two groups implicitly believed. Adherents of the "counter culture" movement called for either a complete disruption of "an insane society" or the rejection of society and a retreat to a separate and simple lifestyle.

FIRST STREAM:
SNCC, BLACK PANTHERS, BLACK CULTURE

"Black Power!"

During a march from Tennessee to Mississippi led by Martin Luther King, Jr., a small knot of young marchers refused to sing the civil rights movement's anthem "We Shall Overcome." Frustrated by the slow pace of civil rights progress, they decided to introduce a new slogan to the vocabulary of protest: "Black Power!" The young black activist Stokely Carmichael led this symbolic break with the older civil rights movement.

A member of the Student Non-Violent Coordinating Committee (SNCC) and eventually its head, Carmichael had soured on the possibilities of Gandhian non-violence to achieve racial equality and on the utility of working with white allies. In the selection below, Carmichael explains the philosophy of black power and its origins. Excerpted from Stokely Carmichael, "What We Want," New York Review of Books 7 (September 22, 1966): 5-7.

One of the tragedies of the struggle against racism is that up to now there has been no national organization which could speak to the growing militancy of young black people in the urban ghetto. There has been only a civil rights movement, whose tone of voice was adapted to an audience of liberal whites. It served as a sort of buffer zone between them and angry young blacks. None of its so-called leaders could go into a rioting community and be listened to. In a sense, I blame ourselves—together with the mass media—for what has happened in Watts, Harlem, Chicago, Cleveland, Omaha. Each time the people in those cities saw Martin Luther King get slapped, they became angry; when they saw four little black girls bombed to death, they were angrier; and when nothing

---

happened, they were steaming. We had nothing to offer that they could see, except to go out and be beaten again. We helped to build their frustration.

For too many years, black Americans marched and had their heads broken and got shot. . . . After years of this, we are at almost the same point—because we demonstrated from a position of weakness. We cannot be expected any longer to march and have our heads broken in order to say to whites: come on, you're nice guys. For you are not nice guys. We have found you out. . . .

An organization which claims to be working for the needs of a community—as SNCC does—must work to provide that community with a position of strength from which to make its voice heard. This is the significance of black power beyond the slogan.

Capturing a central paradox for African Americans in the 1960s, this demonstrator wonders why blacks should fight for a country which continued to deny them basic civil and political rights. In this way, the civil rights movement and the anti-war movement became two sides of the same coin. (Courtesy of Media Image Resource Alliance.)

Black power can be clearly defined for those who do not attach the fears of white America to their questions about it. We should begin with the basic fact that black Americans have two problems: they are poor and they are black. All other problems arise from this two-sided reality: lack of education, the so-called apathy of black men. Any program to end racism must address itself to that double reality.

. . . Thus we determined to win political power, with the idea of moving on from there into activity that would have economic effects. With power, the masses could *make or participate in making* the decisions which govern their destinies, and thus create basic change in their day-to-day lives. . . .

. . . We have no infallible master plan and we make no claim to exclusive knowledge of how to end racism; different groups will work in their own different ways. SNCC cannot spell out the full logistics of self-determination but it can address itself to the problem by helping black communities define their needs, realize their strength, and go into action along a variety of lines which they must choose for themselves. Without knowing all the answers, it can address itself to the basic problem of poverty; to the fact that in . . . [one southern county] 86 white families own 90 per cent of the land. What are black people in that county going to do for jobs, where are they going to get money? There must be reallocation of land, of money.

Ultimately, the economic foundations of this country must be shaken if black people are to control their lives. The colonies of the United States—and this includes the black ghettoes within its borders, north and south—must be liberated. . . . For racism to die, a totally different America must be born.

This is what the white society does not wish to face; this is why that society prefers to talk about integration. But integration speaks not at all to the problem of poverty, only to the problem of blackness. Integration today means the man who "makes it," leaving his black brothers behind in the ghetto as fast as his new sports car will take him. It has no relevance to the Harlem wino or to the cotton-picker making three dollars a day. . . .

Integration, moreover, speaks to the problem of blackness in a despicable way. As a goal, it has been based on complete acceptance of the fact that *in order to have* a decent house or education, blacks must move into a white neighborhood or send their children to a white school. This reinforces, among both black and white, the idea that "white" is automatically better and "black" is by definition inferior. This is why integration is a subterfuge for the maintenance of white supremacy. It allows the nation to focus on a handful of Southern children who get into white schools, at great price, and to ignore the 94 per cent who are left behind in unimproved all-black schools. Such situations will not change until black people have power—to control their own school boards, in this case. Then Negroes become equal in a way that means something, and integration ceases to be a one-way street.

Then integration doesn't mean draining skills and energies from the ghetto into white neighborhoods; then it can mean white people moving from Beverly Hills into Watts. . . .

Whites will not see that I, for example, as a person oppressed because of my blackness, have common cause with other blacks who are oppressed because of blackness. . . .

The need for psychological equality is the reason why SNCC today believes that blacks must organize in the black community. Only black people can convey the revolutionary idea that black people are able to do things themselves. Only they can help create in the community an aroused and continuing black consciousness that will provide the basis for political strength. In the past, white allies have furthered white supremacy without the whites involved realizing it—or wanting it, I think. Black people must do things for themselves; they must get poverty money they will control and spend themselves, they must conduct tutorial programs themselves so that black children can identify with black people. This is one reason Africa has such importance: The reality of black men ruling their own natives gives blacks elsewhere a sense of possibility, of power, which they do not now have. . . .

Black people do not want to "take over" this country. They don't want to "get whitey"; they just want to get him off their backs, as the saying goes. . . .

But our vision is not merely of a society in which all black men have enough to buy the good things of life. When we urge that black money go into black pockets, we mean the communal pocket. We want to see money go back into the community and used to benefit it. . . . The society we seek to build among black people, then, is not a capitalist one. It is a society in which the spirit of community and humanistic love prevail. . . . We can build a community of love only where we have the ability and power to do so: among blacks.

As for white America, perhaps it can stop crying out against "black supremacy," "black nationalism," "racism in reverse," and begin facing reality. The reality is that this nation, from top to bottom, is racist; that racism is not primarily a problem of "human relations" but of an exploitation maintained—either actively or through silence—by the society as a whole.

The Black Panther Party

One of the most spectacular and controversial outgrowths of the Black Power movement was the Black Panther Party. Founded in 1966 by Huey Newton and Bobby Seale in Oakland, the party attracted a great deal of media attention for its commitment to armed self-defense. The image of the Panther dressed in military fatigues and armed became for many white Americans their worst nightmare of Black Power.

The party did not only attract media attention. The Panthers were hounded by the police and the FBI almost everywhere they established chapters. These encounters often led to violent, tragic encounters, many provoked by the police. Panthers were routinely harassed, arrested, and on several occasions, killed.

The media focus on the party's militancy also obscured the positive work many members did in inner-city communities, especially in Chicago where the party ran a successful school breakfast program for needy children.

In this excerpt from a 1973 interview, founder Huey Newton describes the Panther ethos of using armed violence to achieve political goals. His discussion of the "doomed" revolutionary now seems poignantly ironic—Newton died in a drug-related shoot-out in 1989. Taken from "Playboy Interview: Huey Newton," 20 Playboy *(May 1973): 76, 78, 90.*

PLAYBOY: Do you think the *only* way to achieve your revolutionary goals is through armed violence?

NEWTON: Yes, and I think that ultimately it will be through armed violence, because the American ruling circle will not give up without a bitter struggle. But America will not be changed until the world is changed. To say that change will come here just through the ballot box would be a fantasy. We're running for city-council offices today. But if you ask if we would be prepared to fight with armed force when the time is right, I would say yes, when the occasion presents itself—and I think it will come, at some point in the future. . . .

From "Playboy Interview: Huey Newton" *Playboy*, Vol. 20 (May 1973). Reprinted by permission of *Playboy*.

PLAYBOY: So you would feel no hesitation about using violence as a tool, even to the point of killing people, provided it advanced your movement or your principles?

NEWTON: That's right.

PLAYBOY: And you say that without reservation?

NEWTON: The death of any man diminishes me, but sometimes we may have to be diminished before we can reconstruct.

PLAYBOY: That raises our last question: If you're ready to kill for the cause, you must also be ready to die for it. Are you?

NEWTON: I will fight until I die, however that may come. But whether I'm around or not to see it happen, I know we will eventually succeed, not just in America but all over the world, in our struggle for the liberation of all oppressed peoples. The revolution will win. But [Russian revolutionary anarchist Mikhail] Bakunin wrote that the first lesson the revolutionary *himself* must learn is that he's a doomed man. If that sounds defeatist, you don't understand the nature of revolution: that it's an ongoing process and that we don't get out of life alive, anyway. All we can do as individuals is try to make things better now, for eventually we all die. I think Mao's statement sums it up best: "Death comes to everyone, but it varies in its significance. To die for the reactionary is as light as a feather. But to die for the revolution is heavier than Mount Tai."

The Black Panthers achieved the highest profile of any of the militant black power organizations. As a consequence, they often found themselves in conflict with the police. Here volunteers raise money to support Panther members about to go on trial. (Courtesy of Leonard Freed/Magnum Photos, Inc.)

Black Power and Black Culture

Black Power and black pride served as the wellspring for extraordinary cultural, as well as political, achievements. A new-found desire to celebrate black heritage, black history, and black culture helped heal some of the psychological damage inflicted on American blacks by generations of denying or denigrating their traditions. No one articulated this sensibility better than James Brown when he sang: "Say it strong, say it loud / I'm black and I'm proud."

Nikki Giovanni is one of a host of black writers who found their voice in the Black Power struggles of the 1960s. In this poem, written in 1968, she describes how the accumulated effects of violence against leaders for peace and justice transformed her personally. Taken from Nikki Giovanni, Black Feeling, Black Talk, Black Judgement *(New York, 1979), 68-70.*

Adulthood
(For Claudia)

i usta wonder who i'd be
when i was a little girl in indianapolis
sitting on doctors porches with post-dawn pre-debs
(wondering would my aunt drag me to church sunday)
i was meaningless
and i wondered if life
would give me a chance to mean

i found a new life in the withdrawal from all things
not like my image

when i was a teen-ager i usta sit
on front steps conversing
the gym teacher's son with embryonic eyes

---

about the essential essence of the universe
(and other bullshit stuff)
recognizing the basic powerlessness of me

but then i went to college where i learned
that just because everything i was was unreal
i could be real and not just real through withdrawal
into emotional crosshairs or colored bourgeois
intellectual pretensions
but from involvement with things approaching reality
i could possibly have a life

so catatonic emotions and time wasting sex games
were replaced with functioning commitments to logic
and
necessity and the gray area was slowly darkened into
a Black thing

for a while progress was being made along with a certain
degree
of happiness cause i wrote a book and found a love
and organized a theatre and even gave some lectures on
Black history
and began to believe all good people could get
together and win without bloodshed
then
hammarskjöld was killed
and lumumba was killed
and diem was killed
and kennedy was killed
and malcolm was killed
and evers was killed
and schwerner, chaney and goodman were killed
and liuzzo was killed
and stokely fled the country
and le roi was arrested
and rap was arrested
and pollard, thompson and cooper were killed
and king was killed
and kennedy was killed
and i sometimes wonder why i didn't become a

debutante
sitting on porches, going to church all the time,
wondering
is my eye make-up on straight
or a withdrawn discoursing on the stars and moon
instead of a for real Black person who must now feel
and inflict
pain

[Note: Dag Hammarskjöld, United Nations Secretary General, 1961; Patrice Lumumba, Prime Minister of Congo, 1961; Ngo Dinh Diem, President of South Vietnam, 1963; President John F. Kennedy, 1963; Malcolm X, black nationalist leader, 1965; Medgar Evers, NAACP official, 1963; Michael Schwerner, James Chaney, Andrew Goodman, volunteers in Mississippi "Freedom Summer," a black voter registration project, 1964; Viola Liuzzo, white civil rights worker in Alabama, 1965; Stokely Carmichael, SNCC; Leroi Jones, black activist and playwright; H. Rap Brown, SNCC; Martin Luther King, Jr., civil rights leader, 1968; Robert F. Kennedy, Democratic presidential candidate, 1968.]

Second Stream:
Students and the "New Left"

The Port Huron Statement

The Port Huron Statement was the result of a conference held in Port Huron, Michigan, in 1962. Written largely by Tom Hayden, the statement offers a critique of American society and a call to action for America's students. The statement became the founding document for the Students for a Democratic Society, and it announced the arrival of the "New Left" in this country. Excerpted from "An Official Statement of Students for a Democratic Society," in How Democratic Is America? Responses to the New Left Challenge, *ed. Robert A. Goldwin (Chicago, 1969), 1-3, 5-15.*

Introduction: Agenda for a Generation

We are people of this generation, bred in at least modest comfort, housed now in universities, looking uncomfortably to the world we inherit.

When we were kids, the United States was the wealthiest and strongest country in the world: the only one with the atom bomb, the least scarred by modern war, an initiator of the United Nations that we thought would distribute Western influence throughout the world. Freedom and equality for each individual, government of, by, and for the people—these American values we found good, principles by which we could live as men. Many of us began maturing in complacency.

As we grew, however, our comfort was penetrated by events too troubling to dismiss. First, the permeating and victimizing fact of human degradation, symbolized by the Southern struggle against racial bigotry, compelled most of us from silence to activism. Second, the enclosing fact of the Cold War, symbolized by the presence of the Bomb, brought awareness that we ourselves, and our friends, and millions of abstract "others" we knew more directly because of our common peril, might die at any time. We might deliberately ignore, or avoid, or fail to feel all other human problems, but not these two, for these were too immediate and crushing in their impact, too challenging in the demand that we as individuals take the responsibility for encounter and resolution.

While these and other problems either directly oppressed us or rankled our consciences and became our own subjective concerns, we began to see complicated and disturbing paradoxes in our surrounding America. The declaration "all men are created equal . . ." rang hollow before the facts of Negro life in the South and the big cities of the North. The proclaimed peaceful intentions of the United States contradicted its economic and military investments in the Cold War status quo.

We witnessed, and continue to witness, other paradoxes. With nuclear energy whole cities can easily be powered, yet the dominant nation-states seem more likely to unleash destruction greater than that incurred in all wars of human history. Although

---

our own technology is destroying old and creating new forms of social organization, men still tolerate meaningless work and idleness. While two-thirds of mankind suffers undernourishment, our own upper classes revel amidst superfluous abundance. Although world population is expected to double in forty years, the nations still tolerate anarchy as a major principle of international conduct and uncontrolled exploitation governs the sapping of the earth's physical resources. Although mankind desperately needs revolutionary leadership, America rests in national stalemate, its goals ambiguous and tradition-bound instead of informed and clear, its democratic system apathetic and manipulated rather than "of, by, and for the people." . . .

Some would have us believe that Americans feel contentment amidst prosperity—but might it not better be called a glaze above deeply felt anxieties about their role in the new world? And if these anxieties produce a developed indifference to human affairs, do they not as well produce a yearning to believe there *is* an alternative to the present, that something *can* be done to change circumstances in the school, the workplaces, the bureaucracies, the government? It is to this latter yearning, at once the spark and engine of change, that we direct our present appeal. The search for truly democratic alternatives to the present, and a commitment to social experimentation with them, is a worthy and fulfilling human enterprise, one which moves us and, we hope, others today. . . .

We regard *men* as infinitely precious and possessed of unfulfilled capacities for reason, freedom, and love. In affirming these principles we are aware of countering perhaps the dominant conceptions of man in the twentieth century: that he is a thing to be manipulated, and that he is inherently incapable of directing his own affairs. We oppose the depersonalization that reduces human beings to the status of things—if anything, the brutalities of the twentieth century teach that means and ends are intimately related, that vague appeals to "posterity" cannot justify the mutilations of the present. We oppose, too, the doctrine of human incompetence because it rests essentially on the modern fact that men have been "competently" manipulated into incompetence—we see little reason why men cannot meet with increasing skill the complexities and responsibilities of their situation, if society is organized not for minority, but for majority, participation in decision-making.

Men have unrealized potential for self-cultivation, self-direction, self-understanding, and creativity. It is this potential that we regard as crucial and to which we appeal, not to the human potentiality for violence, unreason, and submission to authority. The goal of man and society should be human independence: a concern not with the image of popularity but with finding a meaning in life that is personally authentic; a quality of mind not compulsively driven by a sense of powerlessness, nor one which unthinkingly adopts status values, nor one which represses all threats to its habits, but one which has full, spontaneous access to present and past experiences, one which easily unites the fragmented parts of personal history, one which openly faces problems which are troubling and unresolved; one with an intuitive awareness of possibilities, an active sense of curiosity, an ability and willingness to learn. . . .

We would replace power rooted in possession, privilege, or circumstance by power and uniqueness rooted in love, reflectiveness, reason, and creativity. As a *social system* we seek the establishment of a democracy of individual participation, governed by two central aims: that the individual share in those social decisions determining the quality and direction of his life; that society be organized to encourage independence in men and provide the media for their common participation.

In a participatory democracy, the political life would be based in several root principles:

that decision-making of basic social consequence be carried on by public groupings;

that politics be seen positively, as the art of collectively creating an acceptable pattern of social relations;

that politics has the function of bringing people out of isolation and into community, thus being a necessary, though not sufficient, means of finding meaning in personal life;

that the political order should serve to clarify problems in a way instrumental to their solution; it should provide outlets for the expression of personal grievance and aspiration; opposing views should be organized so as to illuminate choices and facilitate the attainment of goals; channels should be commonly available to relate men to knowledge and to power so that private problems—from bad recreation facilities to personal alienation—are formulated as general issues.

The economic sphere would have as its basis the principles:

that work should involve incentives worthier than money or survival. It should be educative, not stultifying; creative, not mechanical; self-directed, not manipulated, encouraging independence, a respect for others, a sense of dignity and a willingness to accept social responsibility, since it is this experience that has crucial influence on habits, perceptions, and individual ethics;

that the economic experience is so personally decisive that the individual must share in its full determination;

that the economy itself is of such social importance that its major resources and means of production should be open to democratic participation and subject to democratic social regulation. . . .

In social change or interchange, we find violence to be abhorrent because it requires generally the transformation of the target, be it a human being or a community of people, into a depersonalized object of hate. It is imperative that the means of violence be abolished and the institutions—local, national, international— that encourage nonviolence as a condition of conflict be developed. . . .

Almost no students value activity as citizens. Passive in public, they are hardly more idealistic in arranging their private lives. . . . "Students don't even give a damn about apathy," one has said. Apathy toward apathy begets a privately constructed universe, a place of systematic study schedules, two nights each week for beer, a girl or two, and early marriage; a framework infused with personality, warmth, and under control, no matter how unsatisfying otherwise. . . .

But apathy is not simply an attitude; it is a product of social institutions, and of the structure and organization of higher education itself. . . . Tragically, the university could serve as a significant source of social criticism and an initiator of new modes and molders of attitudes. But the actual intellectual effect of the college experience is hardly distinguishable from that of any other communications channel—say, a television set—passing on the stock truths of the day. Students leave college somewhat more "tolerant" than when they arrived, but basically unchallenged in their values and political orientations. With administrators ordering the institution, and faculty the curriculum, the student learns by his isolation to accept elite rule within the university, which prepares him to accept later forms of minority control. The real function of the educational system—as opposed to its more rhetorical function of "searching for truth"—is to impart the key information and styles that will help the student get by, modestly but comfortably, in the big society beyond. . . .

The very isolation of the individual—from power and community and ability to aspire—means the rise of a democracy without publics. With the great mass of people structurally remote and psychologically hesitant with respect to democratic institutions, those institutions themselves attenuate and become, in the fashion of the vicious circle, progressively less accessible to those few who aspire to serious participation in social affairs. The vital democratic connection between community and leadership, between the mass and the several elites, has been so wrenched and perverted that disastrous policies go unchallenged time and again. . . .

TOWARDS AMERICAN DEMOCRACY

Every effort to end the Cold War and expand the process of world industrialization is an effort hostile to people and institutions whose interests lie in perpetuation of the East-West military threat and the postponement of change in the "have not" nations of the world. Every such effort, too, is bound to establish greater democracy in America. The major goals of a domestic effort would be:

1. America must abolish its political party stalemate. . . .
2. Mechanisms of voluntary association must be created through which political information can be imparted and political participation encouraged. . . .
3. Institutions and practices which stifle dissent should be abolished, and the promotion of peaceful dissent should be actively promoted. . . .
4. Corporations must be made publicly responsible. . . .
5. The allocation of resources must be based on social needs. A truly "public sector" must be

established, and its nature debated and
planned. . . .
6. America should concentrate on its genuine social
priorities: abolish squalor, terminate neglect, and
establish an environment for people to live in with
dignity and creativeness. . . .

THE UNIVERSITY AND SOCIAL CHANGE

. . . The civil rights, peace, and student movements are too
poor and socially slighted, and the labor movement too quiescent,
to be counted with enthusiasm. From where else can power and
vision be summoned? We believe that the universities are an
overlooked seat of influence.

. . . Social relevance, the accessibility to knowledge, and internal openness—these together make the university a potential base
and agency in the movement of social change.

1. Any new left in America must be, in large measure, a left
    with real intellectual skills, committed to deliberativeness,
    honesty, and reflection as working tools. The university
    permits the political life to be an adjunct to the academic
    one, and action to be informed by reason.
2. A new left must be distributed in significant social roles
    throughout the country. The universities are distributed in
    such a manner.
3. A new left must consist of younger people who matured in
    the postwar world, and must be directed to the recruitment
    of younger people. The university is an obvious beginning
    point.
4. A new left must include liberals and socialists, the former
    for their relevance, the latter for their sense of thoroughgo-
    ing reforms in the system. The university is a more sensible
    place than a political party for these two traditions to begin
    to discuss their differences and look for political synthesis.
5. A new left must start controversy across the land, if na-
    tional policies and national apathy are to be reversed. The
    ideal university is a community of controversy, within
    itself and in its effects on communities beyond.
6. A new left must transform modern complexity into issues
    that can be understood and felt close-up by every human

being. It must give form to the feelings of helplessness and indifference, so that people may see the political, social, and economic sources of their private troubles and organize to change society. In a time of supposed prosperity, moral complacency, and political manipulation, a new left cannot rely on only aching stomachs to be the engine force of social reform. The case for change, for alternatives that will involve uncomfortable personal efforts, must be argued as never before. The university is a relevant place for all of these activities. . . .

The bridge to political power, though, will be built through genuine cooperation, locally, nationally, and internationally, between a new left of young people, and an awakening community of allies. In each community we must look within the university and act with confidence that we can be powerful, but we must look outwards to the less exotic but more lasting struggles for justice.

THIRD STREAM:
YIPPIES!, COMMUNES, COUNTER CULTURE

The Yippies! in Chicago, 1968

The demonstrations in Chicago during the 1968 Democratic Convention were initially conceived by the Yippies! who sought to turn politics into a theater of the absurd and in doing so attract media attention. Abbie Hoffman, Jerry Rubin, and Paul Krassner founded the Yippies!, and Krassner is credited with coining the name. In his essay "The Birth of the Yippie! Conspiracy," Krassner succinctly described the purpose of the Yippies!: "No more marches. No more rallies. No more speeches. The dialogue is over baby. . . . The goal now is to disrupt an insane society."

In the following selection, Abbie Hoffman describes the goals of the Yippies! and the plans for the demonstrations in Chicago. Taken from Abbie Hoffman, Revolution for the Hell of It *(New York, 1968), 102-3, 106-8.*

Last December [1967] a group of us in New York conceived the Yippie! idea. We had four main objectives:

1. The blending of pot and politics into a potlitical grass leaves movement—a cross-fertilization of the hippie and New Left philosophies.
2. A connecting link that would tie together as much of the underground as was willing into some gigantic national get-together.
3. The development of a model for an alternative society.
4. The need to make some statement, especially in revolutionary action-theater terms, about LBJ, the Democratic Party, electoral politics, and the state of the nation.

To accomplish these tasks required the construction of a vast myth, for through the notion of myth large numbers of people could get turned on and, in that process of getting turned on, begin to participate in Yippie! and start to focus on Chicago. *Precision was sacrificed for a greater degree of suggestion.* People took off in all directions in the most sensational manner possible:

"We will burn Chicago to the ground!"

"We will fuck on the beaches!"

"We demand the Politics of Ecstasy!"

"Acid for all!"

"Abandon the Creeping Meatball!"

And all the time: "Yippie! Chicago — August 25-30."

Reporters would play their preconceived roles: "What is the difference between a hippie and a Yippie?" A hundred different answers would fly out, forcing the reporter to make up his own answers; to distort. And distortion became the life-blood of the Yippies.

Yippie! was in the eye of the beholder. . . .

From *Revolution for the Hell of It* by Abbie Hoffman. The Dial Press, Inc., 1968.

A Constitutional Convention is being planned. A convention of visionary mind-benders who will for five long days and nights address themselves to the task of formulating the goals and means of the New Society.

It will be a blend of technologists and poets, of artists and community organizers, of anyone who has a vision. We will try to develop a Community of Consciousness.

There will be a huge rock-folk festival for free. Contrary to rumor, no groups originally committed to Chicago have dropped out. In fact, additional ones have agreed to participate. In all about thirty groups and performers will be there.

Theater groups from all over the country are pledged to come. They are an integral part of the activities, and a large amount of funds raised from here on in will go for the transportation of street theater groups.

Workshops in a variety of subjects such as draft resistance, drugs, commune development, guerrilla theater and underground media will be set up. The workshops will be oriented around problem-solving while the Constitutional Convention works to developing the overall philosophical framework.

There will probably be a huge march across town to haunt the Democrats.

People coming to Chicago should begin preparations for five days of energy-exchange. Do not come prepared to sit and watch and be fed and cared for. It just won't happen that way. It is time to become a life-actor. The days of the audience died with the old America. If you don't have a thing to do, stay home, you'll only get in the way. . . .

We are negotiating, with the Chicago city government, a six-day treaty. . . . We have had several meetings, principally with David Stahl, Deputy Mayor of Chicago, and there remains but to iron out the terms of the treaty—suspension of curfew laws, regulations pertaining to sleeping on the beach, etc.—for us to have a bona fide permit in our hands.

The possibility of violence will be greatly reduced. There is no guarantee that it will be entirely eliminated.

This is the United States, 1968, remember. If you are afraid of violence you shouldn't have crossed the border.

This matter of a permit is a cat-and-mouse game. The Chicago authorities do not wish to grant it too early, knowing this would increase the number of people that descend on the city. They can ill afford to wait too late, for that will inhibit planning on our part and create more chaos.

It is not our wish to take on superior armed troops who outnumber us on unfamiliar enemy territory. It is not their wish to have a Democrat nominated amidst a major bloodbath. The treaty will work for both sides. . . .

Prepare a street theater skit or bring something to distribute, such as food, poems or music. Get sleeping bags and other camping equipment. . . .

The point is, you can use Chicago as a means of pulling your local community together. It can serve to open up a dialogue between political radicals and those who might be considered hippies. The radical will say to the hippie: "Get together and fight, you are getting the shit kicked out of you." The hippie will say to the radical: "Your protest is so narrow, your rhetoric so boring, your ideological power plays so old-fashioned."

Each can help the other, and Chicago . . . might well offer the medium to put forth that message.

Counter Culture

Some of those who participated in the New Left and the "counter culture" did so as an expression of their thorough disgust with American society. They became increasingly infatuated with Third World liberation struggles and made heroes of revolutionaries like Che Guevara and Mao Zedong. Many, however, had a much more ambivalent relationship to American culture. Indeed, at some level the "counter culture" can be seen as part of a deep strain in American culture that has always valued personal expression over conformity.

This short poem by Jerry Rubin captures this ambivalence. Rubin, a cofounder of the Yippies!, was certainly seen by the public as one of those who disliked what America stood for and advocated its destruction, yet his writing reveals him to be very much in love with American culture despite the alienation he feels because of its corruption. Excerpted from Jerry Rubin, Do It! Scenarios of the Revolution *(New York, 1970), 12-13.*

Child of Amerika

I am a child of Amerika.

If I'm ever sent to Death Row for my revolutionary "crimes," I'll order as my last meal: a hamburger, french fries and a Coke.

I dig big cities.

I love to read the sports pages and gossip columns, listen to the radio and watch color TV.

I dig department stores, huge supermarkets and airports. I feel secure (though not necessarily hungry) when I see Howard Johnson's on the expressway.

I groove on Hollywood movies—even bad ones.

I speak only one language—English.

I love rock 'n' roll.

San Francisco's Haight-Ashbury became one center of America's counter culture. Some came looking for an alternative to a sterile, consumer-based society, others merely looked for sex, drugs and rock and roll. (Courtesy of AP/Wide World Photos.)

I collected baseball players' cards when I was a kid and wanted to play second base for the Cincinnati Reds, my home team.

I got a car when I was sixteen after flunking my first driver's test and crying for a week waiting to take it a second time.

I went to the kind of high school where you had to pass a test to get *in.*

I graduated in the bottom half of the class.

My classmates voted me the "busiest" senior in the school.

I had short, short, short hair.

I dug *Catcher in the Rye*.

I didn't have pimples.

I became an ace young reporter for the Cincinnati *Post and Times-Star*. "*Son*," the managing editor said to me, "*someday you're going to be a helluva reporter, maybe the greatest reporter this city's ever seen*."

I loved Adlai Stevenson.

My father drove a truck delivering bread and later became an organizer in the Bakery Drivers' Union. He dug Jimmy Hoffa (so do I). He died of heart failure at fifty-two.

My mother had a college degree and played the piano. She died of cancer at the age of fifty-one.

I took care of my brother, Gil, from the time he was thirteen.

I dodged the draft.

I went to Oberlin College for a year, graduated from the University of Cincinnati, spent 1 1/2 years in Israel and started graduate school at Berkeley.

I dropped out.

I dropped out of the White Race and the Amerikan nation.

I dig being free.

I like getting high.

I don't own a suit or tie.

I live for the revolution.

I'm a yippie!

I am an orphan of Amerika.

Communes and Alternative Living

The "counter culture" also found some of its members among those for whom New Left politics and the civil rights and anti-war movements had become equally corrupt power struggles. Raymond Mungo was such a wounded veteran of the movement. As the Yippies! prepared to go to Chicago in 1968, Mungo embarked on a personal odyssey that landed him at Total Loss Farm, a commune in Vermont.

*Mungo, and others like him, retreated from the chaotic, and ulti-
mately futile, world of opposition politics to experiment with alternative
ways of living. Often these experiments embraced a "back to the land"
philosophy that manifested itself in the creation of primitive rural communities. Mungo turned his back on American society, but he did so in a
thoroughly American way. His experiences, and the book from which this
selection is taken, were clearly inspired by the journeys of Beat generation author Jack Kerouac and the descent of Henry David Thoreau.
Taken from Raymond Mungo,* Total Loss Farm: A Year in the Life
(New York, 1970), 16-17, 133, 157-59.

When we lived in Boston, Chicago, San Francisco, Washington (you name it, we lived there; some of us still live there), we
dreamed of a New Age born of violent insurrection. We danced
on the graves of war dead in Vietnam, every corpse was ammuni-
tion for Our Side; we set up a countergovernment down there in
Washington, had marches, rallies and meetings; tried to fight fire
with fire. Then Johnson resigned, yes, and the universities began
to fall, the best and the oldest ones first, and by God every 13-year-
old in the suburbs was smoking dope and our numbers multiply-
ing into the millions. But I woke up in the spring of 1968 and said,
"This is not what I had in mind," because the movement had
become my enemy; the movement was not flowers and doves and
spontaneity, but another vicious system, the seed of a heartless
bureaucracy, a minority Party vying for power rather than peace.
It was then that we put away the schedule for the revolution,
gathered together our dear ones and all our resources, and set off
to Vermont in search of the New Age.

The New Age we were looking for proved to be very old
indeed, and I've often wondered aloud at my luck for being 23
years old in a time and place in which only the past offers hope
and inspiration; the future offers only artifice and blight. I travel
now in a society of friends who heat their houses with hand-cut
wood and eliminate in outhouses, who cut pine shingles with
draw-knives and haul maple sugar sap on sleds, who weed potatoes with their university-trained hands, pushing long hair out of
their way and thus marking their foreheads with beautiful penitent dust. We till the soil to atone for our fathers' destruction of it.

We smell. We live far from the marketplaces in America by our own volition, and the powerful men left behind are happy to have us out of their way. They do not yet realize that their heirs will refuse to inhabit their hollow cities, will find them poisonous and lethal, will run back to the Stone Age if necessary for survival and peace. . . .

Over the crest of the hill, for the first time the road descends—walking downhill for a stretch we can catch our breath. That's why we built the road so, that horses pulling loads up the farm could recuperate from the uphill struggle and, freshened, go on. The road dips down to a wooden bridge crossing a stream of many colors in which pickerel, trout, salmon, tuna, and whales have been spotted by the sharpest of eyes. Most folks see only an occasional small trout or sunfish in this Noname Brook, which leads nowhere, but that is because they are all nearsighted. They wear glasses in the faith that the real, or actual, universe is not the one their own eyes can see, but a standard, universal universe dictated by prescription, or politics. You'd certainly be welcome to hang on to your specs here, but this is a place where you *could* take them off without fear of ridicule or violence to your body. Without my glasses, the brook becomes a dazzling pulsating streak of sunlight across the earth, ill-defined and like the great Source difficult to watch for long. They say it can blind you, but how to know which things you might better be blind to? Our great adventure after all is in searching for something not only better but new, nothing less than the next step in the evolution of the race, which may be somewhere we've been before. It goes in spells. And in racing toward the New Age, we can't be expected to carry all the dead weight of the past—all the schools, factories, newspapers, jobs, religions, and movements—which would drag us under. Just do whatever comes to mind, do something you hadn't thought of before, it's bound to get you *somewhere*. And you'll then decide whether you like it and where to move on to. We might stay at the brook all day and be perfectly happy, even dangle our toes in the chilly clear water, but me I'm now anxious to get on up to the farm. Coming? . . .

We *are* saving the world, of course, as the world for us extends to the boundaries of Total Loss Farm and the limits of our own experience; and Total Loss Farm is everywhere now, perhaps under your own rhubarb patch if you looked at it a little closer, and our experience all that anyone could hope to know of life. We were born and raised by parents who loved us at least until they lost us to a certain high-pitched whistle in the wind which they had gotten too old to hear; we work at maintaining ourselves, though our shared labor is seldom very taxing, for it takes little enough work to make plants grow, most of it is out of our hands, and our relationship to the work one of direct gratification and reward, as children insist on; we have children of our own, though they are fully peers by the time they've learned to eat and eliminate without physical help, and soon become more our masters than our students; and we die, sometimes in sulphurous flames, dramatic and shocking, other times silent and mysterious like the gone children wandering Europe with scenes of the parents engulfed in atrocity scrawled across their minds, but never to be spoken: "I come from Auschwitz, or Hué, or Boston, my father was shot for believing in God and hangs limp forever in front of our home as a reminder to the others; my mother was sold to the grim green soldiers for their sport, my brother to be used as a woman; I escaped the country of the somnambulent and blind on the back of a wolf who prowled the ruins and took pity on me; I have come here to begin again."

Our parents must wonder where we are, this story is, as much as anything else, an attempt to fill them in, but it grows harder and harder to speak. Fortunately, it grows simultaneously less necessary. I have clothes on my back, though they are old, and a roof over my head and food for my belly. In this, I am luckier than many. I am surrounded by people who would give their own lives in defense of mine, for they know we will make it together or not at all. I wish to be reconciled with all of my enemies, and to live on the planet and glory in peaches to a ripe old age. I am willing to help you as much as I'm able, as a single person can help another, not as a movement or government can help a mass. I may ask for some help from you as well. If you come to my house with love in your heart and there's room for one more—for there isn't always—you may know I will feed you and house you for the night, if you need it. You may see me walking from town to town with my thumb outstretched to the highway, seeking a lift: don't pass me by.

You have seen me everywhere. I am not asking for the vote. I do not seek to be represented. I do not seek to tear down your buildings or march on your castle or sit at your desk. I am interested neither in destroying what you have put up nor in gaining control of your empire. I demand nothing, and nothing is my inheritance. I live in the world, in the woods, with my friends, where not many people come by and the planet is entire and friendly; we like to be left alone except by those who can help. You can help by giving the planet, and peace, a chance. I ask only that you treat yourself right, give yourself the best of everything; and in so doing, you will be acting for me as well. If you can't stop, at least wave as you go by. Slow down, perhaps stop working: you'll find the time for everything you really want to do.

The "Silent Majority" Responds

In the autumn of 1969 President Richard Nixon, in a nationally televised address, contrasted what he believed to be a minority of Americans engaging in disruptive protest, with what he called "the silent majority"— suburban, law-abiding, conservative, middle-class citizens. It was this majority whose opinion Nixon courted in dealing with protesters and the "counter culture."

Promising to bring the nation together, and heal its wounds, Nixon often tried to play the elder statesman when he publicly discussed demonstrators, leaving it to his vice president, Spiro Agnew, to set a more strident and bellicose tone against protesters. Agnew was surely given this assignment by Nixon, who we now know was enraged at student demonstrators who challenged his policies. Asked by a reporter whether his aggressive posturing differed from the president's attitude, Vice President Agnew responded: "When the president said 'bring us together' he meant the functioning, contributing portions of the American citizenry."

In the speech excerpted below, Agnew calls for a "positive polarization" of the American public. It is an extraordinary gesture for a vice president to announce division as official government policy, but such was the nature of the Nixon administration. Nearly three decades later Agnew's demands for "law and order" strike us as richly ironic. Spiro Agnew was forced to resign for taking bribes, and Nixon, the great champion of law and order, came to think of impeachment before resigning in disgrace because of the Watergate scandal. Taken from Spiro T. Agnew, Frankly Speaking: A Collection of Extraordinary Speeches *(Washington, 1970), 44-49, 51.*

What I said before, I will say again. It is time for the preponderant majority, the responsible citizens of this country, to assert *their* rights. It is time to stop dignifying the immature actions of arrogant, reckless, inexperienced elements within our society. The reason is compelling. It is simply that their tantrums are insidiously destroying the fabric of American democracy. . . .

Last week I was lambasted for my lack of "mental and moral sensitivity." I say that any leader who does not perceive where persistent street struggles are going to lead this nation lacks mental acuity. And any leader who does not caution this nation on the danger of this direction lacks moral strength.

I believe in Constitutional dissent. I believe in the people registering their views with their elected representatives, and I commend those people who care enough about their country to involve themselves in its great issues. I believe in legal protest within the Constitutional limits of free speech, including peaceful assembly and the right of petition. But I do not believe that demonstrations, lawful or unlawful, merit my approval or even my silence where the purpose is fundamentally unsound. In the case of the Vietnam Moratorium [15 October 1969, a day of demonstrations, actions, vigils, and petition drives across the nation], the objective announced by the leaders—immediate unilateral withdrawal of all our forces from Vietnam—was not only unsound but idiotic. The tragedy was that thousands who participated wanted only to show a fervent desire for peace, but were used by the political hustlers who ran the event. . . .

Think about it. Small bands of students are allowed to shut down great universities. Small groups of dissidents are allowed to shout down political candidates. Small cadres of professional protestors are allowed to jeopardize the peace efforts of the President of the United States.

It is time to question the credentials of their leaders. And, if in questioning we disturb a few people, I say it is time for them to be disturbed. If, in challenging, we polarize the American people, I say it is time for a positive polarization.

It is time for a healthy in-depth examination of policies and a constructive realignment in this country. It is time to rip away the rhetoric and to divide on authentic lines. It is time to discard the fiction that in a country of 200 million people, everyone is qualified to quarterback the government. . . .

Now, we have among us a glib, activist element who would tell us our values are lies, and I call them impudent. Because anyone who impugns a legacy of liberty and dignity that reaches back to Moses, is impudent.

I call them snobs for most of them disdain to mingle with the masses who work for a living. They mock the common man's pride in his work, his family and his country. It has also been said that I called them intellectuals. I did not. I said that they characterized themselves as intellectuals. No true intellectual, no truly knowledgeable person, would so despise democratic institutions.

America cannot afford to write off a whole generation for the decadent thinking of a few. America cannot afford to divide over their demagoguery, to be deceived by their duplicity, or to let their license destroy liberty. We can, however, afford to separate them from our society—with no more regret than we should feel over discarding rotten apples from a barrel. . . .

. . . [I]t is time to stop demonstrating in the streets and start doing something constructive about our institutions. America must recognize the dangers of constant carnival. Americans must reckon with irresponsible leadership and reckless words. The mature and sensitive people of this country must realize that their freedom of protest is being exploited by avowed anarchists and communists who detest everything about this country and want to destroy it. . . .

Will we defend fifty centuries of accumulated wisdom? For that is our heritage. Will we make the effort to preserve America's bold, successful experiment in truly representative government? Or do we care so little that we will cast it all aside?

Questions

---

1. *Compare and contrast the"three streams" of dissent.*
2. *To what extent did "culture" play a role in these movements? Can cultural rebellion be the same thing as political rebellion? Why or why not?*
3. *What is the role of violence, or the threat of violence, for each of these groups?*
4. *What is the legacy of each "stream" today?*

Further Reading

For the most complete accounts of SDS and related movements, see Todd Gitlin, **The Sixties: Years of Hope, Days of Rage** (New York, 1987) and James Miller, **"Democracy is in the Streets": From Port Huron to The Siege of Chicago** (New York, 1987). Stewart Burns's **Social Movements of the 1960s: Searching for Democracy** (Boston, 1990) provides a largely sympathetic survey of these movements. One of the best studies of SNCC remains Carson Clayborne, **In Struggle: SNCC and the Black Awakening of the 1960s** (Cambridge, Massachusetts, 1981). Perhaps the most insightful, best-written analysis of the relationship between protest movements and the Nixon administration is Jonathan Schell's **The Time of Illusion** (New York, 1975). For the best contextualization of the drama of the 1960s see Godfrey Hodgson's **America in Our Time** (New York, 1976).